AMERICAN POPULAR CULTURE AND THE BEATLES

FIRST EDITION

AMERICAN POPULAR CULTURE AND THE BEATLES

Kenneth Campbell

Monmouth University

Bassim Hamadeh, CEO and Publisher
Janny Li, Acquisitions Editor
Amy Smith, Project Editor
Casey Hands, Associate Production Editor
Jackie Bignotti, Production Artist
Sara Schennum, Licensing Associate
Natalie Piccotti, Director of Marketing
Kassie Graves, Vice President of Editorial
Jamie Giganti, Director of Academic Publishing

Cover image: Copyright © 2018 Depositphotos/KostyaKlimenko.

Printed in the United States of America.

ISBN: 978-1-5165-4128-7 (pbk) / 978-1-5165-4129-4 (br)

CONTENTS

INTRODUCTION

Virtually every book on the Beatles acknowledges the role that American popular culture and music played in the music and lives of the band and its members. Their authors invariably treat American popular culture as part of the larger story of the Beatles, which is entirely appropriate in any work focused on that iconic group. This book about the relationship between American popular culture and the Beatles brings together the work of various authors to tell a slightly different story—the story of the interactions between American popular culture and the Beatles with as much emphasis upon the former as upon the latter. In other words, although American popular culture is definitely a part of the larger story of the Beatles, so, too, are the Beatles part of a different, larger story—that of the history of American popular culture in the 1950s and 1960s.

In this anthology, I have selected the works of ten authors, myself included, that deal with different aspects of that story. Some focus exclusively on American popular culture and music and mention the Beatles briefly, if at all. Yet Paul Friedlander, David Shumway, Norma Coates, and Gillian Gaar provide essential background for understanding American popular culture and the musical legacy inherited and, to a large degree, transformed by the Fab Four. Their essays constitute the first section of the book, devoted to American influences on the band. The next set of essays, by Brian Ward, Bob Groom, and Andre Millard, provide additional context for that influence in a section specifically devoted to the impact of American rock and roll and popular music in Britain. These two sections also allow for a comparison of the reactions to early rock and roll in Britain and the United States, thus providing insights into the differences between the two cultures. The third and final section of the book explores the impact of the Beatles on American popular culture. The second entry by Andre Millard and an article by Barbara Ehrenreich, Elizabeth Hess, and Gloria Jacobs focus on the phenomenon of Beatlemania and comment on the nature and proposed causes of the enormous popularity of the Beatles from 1963 to 1965. My essay, which wraps up the volume, examines the relationship between the Beatles and American popular culture in the second half of the decade, centering on the theme of the band's relationship to the counterculture and the revolutionary ideals of the late sixties. I offer a few additional thoughts on the subject of this volume in a brief conclusion.

I advise students not to skip over the pre-reading questions included with each of the three sections as these allow you to relate the readings directly to your own experience, and the issues raised by this material are still relevant to us today. The post-reading questions in each section not only test your comprehension of the material read, but also encourage critical thinking about the subject. I firmly hope teachers, professors, students, and general readers will find this particular collection both interesting and enlightening and that it will contribute significantly to your understanding of two of the most important cultural movements of the twentieth-century: the rise of rock and roll in American culture and the phenomenal history of the Beatles and their relationship to that story.

The story originates in the 1950s, when teenagers in both Britain and the United States began to evince a generally healthy disregard for the approval of their parents and began seeking out new forms of entertainment that catered to young audiences. Most notably, white teenagers displayed a readiness to buy records and listen to music by black artists, or black-sounding artists, sometimes referred to as "race music." Even more disturbing to many parents was the histrionic behavior teenagers began to exhibit at dances that featured an upbeat style of rhythm and blues that had developed by the mid-1950s into the music known as rock and roll. Worrying that the sexual rhythms of the music and the dances would corrupt the morals of the youth, many parents especially feared that the mixing of musical genres would lead to miscegenation, or sexual mixing of the races, among the young.

The early years of rock and roll coincided with the beginning of the civil rights movement in the United States. Early rock and roll hits like "Sh-boom" by the Chords, "That's All Right Mama" by Elvis Presley, and "Shake, Rattle and Roll" by Big Joe Turner appeared in 1954, the same year of the landmark Supreme Court decision in Brown v. Board of Education that outlawed school segregation. Elvis, in particular, led the way for both aspiring rock and roll artists and for crossover artists who learned from Elvis that sounding black could provide a ticket to stardom for whites who did not need to conform to the crooner mold set by Frank Sinatra, Bing Crosby, and Perry Como, among others. Together, rock and roll and the civil rights movement shook the placid equilibrium aspired to by fifties society and a world seeking stability after the upheaval of the Second World War.

Those concerned about the future of American youth did not need to look far to find signs of moral decay elsewhere in popular culture. Films such as *Rebel without a Cause* (1955), novels such as *The Catcher in the Rye* (1951) by J.D. Salinger or Jack Kerouac's *On the Road* (1957), and the emergence of young societal dropouts known as beatniks all provided substantial cause for concern. Reality, of course, had more nuance than a stark divide between conformity and rebellion on the part of teenagers or anyone else, but popular culture fed into fears about nonconformity in a decade that particularly valued conformity. It also planted the seeds of rebellion in many young people who would come of age in the following decade.

The Beatles emerged out of a prolific rock and roll scene in England as a whole and their hometown of Liverpool in particular, but they also partook of the general milieu of 1950s culture that shaped their identity as a group and as individuals. The Beatles transformed rock and roll into something new and exciting, helping to ensure that it would not be a passing fad that would die out, as other popular styles of music, such as Big Band and Swing, had done in the preceding decades. They also set a new standard for celebrity status, arriving in the United States in 1964 with more hype than had accompanied the early careers of even the biggest American rock and roll artists, including Elvis. They had grown up listening to American rock and roll through the static on Radio Luxembourg and at listening booths in local record stores, such as the North End Music Store, managed by Brian Epstein, whose protégés the Beatles would become when they agreed to make him their manager in January 1962. Epstein had an enormous impact on the Beatles and their career, dressing them in suits, altering the way they conducted themselves on stage, and securing them a record contract. Toward the end of 1963, he also began arranging for the group to visit the United States early in the following year.

It is easy with hindsight to take for granted what the Beatles went on to accomplish, but as with all truly extraordinary historical events, this does not do justice to the sheer improbability of what actually happened. No matter how popular British groups or singers became in Britain, the success of a British group like the Beatles in the United States was unanticipated and almost inconceivable. Historians of the period have put forward many theories and, clearly, many factors coincided to make it possible, some of them discussed in the readings that follow. You will also read in this volume the extent to which other British artists borrowed or adopted completely American music and culture to forge their own identity. Therefore, their adoption of American popular culture cannot explain by itself the phenomenal success of the Beatles. Yet, one certainly cannot explain their success without understanding the relationship between the Beatles and American popular culture. I hope the readings selected here will help you to do just that, for the merger of the two—culminating in the Beatles' arrival in New York City in February 1964—would ensure that American popular culture would never be the same again.

PART I

AMERICAN INFLUENCES ON THE BEATLES

Rock 'n' Roll and American Popular Culture

Introduction

In many respects, John Lennon, Paul McCartney, George Harrison, and Richard Starkey (aka Ringo Starr) were like millions of other teenagers in the 1950s, searching for an outlet for their youthful energies that would also satisfy their yearning for connecting with something beyond themselves and their immediate surroundings. Like millions of other teenagers, they found it in rock and roll. The pioneers of rock and roll invented a new sound that primarily combined black rhythm and blues with white country and western music, with a dash of swing, jazz, and gospel occasionally thrown in for good measure. The new musical genre benefited from the 1948 invention of the long-playing 33-rpm records and the shorter 45-rpm disks that made hit singles affordable and accessible to a mass teenage audience. Long buried in a haze of nostalgia, the early years of rock and roll generated an excitement among young people at the time that is now difficult to recreate. The selections in this section all contribute key insights to understanding the early years of rock and roll and its significance to American popular culture.

In the first source selected for this section, Paul Friedlander traces the origins of rock and roll music in America from 1953 to 1955 and explains why it resonated so well with teenagers and terrified many of their parents. Rock and roll grew up with the baby boom generation that followed the end of the Second World War, with the legendary Fats Domino recording his first hit as early as 1949. George

Harrison would later identify the big man's "I'm in Love Again" as the first rock and roll record he ever heard. In these early years, Bill Haley scored a tremendous success with hits such as "Rock around the Clock" and "Shake, Rattle, and Roll," but failed to move teenage audiences to the degree that performers such as Elvis Presley and Little Richard soon would. Friedlander goes on to demonstrate the ways in which Chuck Berry raised rock and roll to a new musical art form, without disparaging any of Berry's predecessors. Berry, who turned thirty in 1956, reached teenage audiences and gave voice to their angst in a way that even younger performers failed to capture in their music in this era. Each of these artists would appeal to the four teenage boys from Liverpool who formed the Beatles, but of the early rock and rollers dealt with by Friedlander, Little Richard provided them with special inspiration. As the remaining pieces in this section illustrate, others would come along to further the evolution of American rock and roll, but we can hear the influences of this first generation of rock and rollers in the music of the Beatles and others throughout the 1960s.

No one contributed more to the version of American popular culture that reached Liverpool in the mid- to late fifties than Elvis Presley, the discovery of a Memphis record producer named Sam Phillips who saw the young Elvis as a white performer who could broaden the appeal of black music. Elvis became the idol of the young Beatles, as he did for a legion of youths on both sides of the Atlantic. Therefore, understanding Elvis's appeal is critical to understanding much about the kind of image the Beatles aspired to and later adopted. David Shumway reminds us that people did not only listen to Elvis—that like the Beatles a few years later, he was seen as well as heard and this constituted a large part of his appeal. In fact, when the Beatles started to become famous they changed their look away from a rather tough, masculine image to a more androgynous style that Shumway argues had become central to male fame and celebrity in general and rock and roll in particular by the 1950s. (Pay particular attention in Shumway's piece to the role that Tom Parker played in managing Elvis for suggestive comparisons to Brian Epstein's later management of the Beatles.) In short, Elvis not only influenced the Beatles, he also foreshadowed them. The photo of exuberant young female fans that appears toward the end of Shumway's chapter could easily be mistaken for one taken at the height of Beatlemania.

In the next selection, Norma Coates picks up where Shumway leaves off, expanding on the importance of television to the legacy of Elvis and the first generation of rock and rollers. She argues, however, that television shaped this legacy largely in ways that were at odds with the prevailing ethos of rock and roll. She concentrates on three programs, beginning with *The Ed Sullivan Show*, which featured the most famous television appearances of *both* Elvis Presley and the Beatles, a fact forever entwining the Beatles and American popular culture. Understanding the nature of that show and its prominent role in American popular culture is essential to understanding the meaning and significance of the Beatles' first appearance on it in February 1964. Coates explains this perhaps better than anyone else has. Calling the relationship between rock and roll and television "at the same time complementary and often incompatible," she explores the tensions between two media at odds with one another yet somehow necessary to each other, at least if rock and roll hoped to reach a broader audience. The fact is that television did more to change the image of Elvis and the Beatles than the reverse. Coates also notes how important the teenage girl audience was to marketers interested in capitalizing on what they thought was a short window to attract loyalty to their brands by associating themselves with the rock and roll "fad."

In the final selection in this section, Gillian Gaar successfully shows that girls would not just be consumers of rock and roll, but also artists who played a significant role in the evolution of the genre. She especially challenges the notion that girl groups owed their success to male producers, managers, and songwriters. However, mirroring the disadvantages based on gender in the rest of society, women artists did not garner the same respect or have the same options as male performers, as Gaar amply demonstrates. Still, girl groups such as the Shirelles, the Cookies, and the Marvelettes had a major impact on the American music scene and on an up-and-coming male group from Liverpool. From appearance to lyrical material to the music itself, these girl groups had at least as large an influence on the Beatles as rock icons such as Elvis Presley or Little Richard. In fact, each of the above-named girl groups had hits the Beatles covered. The success of the Beatles and the British Invasion they launched in 1964 would have sweeping effects on American popular culture and energize a generation of American fans. It is unfortunate that they also had the negative effect of hurting the careers of many of the girl groups that they had so admired.

Pre-Reading Questions for Part I

1   Why does music seem to play such a large role in the lives of teenagers? What role would you say it has played in your life to this point?

2   Is there a particular style of music that was popular when you were growing up or that is popular now that might have had a comparable impact to that of rock and roll on teenagers in the 1950s?

3   Does music aimed at young people inevitably encourage rebellion and disobedience toward parents and authority figures? Do parents and authority figures always object to music aimed at the young for this reason?

4   What stereotypical images do you have of American society and culture in the 1950s? Has this period received special attention or been relatively ignored in your prior education?

Classic Rockers—The First Generation

Just Give Me Some of That Rock and Roll Music

Paul Friedlander

Rock and roll in the 1950s attacked, often indirectly, many of the institutions that helped to control young people. ... During the otherwise silent years of the Eisenhower administration's authoritarian attitudes, rock and roll's suggestive stage manner, guttural vocals, double entendre lyrics were seen as attackers of sexual decency and the stable family. Rock and roll fostered the separation of youth from parental control.

> —Steve Chapple and Reebee Garofalo, *Rock and Roll Is Here to Pay: The History and Politics of the Music Industry*

Rock and roll is poison put to sound.
> —Cellist Pablo Casals

Figure 1.1 Chuck Berry

Combine a traditional European ballad form with an irregular Afro-American rhythm, a vocal and/or instrumental ejaculation to break up or distort the melody, and in 1955, you have a new sound.

—Rock historians Don J. Hibbard and
Carol Kaleialoha, *The Role of Rock*

Rock and roll is just rhythm and blues. It's the same music I've been playing for 15 years in New Orleans.

—Fats Domino, from an interview on *Heroes of Rock and Roll*, a 1981 ABC-TV special

I Found My Thrill

In 1954 teens growing up in Springfield—whether in Maine, Missouri, Oregon, or Illinois—had probably never heard of rock and roll. The local radio station and television's *Your Hit Parade* were playing the same old pop songs—conformist, fantasy-oriented lyrics and soporific, beatless music. This popular music appealed to both parents and their kids and featured a mixture of artists: older song stylists like Perry Como, Frank Sinatra, and Nat "King" Cole; newcomers like Eddie Fisher, Patti Page, and Rosemary Clooney; and the slightly more emotional singers like Frankie Laine, Guy Mitchell, and Johnnie Ray.

Public awareness of rock and roll grew slowly. Although rhythm and blues was becoming popular in cities with large black populations, also developing a "cult" following among some white teens, most young white Americans were unaware of their impending musical liberation. Once rock and roll did emerge, it so threatened the prevailing societal equilibrium that Columbia University's Dr. A. M. Meerio was moved to conclude at the time, "If we cannot stem the tide of rock and roll with its waves of rhythmic narcosis and vicarious craze, we are preparing our own downfall in the midst of pandemic funeral dances."[1]

Rock and roll music was not musically complex—it contained elements from rhythm and blues, blues, and gospel mixed with varying amounts of country music and pop. There were emotion-laden vocals. There was an emphasis on the two and four beats of the measures (one-TWO-three-FOUR); listeners rocked on the one and three and rolled on the TWO and FOUR. Young people reacted emotionally to the music, moving their bodies in sympathetic vibration as the performers moved theirs. The lyrics told teen tales about romance, dance, school, music, and sex—just simple stories about everyday life.

In an era of the organization man, when dutiful parents strove to belong and conform, rock music became a catalyst for teens to form their own group identity—a comradeship of those who felt good about, and identified with, the music. Many youth of the fifties viewed rock and roll as an expression of both rebellion against and a growing uneasiness with the perceived rigidity and banality of an era dominated by conservative Republican politics and Mitch Miller musicality. It gave them a sense of community, as would the antiwar protests of the next generation.

To most adults, however, there was something unnerving about the music. To parents, many of whom were socialized by training in the military, the hierarchical structure of workplace and home, and the conformist societal climate, this music produced a frighteningly spontaneous and sensual reaction in their children. Their offspring reacted in an unauthorized manner. And adult antagonism toward rock music also reflected the inherent racism of the era. Having correctly perceived rock music as fundamentally black in both origin and nature, most white parents judged it bestial and subhuman. For example, the Alabama White Citizens Council announced a campaign to rid the country of this "animalistic, nigger bop." Many government, religious, and educational spokespersons echoed those sentiments, characterizing the music as immoral and sinful—and its purveyors as lazy and shiftless juvenile delinquents.

So young people had a problem. Father, teacher, and parson all said that rock and roll was bad for them. But, lying in bed cuddling their radios or after school at a friend's house, young people knew that listening to rock music made them feel good. Dad and Mom, if they talked about it at all, said that songs with double-entendre lyrics about sex and romance were wrong. However, since parents seemed to be involved in the sexual activity that they prohibited for their teenage offspring, it appeared like a "Do as I say, not as I do" scenario. Life for teens was beginning to lose its safe predictability. The infallibility of the family and the honor of society were at stake, and maybe, just maybe, father didn't know best.

Like their audiences, the classic rockers sought musical and emotional outlets. Having been exposed to both black and white musical roots, these rock pioneers forged a fusion of styles. There emerged two distinct generations: predominantly black artists who became popular before 1956, and the Elvis-led, white, country-rooted group who parlayed the genre into its extraordinary commercial success. The first generation of classic rockers—Fats Domino, Bill Haley, Chuck Berry, and Little Richard—rose to prominence between 1953 and 1955. They led the rock and roll explosion, establishing the classic rock genre as a viable commercial force in popular music. Their music remained close to its roots in rhythm and blues, blues, and, in Haley's case, country, creating mostly upbeat rock songs about dance, romance, and teen lifestyles. Yet their stories show how they were just ordinary folks who exhibited an abundance of creative talent and a passion for their music.

Antoine "Fats" Domino

He was a performer of great charm but little charisma. … [His musical style] was dominated by a warm vocal style and a thick, chunky, boogie-woogie bass New Orleans piano.

—Rock Historian Peter Guralnick, *Feel Like Goin' Home:*
Portraits in Blues and Rock 'N' Roll

In 1949 Antoine "Fats" Domino recorded his first rhythm and blues hit, "The Fat Man," which sold 1 million copies by 1953. Yet Domino didn't become rock and roll's first superstar. Though he was an accomplished pianist and he cocomposed most of his hit songs, his stage show, and consequently much of his public persona, lacked the explosive rebelliousness of Elvis or Little Richard. Domino and his music were too easygoing. White America would have to wait for its king of rock and roll.

One of nine children, Domino was born in New Orleans on February 26, 1928. His family spoke mostly French Creole at home and was steeped in the rich musical tradition of the city. His father was a well-known violinist, but Domino learned to play mostly from his uncle, jazz guitarist Harrison Verrett. Verrett, who had worked with jazz pioneers Kid Ory and Papa Celestin, taught the nine-year-old Domino by writing note letters on the white piano keys with black ink. Within a few years the youngster was playing in local honky-tonks for tips, and earning $1.50 a day mowing lawns.

In December 1949 New Orleans bandleader and trumpeter Dave Bartholomew suggested to Lew Chudd (president of Los Angeles-based Imperial Records) that they go see Domino perform. Chudd was impressed, and Domino, with Bartholomew's band, went into the studio to record "The Fat Man." This began a collaboration that lasted into the sixties. The combination of performer-composer Domino and bandleader-arranger-producer-composer Bartholomew is credited with more charted rock music hits than any classic rock artist except Elvis Presley.

The studio, in this case, was J&M Studios, located behind a furniture store at the corner of Rampart and Domaine in New Orleans. Like many other studios (Sun and Stax in Memphis, Motown in Detroit, Chess in Chicago, and Atlantic in New York), J&M was a place that captured the sound of a region—the New Orleans R&B sound. It featured a specific group of musicians, led by Bartholomew; the studio sound was engineered by owner Cosimo Matassa; and local recording stars like Domino, Lloyd Price, and Huey "Piano" Smith charted new waters.

By today's standards, recording conditions at that early J&M location were primitive. Producer Robert "Bumps" Blackwell once described it this way:

> The studio was just a backroom in a furniture store, like an ordinary motel room, for the whole orchestra. There'd be a grand piano just as you came in the door. I'd have the grand's lid up with a mic in the keys and Alvin Tyler and Lee Allen (saxes) would be blowing into that. Earl Palmer's drums were out of the door, where I had one mic as well. The studio bass man would be over on the other side of the studio. You see the bass would cut and bleed in, so I could get the bass.[2]

"The Fat Man" entered the R&B charts in April 1950 and rose to #6. The title was no anomaly; although only five-foot-five, Domino weighed 224 pounds. He released five more gold (million-selling) records before 1955. In July 1955 "Ain't It a Shame" (#10) reached the top-40 popular music charts, allowing Domino his first major access to teenage America. Pat Boone's cover of the same tune hit the charts simultaneously and eventually climbed to #1.

Throughout the 1950s and into the early 1960s, the team of Domino, Bartholomew, and the "Cosimo" sound created a series of thirty-five top-40 hits. Based on the traditional R&B ensemble of drums, bass, piano, electric guitar, and saxophone(s), Domino's sound, called rhythm and blues in 1954, was heralded as rock and roll by 1956. Although Domino never had a #1 hit, his ten top-10 hits included: "Blueberry Hill" (#2, 1956); "Blue Monday" (#5, 1957); "I'm Walkin'" (#4, 1957); "Whole Lotta Loving" (#6, 1958); and "I Want to Walk You Home" (#8, 1959).

Like most classic rockers, Fats Domino came from humble beginnings in the South. The rich musical tradition of New Orleans provided him with a variety of influences. His piano style drew from boogie-woogie players such as Meade Lux Lewis, Albert Ammons, and Pete Johnson. Domino's recording band (Dave Bartholomew's group) contained some of the finest R&B players available in New Orleans. His musical blend included Domino's own Creole-accented lilting vocal style—"I found my three-ill on Blueberry he-ill"—strong drums and bass; jazz-flavored, melodic saxophone solos; and that syncopated honky-tonk piano.

Despite Domino's failure to score a #1 hit on the pop charts, he was still one of the most commercially viable of the classic rockers. Early in his career, Domino took his uncle's advice and retained the songwriting royalties to his compositions. Thus, Domino received substantial sums of money, whether songs he penned gained popularity through his own recording or were covered by other artists.

Rock and roll artists who achieve a top level of commercial success do so not only because of individual talent but also because they are surrounded by a team of gifted, highly motivated individuals working in support. Fats Domino had such a team. Cocomposer Dave Bartholomew was a skilled musical director and record producer, Cosimo Matassa's studio and engineering blended perfectly with the "New Orleans sound," and Lew Chudd's Imperial Records was one of the largest independent record companies in the nation—with sufficient resources, motivation, and talent to market its stable of artists. Although Domino didn't have an influential manager the caliber of Elvis's infamous "Colonel" Tom Parker, Harrison Verrett provided him with sound business advice and direction. This "team" of support personnel is absent for many of the less successful artists of the era.

Fats Domino's legacy is a musical smile—the sound and feeling that come with his "good time" rock and roll. His music was bouncy, attributable in part to that wonderfully syncopated honky-tonk piano. His lyrics, which portrayed an unspoiled, romantic lifestyle and were reinforced by his relaxed delivery and stylish drawl, presented a relatively asexual, nonthreatening vision for youth and parents. Domino fostered this safe image by remaining seated at the piano during his live performances. Although he lacked the charisma and sexual energy of Little Richard and Elvis, Domino was the era's second most successful recording artist—collecting eighteen gold awards and selling more than 30 million records. He has survived rock's first five decades and continues to perform into the twenty-first century.

Bill Haley

In the spring of 1955 Bill Haley had everything going for him. His third top-20 hit, "Rock Around the Clock," had gone #1, he fronted an exciting rock and roll band, and he had an entrée into mainstream success because he shared the same skin color as his (mostly) white audiences. Yet Haley would fail to emerge as rock and roll's first teenage heartthrob. At twenty-eight, he lacked the youthful charisma and sexual swagger to become the king of rock and roll. The world would have to wait for Elvis Presley. Haley was, however, one of rock and roll music's pioneers. Incorporating his intuitive feel for, and experience with, country music, blues, jazz, and rhythm and blues, Haley consciously created a collage of up-tempo, beat-driven dance music chronicling the rocking and rolling of fifties teens.

William Haley was born in Highland Park, Michigan, on July 6, 1925. His father had moved from Kentucky to the Detroit area to find work, but when the Great Depression hit he settled his wife and two children near Chester, Pennsylvania. Haley Sr. found steady work in the Sun Shipyards, which gave his family a reliable income at a time when rural neighbors barely got by.

When Bill was seven, he taught himself guitar and entered amateur contests in an outdoor country and western park near his home. Haley came from a musical family—his mother taught piano, and his father played mandolin. Starting out as a country and western singer, he soon met Hank Williams: "Hank taught me a few chords and he did influence me. He was a great blues singer and he stimulated my interest in rhythm and blues music, race music as it was called then."[3] Haley was also listening to the jump-band jazz of Louis Jordan, Lionel Hampton, and Lucky Millender.

By age fifteen Haley had joined Cousin Lee, a group with a regular radio show on WDEL in Wilmington, Delaware. Haley became a professional country and western musician and traveled widely in the Midwest, but he eventually quit the road, got married, and returned to Chester, where he worked at WPWA as a disc jockey, sports announcer, and emcee of his own live music show. Onstage, the yodeling, guitar-strumming singer was shy and reserved, which stemmed from the self-consciousness of being blind in one eye.

Chester, Pennsylvania, contained a thriving music scene. Not only did the Four Aces and Frankie Avalon hail from that area, but Haley also worked clubs in the black section. "Back then, we worked colored nightclubs and there was no problem with either the musicians or the patrons. And I worked on the same bill at Pep's Music Barn with B. B. King, Fats Domino, Lloyd Price, Ray Charles, Nat King Cole—no hang-up whatsoever."[4]

Haley was a visionary, in that he made a conscious effort to integrate his country roots with rhythm and blues. "I felt that if I could take, say, a dixieland tune and drop the first and third beats, and accentuate the second and fourth, and add a beat that the listeners could clap to as well as dance, this could be what they were after."[5]

Thus, Bill Haley was a sideburned, cowboy-booted country and western singer when, in 1952, he recorded an R&B tune titled "Rock This Joint" on the small independent Essex label. His band, the Saddlemen, was a country band that contained an accordion and a steel guitar, along with bass, drums, guitar, and piano. Haley had written "Rock-a-Beatin' Boogie" for another group and found out that disc jockey Alan Freed was using it to open his radio show in Cleveland. The words "Rock, rock, rock everybody / Roll, roll, roll everybody" were infectious.

The time for Haley's personal transformation was clearly at hand; off came the sideburns, boots, and country name, out came the tuxedos. Bill Haley and the Saddlemen became Bill Haley and His Comets. The country group became a powerful rock and roll ensemble consisting of drums, bass, two electric guitars, piano, steel guitar, and tenor saxophone. Haley began to instill more emotion in his vocals, and Rudy Pompelli's saxophone solos and R&B-derived "down on your knees" stage antics drove the audience wild. They recorded "Crazy Man Crazy," which sold more than 1 million copies and reached the Billboard top 20 in 1953. The group garnered interest from all three majors (Columbia, RCA, and Decca); it signed with Decca.

In April 1954 the group assembled at New York's Pythian Temple for their first Decca session. Rarely has there been a more auspicious first session. They recorded "Rock Around the Clock," a song written by a pair of white middle-aged music-business veterans.[6] Although it sold a healthy 75,000 copies, the record failed to make much of an impact. The band also recorded their musically and lyrically sanitized cover version of Big Joe Turner's R&B hit "Shake, Rattle, and Roll," and it reached #12. The decision to use "Rock Around the Clock" behind the opening credits of the 1955 movie *Blackboard Jungle* secured the song, and Bill Haley, a place in the history books. Teens acquired an anthem of rebellion, as they added the words "whether you like it or not" to the title—and parents found a target. The song rose to #1 and stayed there for an incredible eight weeks. It has since sold 30 million copies.

Haley became the first white rock and roll star. He toured with the major package shows, headlined concerts, and became a rock idol in Europe. At the end of 1955, Haley was named *Downbeat* magazine's Rhythm and Blues Personality of the Year, which evidenced that Haley was also popular in the black music community. He reached the top 20 once more in early 1956 with "See You Later, Alligator" (#6). But America was still looking for a teen idol, and the slightly balding, pudgy, somewhat shy Haley didn't fit the bill. Consequently, other white artists, including Elvis Presley, surged past him in popularity. Haley continued to tour for the next two decades, becoming a star in the rock nostalgia movement of the late 1960s. By the late 1970s he was in severe physical and financial distress. His sax player and musical director, Rudy Pompelli—who had stayed loyal through it all—died in 1976. Bill Haley lived his last years in Harlingen, Texas. He drank heavily, slipping in and out of reality. On February 9, 1981, he died alone.

Bill Haley was the first white musician of the fifties to synthesize black and white musical styles and have a major impact on popular music. He combined a strong backbeat with a clear and forceful vocal style, Rudy Pompelli's outstanding tenor saxophone solo work, and a lyrical content that reinforced the joys of dancing to rock and roll. Before Elvis, Chuck Berry, and Buddy Holly, there was Bill Haley, who introduced teenage America to classic rock and roll.

Chuck Berry

> Berry was the first performer to demonstrate that rock and roll could be philosophically and artistically worthwhile as well as good to dance to. ... [Berry put] a measure of quality into rock and roll.
>
> —Rock Historian Loyd Grossman, *A Social History of Rock Music*

> Hail, hail rock and roll
> Remember it from the days of old. ...
> Long live rock and roll
> The feelin' is there, body and soul.
>
> —Chuck Berry's "School Days" (Chess Records, 1957)

Charles Edward Anderson Berry was the father-poet of classic rock and roll. He chronicled the fifties teenage experience with a literacy and musical creativity unmatched by his contemporaries. His stories of struggle, romance, and dance provided the listener with a lyrical pastiche reflecting the first stab at self-sufficiency by the era's youth. Chuck Berry the person, however, remains somewhat of an enigma. His struggles with the law have left him embittered and uncommunicative—so much so that, until the release of his autobiography in 1987, even the year and place of his birth were in doubt. Now we know that Berry was born on October 18, 1926, in St. Louis, Missouri, the second of three boys in a family of six children. Although these were the Depression years, his father was a building maintenance contractor, ensuring his family a relatively comfortable existence. Both parents were active in the Baptist church, and young Charles sang in the choir at age six.

In addition to his church music, Berry's vocal interests lay in the era's popular music: "My favorite singers ... are Nat [King Cole] and Frank [Sinatra], in that respect, because I'm moody, and Nat sang moody music."[7] His clear enunciation on his material reflects these pop vocal influences. St. Louis was perfectly positioned, geographically speaking, as a musical crossroads. It was close to Kansas City, the jazz mecca of the big-band era, and astride the Mississippi River; the city also was an important way station for the railroad and river traffic that brought southern blues musicians to the industrial North. Making his home along these routes, Berry was inundated with various styles of music throughout his youth.

Berry was a self-taught musician, proficient in guitar, saxophone, and piano. As the father of rock and roll guitar, he would fuse elements from the blues (repetition, choke, and bend) with country-derived speed and slides. His developing guitar style was clearly influenced by regional black jazz and blues artists as well as by the country and western music that he followed avidly on the radio. When asked about his guitar influences, Berry cited "a person named Charlie Christian, guitarist for Benny Goodman, T-Bone Walker, and Carl Hogan (Louis Jordan's guitarist)."[8] One important innovation, often overlooked in chronicling the development of rock guitar, is Berry's rhythm-guitar style. Using E-fingering bar chords, Berry would strum an eighth-note pulse on the bass strings of the guitar while alternating with his pinkie every two beats four frets above the bar. This created a forceful, driving foundation to Berry's material that continues to be used by modern rock guitarists.

Berry's first brush with the law occurred in 1944. He and two companions were arrested for auto theft and robbery, and Berry spent nearly three years in reform school. Later, Berry obtained a job at the General Motors plant while he and his sister studied to become hairstylists at the Poro School of Beauty Culture. In the early 1950s, with a wife and two children to support, Berry supplemented his income by leading a small blues combo. A local piano player named Johnny Johnson invited guitarist Berry to replace a departed sax player, and the quartet eventually became popular enough to rival larger local combos such as Ike Turner and the Rhythm Kings.

Berry's rise to fame is steeped in legend. Mythology has it that Berry, ostensibly in town for vacation, stepped onto a Chicago stage to join blues great Muddy Waters during a jam session. Berry disputes this but acknowledges that Waters did recommend that Berry visit Chess Records head Leonard Chess. By 1954 Chess Records was the premier proponent of the Chicago urban blues sound; its artist roster included Waters, Howlin' Wolf, Willie Dixon, and many others. Berry viewed himself as a blues artist, but Leonard Chess was more interested in a medium-tempo song named "Ida May" (also identified as "Ida Red"). He instructed Berry to rework the tune at a faster pace and change the name.

Returning to Chicago, Berry recorded the song, now titled "Maybellene," on May 21, 1955. Leonard Chess rushed "Maybellene" to New York and disc jockey Alan Freed. The country's most prominent rock and roll disc jockey gave it his enthusiastic support—and Chess gave Freed one-third of the songwriter's royalties. With the assistance of New York airplay, "Maybellene" reached #1 on the R&B charts and #5 on the pop charts that summer.

Whereas most classic rockers wrote tales of love, Berry wrote tales of teen existence that exhibited a freshness, humor, and literacy reminiscent of Tin Pan Alley professionals. It is para-doxical that a man who was already thirty years old by the time "Roll Over Beethoven" was a hit in 1956 could so accurately speak for a generation of teens that was tasting rebellion for the first time. Perhaps the indelibly etched experience of being a black youth from the border South gave Berry insight into the oppression and frustration felt by a new generation of adolescents. A man with a high school education became rock's first poet laureate.

Chuck Berry recorded eight more top-40 hits during the next four years. "Roll Over Beethoven" (#29, May 1956) alerted the nation to the excitement of the new sound, chiding classical music composers Beethoven and Tchaikovsky to vacate the scene and make way for rhythm and blues (that is, rock and roll). In 1957 "School Days" (#3) chronicled a typical school-day experience from "Up in the morning and out to school" to day's end at the local gathering place, where they all "hail, hail rock and roll." Of special note in "School Days" is the call and response between the vocal and the guitar during the verses. In an era of live recordings, this almost perfect call-and-response synchronization of the guitar to the meter and pitch of the vocal melody and phrasing was a marvelous accomplishment.

Berry once again celebrated the new sound with "Rock and Roll Music" (#8, November 1957) and introduced his audience to their first teenybopper in "Sweet Little Sixteen" (#2, February 1958). "Johnny B. Goode" (#8, May 1958) was one of rock and roll's first biographies—the story of a young Louisiana guitarist out to make it big. I don't know of another song that has permeated live rock and roll to a greater extent. Request "Johnny B. Goode" at any rock and roll club, and you're likely to get it played on the spot; its anthemic "Go, Johnny, go!" has become a rallying cry for the entire genre of rock and roll.

Berry developed a performance style that excited his audiences (though he was not as wild onstage as Jerry Lee Lewis and Little Richard). Bent over in a crouch, his head bobbin' and weavin', Berry would strut across the stage doing his famous duckwalk. Down through the years, this and other Berry performance practices have been emulated by rock guitarists.

Berry's strong sense of artistic and personal integrity was challenged the first time he appeared on Dick Clark's network TV show, *American Bandstand*. Like all other performers, Berry was expected to lip-synch (move his mouth without singing) the words to his song while the record played on the air. Berry balked. Luckily for Berry, Leonard Chess was present to point out the potentially cataclysmic results of a standoff with Dick Clark. Berry eventually saw the economic wisdom of this argument, lip-synched, and later even named his St. Louis club Chuck Berry's Bandstand.

Movies were another medium where rock music received additional exposure. With the success of "Rock Around the Clock" in *Blackboard Jungle*, Hollywood jumped on the rock and roll soundtrack bandwagon. Berry's first movie effort was *Rock, Rock, Rock*, which was followed by *Mr. Rock and Roll* and *Go Johnny Go*. During this era, approximately twenty-five major movies were devoted to the subject of rock and roll.

As with many of the other classic rockers, Berry's career and financial security were illusory. In December 1959 Berry was charged with a violation of the federal Mann Act, which prohibited transporting a minor across state lines with intent to commit prostitution. According to Berry, he added a twenty-one-year-old woman to his entourage during an El Paso tour date and gave her a job as a cigarette girl in his club. She began turning tricks as a prostitute, was assaulted by a customer, and possibly traded testimony against Berry in exchange for the goodwill of the authorities. The prosecution contended she was only fourteen years old.

The first trial verdict (a conviction) was vacated on appeal due to the blatant racial prejudice of the presiding judge. The second trial sealed Berry's fate. Again convicted, he entered federal prison in Terre Haute, Indiana, in February 1962. By the time of his release in the fall of 1963, he had lost his club and found his career in shambles. The experience changed him. Carl Perkins noted that the man who had once seemed so friendly and easygoing was now terse and moody. In Patrick Salvo's 1972 *Rolling Stone* interview, Berry even denied that he went to jail.

In 1964 Berry went head-to-head with the British invasion. Although he had three top-40 tunes—"Nadine," "No Particular Place to Go," and "You Never Can Tell"—it was a losing battle. Many sixties groups recorded Berry's songs and often cited him as a major influence in their development, but he never again achieved his previous popular status. Ironically, in 1972, a live recording of the suggestive "My Ding-a-Ling" became Berry's only #1 chart hit. Fifty years after his first hit record, he continues to perform, thrilling fans with his masterful version of classic rock and roll.

Chuck Berry created the most literate, stylistically innovative, and original music of the era—he was a complete musician who was not only a vocal stylist like Elvis but also a composer, instrumentalist, and bandleader. Whereas most other performers limited their scope to various permutations of the boy-girl romance formula, Berry's songs dealt with important adolescent concerns such as romance, sex, work, school, cars, dancing, parents, and rock and roll music. As a guitarist, he created the baseline for the genre. But Berry, the era's "brown-eyed, handsome man," fell from grace, as did many other classic rockers. However, his massive legacy and the man himself are still a vibrant part of the rock and roll community.

Little Richard

> When Jerry Lee [Lewis] hits the piano keyboard with his butt, bangs the keys with the boot of his heel of an outstretched leg and leaps on top, it's Little Richard. When Presley chokes-gasps-gulps his words and swivels his pelvis, it's Little Richard. When the Beatles scream "yeah, yeah, yeah" and gliss into a high falsetto, it's Little Richard.
>
> —Pop Music Scholar Arnold Shaw,
> *The Rockin' '50s: The Decade that Transformed the Pop Music Scene*

Richard Pennimen always wanted to be acknowledged as the king of rock and roll. He exploded into the first era of rock and roll with a string of top-40 hits. His unique stage appearance and live performance style were imitated by many of his contemporaries. His persona and penchant for a controversial lifestyle were unmatched. But Richard was simply too outrageous, too raw, and too black to capture the crown he so desperately wanted. America would await another's ascendance to the throne.

Little Richard was born on December 5, 1932, at his home in the comfortable Pleasant Hill neighborhood of Macon, Georgia. He was the third child, and second boy, in a family that eventually numbered twelve children. His father, the son of a preacher, was a brick mason and sold moonshine on the side. His mother, Leva Mae, was probably being kind when she stated once that "Richard was the most trouble of any of them." Richard was rambunctious, a practical joker, and uncontrollable into his teens. As an adolescent, he claims to have been "experienced" with men, boys, women, and girls.

At age thirteen, Richard's wild behavior landed him on the streets. He hit the road as a vocalist for Dr. Hudson's Medicine Show selling "tonic." Upon his return to Macon, Richard was taken in by a white couple, Ann and Johnny Johnson, who ran a nightclub called the Tick Tock Club. From this point on, Richard set his sights on a career in music.

Figure 1.2 Little Richard

The outstanding feature of Little Richard's music was his unique vocal style. This highly emotive singing, soaring falsetto, and screams of praise all came from his gospel background— singing in choirs, contests, and revival and camp meetings. Whether it be the Pentecostal, AME Methodist, or Holiness Temple Baptist Church, the gospel style was emotional and musical. Richard was apparently good enough to become lead vocalist in a number of church-affiliated singing groups, including Ma Sweetie's Tiny Tots. These roots are evident not only in his vocal style but also in his active performance style.

In 1951 at the age of eighteen, Richard won a recording contract with RCA Records in a talent contest. The eight sides that he cut had little impact but enabled Richard to assemble a fine rhythm and blues band, the Upsetters. The core rhythm section and powerful saxophones created a potent sound that later included Georgia natives James Brown and Otis Redding as Upsetter vocalists. Richard recorded additional tunes with the Peacock label in 1953 while developing a regional following.

According to rock legend, Little Richard was washing dishes in Macon's Greyhound Bus terminal when "the call" came from Art Rupe of Los Angeles–based Specialty Records. What the legend omits is that Richard was already an established regional artist with a top-notch band who had pestered Rupe unmercifully about the demo tape he had submitted seven months earlier. Specialty sent Little Richard to J&M Studios in New Orleans to record with producer Bumps Blackwell (the musical mentor of Quincy Jones and Ray Charles). Blackwell described the session this way: "When I walked in, there's this cat in this loud shirt, with hair waved up six inches above his head. He was talkin' wild, thinkin' up stuff just to be different, you know. I could tell he was a mega-personality."[9]

Richard's first time through "Tutti-Frutti" left Blackwell in a quandary; the music and feeling of the song were explosive, but the words were beyond suggestive: "Tutti frutti, good booty / If it don't fit, don't force it / You can grease it, make it easy." New Orleans blues writer Dorothy La Bostrie was called in to rework the lyrics, and Richard, with backing from Bartholomew's studio band, recorded the tune in fifteen minutes. By January 1956 the song was #2 on the R&B charts and #17 on the pop charts. During the next two years, Little Richard had eight more top-40 hits. His chart success was followed, like that of Chuck Berry and others, by inclusion on the star-laden package tours that crisscrossed the United States.

If the lyrics of Richard's songs were any indication of his life, it was pretty unidimensional. He simply enjoyed "rocking," "rolling," and "balling" with his coterie of R&B belles. They ranged from Sue and Daisy, representing the sanitized version of "Tutti-Frutti," to Miss Molly, Long Tall Sally, Lucille, Jenny, and more. Either white society was oblivious to the sexual double entendres in these songs or it relished the thrill of those intemperate references.

The Hollywood Little Richard of "Don't Knock the Rock," "The Girl Can't Help It," and "Mr. Rock and Roll" was fairly sedate. Live audiences were treated to his megapersonality onstage. His appearance was outlandish. There were silver lamé or multicolored suits, boots, and capes. His processed hair (straightened and shaped) stood anywhere from six inches to a full foot above his forehead. He wore pancake makeup, mascara, and eyeliner. Charlie Gillett describes a Richard who was "dressed in shimmering suits with long drape jackets and baggy pants, his hair grown long and slicked straight, white teeth and gold rings flashing in the spotlights, he stood up, and at times on, the piano, hammering boogie chords as he screamed messages of celebration and self-centered pleasure."[10]

During the fall of 1957, at the peak of his career, Little Richard announced that he was giving up secular music and enrolling in Oakwood College in Huntsville, Alabama. At this Seventh-Day Adventist school he would pursue a course of Bible study to ready himself for the ministry. He had reached this conclusion, according to rock mythology, while on tour in Australia. The details are cloudy, but Richard saw, heard, or felt a sign from God. According to legend, this sign came in the form of an apocalyptic vision, an engine fire on a tour charter aircraft, news that the Soviet Union had just launched Sputnik, a fireball over the concert stadium, or some or all of the above.

This abdication from rock music took Specialty Records by surprise. They weathered the storm by releasing previously recorded sessions, including "Good Golly Miss Molly," well into 1958. Richard studied, sang, and recorded gospel music. But while on tour in England in 1962, he reversed his direction, performing many of his old hits to the delight of his fans (who included another group on the bill, named the Beatles). This jumping between two genres (classic rock and gospel) continued into the eighties.

Little Richard attempted a major comeback in the late 1960s, recording soul-flavored material on the Okeh label. He later cracked the top 100 twice on Reprise in 1970. This was the time of mirrored costumes, talk-show tiffs, and the revelations of Richard's bisexuality. However, no matter how outlandish his behavior became, Richard maintained that the effect of his music was a healing one: "I believe my music is healin' music ... because it inspires and uplifts people."[11]

Although his song catalog didn't have as much impact on subsequent rock generations as those of Berry and Holly, Little Richard's live performance style and emotive vocal style were major building blocks of sixties rock and roll. Richard's androgynous stage persona is reflected in the performance styles of Mick Jagger, David Bowie, Jimi Hendrix, Prince, and others. Teens of the fifties may not have been ready for a scabrous black rock messiah, but, even in the twenty-first century, Richard is still making the congregation rock.

***

Between 1953 and 1955, the first classic rock and roll generation (Fats Domino, Bill Haley, Chuck Berry, and Little Richard) appeared on the popular music charts. Three of the four were black, and all played a music that reflected primary roots in blues or rhythm and blues. Domino's lilting visions of courtship and dire straits were driven by a pulsating piano and the beat of a forceful rhythm and blues band. Haley shouted his calls of dance and romance over his own driving country- and R&B-rooted ensemble. Chuck Berry was an exceptional innovator. Firmly rooted in blues, Berry defined certain elements of rock music. He focused the instrumental solo on guitar, then created its stylistic parameters. His lyrical vision included most of the major concerns of the adolescent audience. Finally, Little Richard brought the most bawdy parts of the rhythm and blues legacy—the howl, the harem, the musical power—to his rock audience.

As a group, they were pioneers of rock and roll. Each paid his dues in another style before crossing over to the popular charts—their average age was twenty-six at the time of their first pop hits. Staying close to their black musical roots, they maintained that unrestrained, rebellious exhortation in their lyrics. In addition to songs about romance, there were also some about sex, school, dancing, and rock and roll music itself.

Though some of the lyrics were subliminally "wicked," few songs were overtly critical of the system. It wasn't until the sixties that some rock lyrics called decisively for change. Lyrics and music of the classic rock era redefined adolescent lifestyles. They opened a Pandora's box—filled with both a spontaneous, emotional response to this essentially black music and an evolving sense of teen identity and community.

By 1955 young, white, country-rooted musicians populated the South, listening to rock's first generation and adapting those sounds to their own creative visions. Soon, these men—Elvis, Buddy Holly, Jerry Lee Lewis, and the Everly Brothers—would explode on the scene. As classic rock's second generation, they would bring guitars to the forefront, return to an almost exclusive emphasis on romance, and reap commercial success and economic rewards beyond their wildest dreams.

Notes

1 Jerry Hopkins, *The Rock Story* (New York: Signet Books, 1970), 31.

2 Charles White, *The Life and Times of Little Richard* (New York: Pocket Books, 1984), 47–48.

3 Arnold Shaw, *The Rockin''50s: The Decade That Transformed the Pop Music Scene* (New York: Hawthorne Books, 1974), 139.

4 Ibid., 143.

5 Charlie Gillett, *The Sound of the City* (New York: Dell Publishing, 1972), 34.

6 Decca executive and Haley producer Milt Gabler had suggested that part of the success of "Rock Around the Clock" was due to the fact that it was a rewrite of an old blues tune, "My Daddy Rocks Me with a Steady Roll." He claimed that the words *rock and roll* came straight from the lyrics of that song.

7 Chuck Berry, 1969 interview with Greil Marcus, *The "Rolling Stone" Interviews: 1967–1980* (New York: Rolling Stone Press, 1981), 175.

8 Ibid.

9 White, *The Life and Times of Little Richard*, 47.

10 Gillett, *The Sound of the City*, 37.

11 Little Richard, 1969 interview with David Dalton, *"Rolling Stone" Interviews*, 366.

Discography

Fats Domino: *Jukebox/20 Greatest Hits the Way You Originally Heard Them,* Capitol
Bill Haley: *From the Original Master Tapes,* MCA
Chuck Berry: *The Great Twenty-Eight,* Chess
Little Richard: *The Essential,* Specialty

Bibliography

Brackett, Nathan. *The New* Rolling Stone *Album Guide: Completely Revised and Updated, 4th Edition.* New York: Fireside, 2004.

Carson, Mina, Tisa Lewis, and Susan M. Shaw. *Girls Rock: Fifty Years of Women Making Music.* Lexington, KY: University Press of Kentucky, 2004.

Chapple, Steve, and Reebee Garofalo. *Rock and Roll Is Here to Pay: The History and Politics of the Music Industry.* Chicago: Nelson-Hall, 1977.

Charlton, Katherine. *Rock Music Styles: A History.* 2d ed. Madison, WI: W. C. B. Brown and Benchmark, 1994.

Dannon, Fredric. *Hit Men.* New York: Random House, 1990.

Davis, Clive, with James Willwerth. *Clive: Inside the Record Business.* New York: Ballantine Books, 1974.

Frame, Peter. *Rock Family Trees.* New York: Quick Fox, 1979.

_____. *Rock Family Trees.* Vol. 2. New York: Omnibus Press, 1983.

Frith, Simon. *Sound Effects: Youth, Leisure, and the Politics of Rock 'n' Roll.* New York: Pantheon Books, 1982.

_____. *Performing Rites: On the Value of Popular Music.* Cambridge, MA: Harvard University Press, 1996.

_____, ed. *Facing the Music.* New York: Pantheon Books, 1988.

Frith, Simon, and Andrew Goodwin, eds. *On Record.* New York: Pantheon Books, 1990.

Gambaccini, Paul. *Critics' Choice: The Top 100 Rock 'n' Roll Albums of All Time.* New York: Harmony Books, 1987.

George-Warren, Holly, and Patricia Romanowski. *The New* Rolling Stone *Encyclopedia of Rock and Roll.* New York: Fireside, 2001.

Gitlin, Todd. *The Sixties: Years of Rage, Days of Rage.* New York: Bantam Books, 1987.

Guitar Player Magazine. *Rock Guitarists.* New York: Guitar Player Books, 1975

_____. *Rock Guitarists.* Vol. 2. New York: Guitar Player Books, 1978.

Goodman, Fred. *The Mansion on the Hill.* New York: Vintage, 1998.

Hammond, John, with Irving Townsend. *John Hammond on Record: An Autobiography.* New York: Penguin Books, 1981.

Hart, Mickey, with Jay Stevens. *Drumming at the Edge of Magic.* New York: Harper, 1990.

King, Thomas R. *The Operator: David Geffin Builds, Buys, and Sells the New Hollywood.* New York: Broadway, 2001.

Kooper, Al, with Ben Edmonds. *Backstage Pass: Rock 'n' Roll Life in the Sixties.* New York: Stein and Day, 1977.

Lull, James, ed. *Popular Music and Communication.* Newbury Park, CA: Sage, 1992.

Marcus, Greil. *Mystery Train: Images of America in Rock N' Roll Music.* New York: Plume, 1997.

Marsh, Dave, and Kevin Stein. *The New Book of Rock Lists.* New York: Simon and Schuster, 1994.

Negus, Keith. *Popular Music in Theory.* Hanover, NH: Wesleyan University Press, 1997.

Ochs, Michael. *Rock Archives: A Photographic Journey through the First Two Decades of Rock and Roll.* Garden City, NY: Doubleday, 1984.

Peellaert, Guy, and Nik Cohn. *Rock Dreams.* New York: Popular Library, 1973.

Pichaske, David. *A Generation in Motion: Popular Music and Culture in the Sixties*. New York: Schirmer Books, 1979.

Rolling Stone. *The "Rolling Stone" Interviews: Talking with the Legends of Rock and Roll, 1967–1980*. New York: St. Martin's Press, Rolling Stone Press, 1981.

_____. *The "Rolling Stone" Interviews: The 1980s*. New York: St. Martin's Press, Rolling Stone Press, 1989.

Stokes, Geoffrey. *Star-Making Machinery: Inside the Business of Rock and Roll*. New York: Vintage Books, 1977.

Strong, Martin C. *The Great Rock Discography: Complete Discographies Listing Every Track Recorded by More Than 1,200 Artists, 7th Ed*. Edinburgh: Cannongate Books, 2004.

Wade, Bonnie C. *Thinking Musically: Experiencing Music, Expressing Culture*. New York: Oxford University Press, 2004.

Ward, Ed, Geoffrey Stokes, and Ken Tucker. *Rock of Ages: The* Rolling Stone *History of Rock and Roll*. New York: Rolling Stone Press, Summit Books, 1986.

Whitburn, Joel. *The Billboard Book of Top 40 Albums*. New York: Billboard Books, 1991

_____. *The Billboard Book of Top 40 Hits*. New York: Billboard Books, 1992.

Classic Rockers—The First Generation

Berry, Chuck. *The Autobiography*. New York: Harmony Books, 1987.

Friedlander, Paul. "A Characteristics Profile of the Eight Classic Rock Era Artists, 1954–1959." PhD diss., University of Oregon, 1987.

Guralnick, Peter. *Feel Like Goin' Home: Portraits in Blues and Rock 'n' Roll*. New York: Outerbridge and Dienstfrey, 1971.

Pegg, Bruce. *Brown-Eyed Handsome Man: The Life and Hard Times of Chuck Berry*. New York: Routledge, 2002.

Swenson, John. *Bill Haley: The Daddy of Rock and Roll*. New York: Stein and Day, 1983.

White, Charles. *The Life and Times of Little Richard*. New York: Pocket Books, 1984.

Watching Elvis

David R. Shumway

> You could make an argument that one of the most socially con-
> scious artists in the second half of this century was Elvis Presley,
> even if he probably didn't start out with any set of political ideas
> he wanted to accomplish. He said, "I'm all shook up and I want to
> shake you up," and that's what happened.
>
> *Bruce Springsteen*

Television was essential to the rise of rock & roll and its transformation of American popular music. Because TV could convey the visual excitement of rock & roll performances, popular music shifted from a primarily aural mass experience to one in which the visual field held equal primacy. Television had a profound impact on everyday life in America; its rapid penetration of American homes was unprecedented, the number of households with TV increasing from 0.66 percent in 1948, to 64 percent in 1955, and to 90 percent by the end of the decade.[1] Moreover, those TVs were fed by national networks, meaning that Americans of all regions experienced the same entertainment simultaneously, or nearly so. Television was thus the major factor in producing what Lynn Spigel has called "an odd sense of connection" in the disconnected new suburbia in which "people could keep their distance from the world but at the same time imagine that their domestic spheres were connected to a wider social fabric."[2] Television kept more people at home and out of taverns and movie theaters, but it gave them more or less the same experiences as their neighbors and counterparts across the nation.

The profound changes wrought by TV are part of a larger transformation of American culture that was occurring during the 1950s. While the decade has long been misunderstood as a period of normalcy from which the United States began to deviate in the 1960s, the idea that the 1950s were placid, or "tranquilized," to quote Robert Lowell, is no longer the standard assumption, and indeed is now considered part of the period's misrecognition of itself.[3] Television played a significant role in disseminating this ideology through situation comedies such as *The Adventures of Ozzie and Harriet* and *Leave It to Beaver*. Popular memory of the decade was later influenced by re-creations such as the film *American Graffiti* (directed by George Lucas, 1973) and the 1970s TV series *Happy Days*. But television was not only a reassuring diversion; it also brought political controversy and the dangers of the Cold War into the living room. [...] [M]ovies became more controversial and politicized during the period, partly in response to the blandness of television entertainment. Television, however, was instrumental in spreading the threat of nuclear war and of a communist conspiracy, even as it was also instrumental in bringing down Senator Joseph McCarthy.[4] Television news brought pictures of the growing civil rights movement into homes throughout the land, helping to fracture the acquiescence of northern whites to segregation in the South. And it was television that made Elvis Presley a national star and the first rock icon.

No one benefited more from television than Elvis, who appeared on national programs at least twelve times from January 1956 to January 1957. This chapter looks at Elvis's televised performances and argues that the controversy he generated had much more to do with what people saw than what they heard. While it is well known that Elvis transgressed racial boundaries that still largely separated white and black culture in the 1950s, his appearance and behavior on the tube also threatened class hierarchies and reminded people that America's youth were defining themselves against adult norms. Elvis redefined popular music stardom by his failure to conform to accepted conventions of performance decorum, and the most threatening aspect of his performance was his violation of gender codes. Elvis crossed gender boundaries in several ways, but it is my contention that his most troubling transgression was to call attention to his body as a sexual object. In the history of mass culture, Elvis may be the first male star to display his body in this way overtly and consistently. In violating this taboo, Elvis became, like most women but unlike most men, sexualized. In adopting an explicitly sexualized self-representation, Elvis played out the implications of becoming the object of the gaze. In so doing, he both exploited and provoked cultural anxiety over the changing construction of gender.

The Fraught Fifties

The strong reactions to Elvis, both positive and negative, show that social divisions that had previously been taken for granted were now coming into question. The most fraught division in the 1950s was race. In 1954, the U.S. Supreme Court ruled in *Brown v. Board of Education* that segregated public schools were unconstitutional. That decision "marked the dawn of the modern civil rights movement and a new phase of mass black struggle in the southern states and beyond."[5] Elvis Presley famously was a white singer who sounded black, as Sam Phillips, the man who first recorded him, recognized. In the early 1950s, the popular music world was nearly as segregated as southern schools. "In 1950, for example, only three records which made the national Rhythm and Blues charts also crossed over into the pop field."[6] Beginning in 1954, however, R&B records began to have significant impact on the pop charts. So just as Jim Crow laws began to come under threat legally, musical apartheid also began to break down. Neither the Brown decision nor increased white interest in black music caused an immediate reaction, but by 1956, "throughout the South, opposition to black and black derived styles of music quickly escalated."[7] One factor in this was the "improved chart performance of original black recordings against white covers," while another "was the enormous commercial success of Elvis Presley."[8]

That whites would be troubled by the popularity of black entertainers is perhaps not surprising, but the long history of minstrelsy suggests that whites performing in black styles should not have been threatening. Yet as Eric Lott has observed in his study of blackface entertainment, "Certain kinds of cultural conquest—Jackie Robinson's entrance in major league baseball, Elvis Presley's explicit dismantling of 'racial' music—are far from harmless allowances on the part of white-supremacist capital."[9] And Elvis clearly did threaten—and not just southerners. One difference is that nothing in Elvis's performance suggests that he was mocking his black sources. Had he appeared in blackface and used an exaggerated African American dialect, his act would have been familiar and unthreatening. As it was, Elvis's performance seemed more like an homage to black music than a parody of it, largely because his approach was not mere imitation. The black songs he recorded he made his own, just as his vocal style was a distinctive reworking of black and white influences. Had white supremacy not appeared to be under attack, perhaps none of that would have mattered, but under the circumstances, Elvis stood for the "mongrel" culture that racists feared.

The threat posed by Elvis's transgression of the racial divide was exacerbated by his violation of the class divide. Although offspring of the white working class had long dominated American popular music, they seldom retained a distinct class identity. They adopted middle-class or even bourgeois dress and manners, reflecting the upward mobility of which their success became emblematic. Elvis, on the contrary, showed no inclination—or maybe lacked the ability—to hide his class origins. He all too clearly remained the son of a "common laborer" from Tupelo. While most other early rock & rollers, black and white, observed concert conventions of performance attire, wearing suits and ties, if not tuxedos, Elvis dressed somewhat but noticeably down. He typically sported tight pants and pointy-toed boots. He often did not wear a tie or suit, and when he did wear a suit it was not something you would expect to see on a banker. More important, his pompadour hairstyle, long sideburns, and pouty demeanor made him look like someone from the other side of the tracks. This was especially troubling because his music appealed to young people of all classes and America was then in the midst of a juvenile delinquency crisis that was blamed on, among other causes, the evil influence of the mass media.[10]

Like race and gender, the traditional class divisions were being challenged, as the working class benefited from the new power of labor unions. Where classes were once separated by neighborhoods, the large-scale exodus of workers to the suburbs produced the mixing of classes and seemed to portend the leveling of class distinctions. High schools, which once were safe havens for middle-class youth, became increasingly populated by working-class kids now encouraged—or forced—to stay in school, and the consequences were illustrated in the film *Blackboard Jungle* (1954), featuring the first rock & roll hit, Bill Haley and the Comets' "Rock Around the Clock." As another film, *Rebel without a Cause* (1955) revealed, the juvenile delinquency crisis represented the fear that middle-class youth were beginning to behave like those of the lower classes. The recently coined term *teenager* reveals the breakdown of previously assumed class distinctions. "The middle-class adolescent and the juvenile delinquent from the 'the other half' had once functioned as a normative binary, with clear class and ethnic lines separating them. The teenager, however, could not be so easily distinguished from the juvenile delinquent, for s/he had incorporated a degree of freedom from adult supervision previously associated with lower-class youth."[11] The very fact that teenagers bought Elvis's records was an indication to worried parents of the dangers of this new freedom.

Elvis's challenge to racial boundaries is well known, and his class associations are unlikely to come as a surprise. His challenge to gender norms, however, was largely unremarked at the time. The 1950s have traditionally been characterized by a reversion to prewar patterns, and they are sometimes said to have imposed even more rigid limits than had been typical of the 1920s and 1930s. But Beth Bailey, Barbara Ehrenreich, and others have observed important changes in the construction of sexuality and gender during the 1950s and noted the cultural tensions and anxieties that these changes produced. One change is the development of what has been called "a highly sexualized society," in which "the number of explicitly sexual references in the mass media doubled between 1950 and 1960." Yet it was a society that continued to demand that "teen and preteen girls ... be not only 'good' and 'pure' but to be the enforcers of purity within their teen society."[12] Thus conditions were ripe for these girls to participate in communal fantasies that were at once sexually charged but not sexually explicit. Such fantasies are the stuff that fueled Elvis's rise.

It was not just teens who felt confusion, however. Changes in the social relations of the genders produced a crisis of gender roles. During the war a large number of women entered what had been a largely male workforce, threatening the definition of masculinity, which was also called into question because an increasing number of men found themselves in a job and in a home life that did not permit them to exhibit such masculine qualities as power, dominance, aggression, and ambition.[13] These changes permitted and were abetted by an increasing awareness that gender was not a natural expression of biology. The notion that gender is a cultural construction was spread in popularized form, at least partly as a result of equally popularized versions of Sigmund Freud. The result was a perception of the "fragility of gender," which was given expression in a deluge of articles about a "crisis of American masculinity" that in turn often seemed to be caused by a crisis in femininity.

The crisis—or crises—was attributed to two causes. The first had to do with the changing roles men played in American society. Previously, masculinity had been identified with independence and aggression, and it had been given its own spaces in society, the many forms of work and leisure that excluded women. According to Bailey, however, "In the postwar era Americans were coming to grips with changes in their economy and society that, they feared, had rendered 'traditional' masculinity obsolete and threatened the vitality of American culture. In the world of the corporation, the 'organization,' men needed different qualities to succeed. Teamwork, conformity, cooperation, the 'social ethic'—these were functional behaviors for corporate success. But they were traditional *feminine* behaviors—the antithesis of aggressive masculinity. To continue to provide well for his family, many feared, a man would have to act like a woman."[14] It was not just men's roles that were changing, however. In spite of the postwar ideological effort to return women to traditional roles, there were more married women in the labor force of the 1950s than before the war.[15] As more women entered the economy, critics charged "that women were robbing men of their masculinity by adopting masculine (aggressive) roles." These changes threatened three perquisites the American male had assumed as his right: his role as economic provider, his separate subculture of work and leisure, and aggressiveness, the definitive character of masculinity itself. As Bailey notes, there is a crisis of femininity implicit here: "The fragility of gender was the root of the trouble. The necessary barriers had broken down and women were exercising too much power—whether by stifling masculinity or by assuming masculine traits themselves."[16]

The Male Star as Object of the Gaze

The very perception that gender roles are fragile both made Elvis's transgressions all the more threatening and made them a cultural force that others would exploit. Elvis crossed gender boundaries in several ways, but it is my contention that his most troubling violation was to call attention to his body as a sexual object, which initiated a certain kind of visual presentation of male rock & roll stars that I call feminization. Not all rock stars exhibit themselves in this way, but enough have—and they represent a relatively wide spectrum of rock forms—that feminization cannot be regarded as merely an accident of individual expression. To say that rock stars have been feminized is to say that in their appearance and performance they have violated traditional male gender codes by adopting some that are normally female codes. But feminization does not, as Marjorie Garber contends, render Elvis a transvestite.[17] Transvestism, or female impersonation, might be seen as one extreme toward which feminization has developed, but the phenomenon on which I will focus here is not mainly a matter of cross-dressing. Elvis and other feminized rock stars retain many traditionally male characteristics in their appearance and behavior. They remain, for example, aggressive and even violent in their performances. Thus such cross-dressers as David Bowie or Boy George should not be understood primarily as examples of feminization, although the phenomenon might explain the conditions for their public acceptance. Transvestite rock has been more directly influenced by gay subcultures.

In describing Elvis's feminization, my aim is to try to account for the process in terms of a violation of a gender distinction that is at least as fundamental as dress but much more subtle: my claim is that Elvis becomes feminized because he displays his body as a sexualized object. The feminized rock star does not pretend to be a woman but rather takes up some of the markers usually reserved for women. As a result the rocker is perceived as feminine because of the rigidity of the gender system; were it not so rigid, he might be perceived as redefining masculinity. Moreover, unlike the transvestite, the rock star may or may not be aware that he is transgressing gender codes. Elvis, I think, was largely unaware that his performances violated a gender boundary. That may be because Elvis's violation was not so much his behavior but the relation of that behavior to the gaze, a relation that Elvis might not have comprehended, though later rock stars made explicit use of it.

Some of Garber's case for Elvis as a cross-dresser does refer to his costumes—his use of eye shadow, his 1950s gold-lamé suit, and his 1970s jumpsuit (though, of these, only eye shadow is unambiguously feminine). But much of it rests on the perception of Elvis's feminization. As she puts it, "Critic after critic notices that his sexuality is subject to reassignment. ... This male sex symbol is insistently and paradoxically read by the culture as a boy, a eunuch, or a 'woman'— anything but a man."[18] The issue, as we will see, is even more complicated than Garber makes it, since Elvis is often perceived not merely as a man but as something of a superman. In spite of this, Elvis has been feminized. Biographer Albert Goldman offers the most extreme expression of this, providing Garber with an image of Elvis in his Las Vegas jumpsuit as a transvestite successor to Marlene Dietrich.[19] Goldman himself describes Elvis's postarmy appearance on a television program with Frank Sinatra as "queer. ... When he confronts the smaller but more masculine Sinatra, Elvis's body language flashes, 'I surrender, dear.'"[20] Goldman's view is suspect, because he is an "Elvis debunker" and because his reading reflects the perceptions of 1981 far more than it does those of 1956. If few in the 1950s perceived Elvis as a "woman," he did seem in some odd way feminine.

I understand the gaze as a power relation or as a sign of that relation. One instantiation of male dominance exists in the unequal exchange of looks that men and women direct at each other. As many theorists have argued and empirical studies have demonstrated, men gaze at women far more often than the reverse.[21] This fact of social behavior is represented, enacted, and reinforced in all forms of visual media. The propensity for male film characters to gaze at their female counterparts is well known, and feminist film scholars since Laura Mulvey have argued persuasively that the camera's gaze usually duplicates the male character's, so that the female is the object of the viewer's gaze as well.[22] But we also have the history of painting and still photography, especially advertising, where women's bodies are displayed to sell everything from women's clothing to motor oil. As John Berger puts it, "Men look at women. Women watch themselves being looked at."[23] The power relations implied in this gaze are not a matter of voyeurism, at least as it has been defined in the psychoanalytic tradition. It is not the illusion of a surreptitious control that the gaze enacts; it is, rather, a direct assertion of dominance. The gaze is a gesture that, in modern American and European societies, is similar to gestures in animal social groups that mark and reinforce their hierarchical relations.

The gaze does more than merely assert simple dominance, however. By demarcating the female body as sexual, the gaze is central to the construction of sexuality. It is not just the one-way direction of the gaze that matters but that the female body is gazed at precisely as a sexualized object. My point here is that to be gazed at as a sexualized object is to be put into a role that until recently only women have played in our culture. As Steve Neale has observed, when males are presented as the object of an erotic look, as Rock Hudson is in Sirk's melodramas, the male's "body is *feminized* ... an indication of the strength of those conventions that dictate that only women can function as objects of an explicitly erotic gaze."[24] The image or persona that many male rock stars present in performance is the product of the same process of feminization. In other words, these stars have been constructed by dominant relations of visibility.

The cinema, however, is a place where rupture in these relations could occur. Merely to be represented, to act in a film, is already to step to the other side of the gaze. Most male stars in Hollywood cinema have avoided feminization by controlling the look within the filmic narrative. As Mulvey has explained, the camera's point of view is associated with the male hero, and the audience is thereby made to identify with his gaze.[25] Moreover, male movie stars typically played roles that conformed to ideas of traditional masculinity. Rudolph Valentino, however, does represent a rupture in visual relations. His appeal, according to Miriam Hansen, depends "on the manner in which he combines masculine control of the look with the feminine quality of 'to-be-looked-at-ness.' ... To the extent that Valentino occupies the position of primary object of spectacle, this entails a systematic feminization of his persona."[26] Outside of his films, in photographs and performances as a dancer, Valentino was even more feminized, because in these he lacks the masculine control of the look and his body becomes solely the object of the gaze.[27] Like later rock stars, however, Valentino insisted on his masculinity, even to the point of challenging to fight anyone who questioned it.

Valentino, though, is the exception rather than the rule. We can find instances of male stars' bodies as objects of the gaze in the films of the classic period, but they are not common. Clark Gable, for example, does something of a striptease for Claudette Colbert in *It Happened One Night,* but this scene must be read against his dominance, in visual and all other relations, in the rest of the film. Only the faces of male stars are regularly the objects of the camera's gaze during the classic period of Hollywood, yet the convention dictates that a male face will appear to be watching someone else, revealing spiritual depth or intellectual activity. Cary Grant may have defined a certain image of the handsome male, and as such was certainly an object of desire, but seemingly without our noticing anything in particular about his body except his face.

Jon Savage points out that, after Valentino, James Dean is the next instance of a major male star who is presented as the object of the gaze and who, like Valentino, became the object of cult worship. In *Rebel without a Cause* Dean was the "uncanny enactment of 'the passivity of the adored object' that was the new condition of male stardom. Masculinity was now being defined by the female gaze."[28] But it is precisely "masculinity" that is put in question by this relationship.

Savage describes Dean's sexuality in that film as "highly androgynous," which is to acknowledge Dean's feminization.[29] That both the Sal Mineo and the Natalie Wood characters appear to take Dean as an object of desire only reinforces this feminization. If being the object of the female gaze is feminizing, then a fortiori, so is being the object of the male gaze.

Valentino, Dean, and Elvis are routinely described as androgynous, but that problematic term deserves a bit of digression. A simple definition of the word is the combination of male and female in one being, and the dictionary gives *hermaphroditic* as a synonym. The latter term, however, is most often applied to the existence of both male and female genital organs in the same individual, whether such an arrangement is functional and biologically normal, as in earthworms, or is a nonfunctional defect, as in humans. Androgyny, on the other hand, is most often applied to the appearance and, less frequently, the behavior of people and thus concerns secondary sexual traits such as beards or breasts. Yet the term is often used as if physical features beyond these were also sexually differentiated. Thus Valentino is said to have a feminine face, while Elvis Presley and Mick Jagger are said to have female eyes or lips. In this conception, androgyny seems to be, like hermaphroditism, a kind of birth defect. Dean's androgyny, however, doesn't fit this model. His face and body are quite ordinary in their appearance and his blue jeans and T-shirts are usually markers of masculinity; nor is his behavior stereotypically feminine. It is, rather, that Dean's body is displayed for others, that it has "to-be-looked-at-ness," which leads us to experience him as androgynous. Similarly, a rock star's lips become a gender marker because of the way they are constituted in visual relations.

Valentino and Dean were cult objects of desire, but their onscreen sexualization is relatively subtle. Neither prepares us for Elvis Presley, who was a fan of both, nor does Frank Sinatra, who had a following of teenage girls in the 1940s. Because Elvis's androgyny, like Dean's, cannot be ascribed to dress or to what we would normally call feminine gestures, it can only be produced by his position within the structure of the gaze. Yet the passive/active opposition that has been held to structure the politics of looking in narrative films cannot operate in the same way in the concert setting. The singer is both active and passive, an object of adoration and at the same time someone engaged in demanding physical work. To be the object of mass adoration confers a sense of enormous power on the star. That power compensates to some extent for the lack of the control of the look, but it does so only ambiguously, for as Sue Wise has pointed out, the star is precisely an object to his fans and is thus in their power.[30] Moreover, "to be a performer is to be at one's most vulnerable."[31] Unlike most male stars, but like Valentino and Dean, Elvis consistently revealed that vulnerability.

Elvis on Television

The major factor in Elvis's feminization was the sexual suggestiveness of his dancing. This dancing was a source of shock when it was first presented on national TV. Yet it is important to keep in mind that when Elvis was performing in small clubs in the South, his dancing provoked no outrage. Even his first TV appearances on the Dorsey Brothers' *Stage Show*, which included some of his dancing, produced little outcry, perhaps because the shows were seen by smaller audiences or because Elvis's dancing was shot from a high angle, lasted for only a short time, and was relatively tame. But after Elvis's performance of "Hound Dog" on the *Milton Berle Show* in June 1956, things changed. One difference was that the TV cameras met Elvis head-on. Another is that he performed without a guitar, and as his biographer describes it,

> Perhaps to make up for its absence he seemed to have carefully worked out new moves, wrists splayed out almost limply in seeming contrast to the ferocity of his vocal attack, fingers fluttering, arms outspread. With Scotty's solo, he lurches backward in what might be interpreted as an upbeat adaptation of the shrugging, stuttering, existential hopelessness of a James Dean, there is a jittery fiddling with his mouth and nose, and as the song comes to an end he is dragging the microphone down to the floor, staggering almost to his knees. ... He points at the audience and declares emphatically, *You* ain't nothin' but a hound dog, then goes into his patented half-time ending, gripping the mike, circling it sensuously, jackknifing his legs out as the audience half-scream, half laughs, and he laughs too—it is clearly all in good fun.[32]

Those in the TV studio that day may have experienced Elvis's performance as good fun, but many in the television audience did not. Elvis had given them a little peek at what they might have witnessed in a Beale Street club, and they were not amused. The reaction of both professional critics and of self-appointed guardians of morality was swift and harsh. According to *New York Times* critic Jack Gould, "He is a rock-and-roll variation on one of the most standard acts in show business: the virtuoso of the hootchy-kootchy. His one specialty is an accented movement of the body that heretofore has been primarily identified with the repertoire of the blonde bombshells of the burlesque runway."[33] *Life* called him "a disturbing kind of idol," and *Look* called him "vulgar."[34] The reaction went beyond Elvis to encompass all rock & roll, the live performance of which was banned by cities from Santa Cruz, California, to Jersey City.[35]

Although from a ratings point of view, "the broadcast was an unmitigated success," the negative reactions had an impact.[36] The public outcry nearly caused NBC to drop Elvis's next scheduled appearance on the *Steve Allen Show*. Rather than cancel the appearance, however, the network devised a plan to contain Elvis. Allen dressed him up in tails and had him sing "Hound Dog" to a live basset hound—while standing more or less still. Later in the same year, Elvis was restrained by court order from making any offensive gyrations onstage in Jacksonville, Florida. Early in 1957, in what was Elvis's third appearance on his show, Ed Sullivan insisted that Elvis be photographed only from the waist up.

Figure 2.1 Elvis performs "Hound Dog" on the *Milton Berle Show*, with D. J. Fontana and Bill Black, 1956. (courtesy Photofest)

Why did Elvis's dancing cause such an outcry? People were not used to seeing such overt male self-display. Precursors, such as Valentino, whose dance performances and still photographs were read in much the same way, reached relatively few viewers when compared either to Valentino's more conventional film roles or Elvis's television performances. Fred Astaire, Gene Kelly, and other film dancers also bear comparison to Elvis, and Steven Cohan has argued that song-and-dance men were feminized as a result of the way they displayed their bodies before the camera.[37] Yet Astaire and his ilk never produced the cultural anxieties that Elvis did. While the dancer's body is much more the object of the gaze than that of the dramatic leading man, he is not presented as the object of an explicitly sexual gaze. In part this is because a song-and-dance man like Astaire usually played a conventional male role in the films in which he danced. More important, however, the dancing itself is a highly conventionalized spectacle, the performance of which is understood as an art or craft of which the dancer is master. Moreover, the dancer's body is usually covered in formal wear or other conventional garb, making it much less the object of the gaze than is the male ballet dancer's. In fact, the song-and-dance man's dance diverts attention from his body as a sexual object, perhaps in the same way that athletic contests can display men's (and women's) bodies without such display being perceived as sexual.[38]

Figure 2.2 Disciplined Elvis on Steve Allen with bassett hound, 1956. (courtesy Photofest)

But if Elvis represents a break with male performance in mass culture, it does not mean that he invented the style of performance he displayed. On the contrary, there is good reason to believe that Elvis's dancing, like his singing, was an adaptation of black performers' styles. T-Bone Walker and Wynonie Harris are often mentioned as precursors. Harris's producer, Henry Glover, said, "When you saw Elvis, you were seein' a mild version of Wynonie."[39] Some who knew Elvis in his prerecording days say that he learned his style from performers on Memphis's Beale Street: "He would watch the colored singers, understand me, and then got to doing it the same way as them. He got that shaking, that wiggle, from Charlie Burse ... right there at the Gray Mule on Beale. Elvis, he wasn't doing nothing but what the colored people had been doing for the last hundred years."[40] The question of just what, if anything, Elvis did bring to this style can probably never be settled, because the black musicians whom he imitated were seldom filmed. But that is my point. Black blues musicians were part of a subculture; their music did reach a mass audience, but their live performances did not. What distinguished Elvis's performances was that they were televised, and, in the cases of the *Milton Berle Show* and *Ed Sullivan Show,* they were watched by enormous audiences consisting mainly of whites who had never seen R&B singers perform.

It was not just the size or racial composition of the audience that is significant here, however. The context in which Elvis performed gave the dancing he learned from black performers a new meaning, as did the persona he developed in collaboration with his manager, Colonel Tom

Parker, and the entertainment industry. It is first worth considering what that persona was not. Elvis did not present himself as a typical blues or R&B figure. Elvis did not cultivate the image of a sexual athlete or lady-killer as Wynonie Harris, Robert Johnson, and Muddy Waters had in different ways. The lyrics to the latter's most famous songs—"Mannish Boy," "I'm Your Hoochie Coochie Man," "Rollin' Stone," "I'm Ready"—are celebrations of the singer's sexual prowess that brag about both his conquests and his abilities. There is not a hint in these songs of the vulnerability characteristic of many blues songs, including those of Johnson. Johnson's persona developed less in his lyrics than in his behavior and in the legends that spread after his death. By virtue of his reputed pact with the devil, Johnson *was* the hoochie coochie man whom Muddy Waters merely sang about. Elvis, on the other hand, was in his early years the antithesis of such Faustian characters. The lyrics of his major early hits almost invariably present a wounded or vulnerable lover—"Heartbreak Hotel," "Don't Be Cruel," "I Want You, I Need You, I Love You," "Love Me Tender." Big Mama Thornton's "Hound Dog" was, in her version, the female equivalent of a Muddy Waters song. Elvis's version of the Jerry Leiber and Mike Stoller song, on the other hand, doesn't transform the material back into the male original (as Rufus Thomas had in "Bear Cat"). Elvis's "Hound Dog" is best understood as an inspired piece of scat singing or as a novelty song, sexual in attitude or presentation but not in content. The failure to occupy an unambiguous male subject position here corresponds to other, less subtle violations of the gender system we find in Elvis's visual presentation.

Elvis borrowed his performance style from another kind of blues—that of the singers and shouters who had fronted for bands—but he didn't imitate their personas, either. Wynonie Harris, for example, was explicit about the image he used to attract women: "I play to create impressions," Harris said, "women can get stirred up by a man who seems cruel, ornery, vulgar, and arrogant."[41] Charlie Gillett describes the performances of blues shouters, such as Harris and Joe Turner as "intimate, relaxed, loaded with sexual references and suggestive plays on words." "But it wasn't just the words—the whole character of the shouted blues was adult, in the tone of voice used by the singers, the assumptions behind the songs, and the sophistication of the musical arrangements."[42] Although Elvis may not have been at first understood mainly as a teen performer, it quickly became apparent that teenagers would be his major market. Cause and effect are hard to disentangle here, and we can't safely assert either that Elvis's persona was designed to attract his teen audience or that the audience was attracted to a persona that emerged without conscious design. In any case, some elements of Harris's style—orneriness, vulgarity—doubtless appealed to teens, and we find these in Elvis's performance. Nevertheless, Elvis does not act cruel in spite of the aggression of his performances, and he certainly doesn't come across as the sophisticated and insinuating adult. Innocence, rather, is the dominant characteristic of the Elvis of the 1950s. That quality has been apparent to many interpreters of his music, for example, Peter Guralnick on "That's All Right," Elvis's first release from Sun Records: "It sounds easy, unforced, joyous, spontaneous. It sounds as if the singer had broken free for the first time in his life. The voice soars with a purity and innocence."[43] In his seminal essay, "Elvis: Presliad," Greil Marcus describes Elvis in much the same terms that Richard Dyer would later apply to Marilyn Monroe: "Elvis embodies ... a delight in sex that is sometimes simple, sometimes complex, but always open."[44]

This side of Elvis may have gotten lost in the late 1960s, when the first generation of rock critics described him as if he were the white incarnation of the bluesman's sexuality. This reading of Elvis ignores not only the image he presented in his music but his larger public persona as well. "The official Elvis," as Guralnick observes, is marked by "modesty, ... deferential charm, [and] the soft-spoken assumption of commonsense virtues."[45] One sees this Elvis much in evidence in the TV appearances of the period, in the still photos, and the interviews. And, there is a particular sense of vulnerability to Elvis, especially in the way he responds to various figures of authority, such as television host Steve Allen. On Allen's show, Elvis was being disciplined by being made to perform as a clown, and he responded to the humiliation with perfect submission. Compare Mick Jagger's mocking expression while singing bowdlerized lyrics to "Let's Spend the Night Together" on the *Ed Sullivan Show* in 1967. Unlike the Rolling Stones or the Beatles, Elvis always seems to play the good son to the show business fathers, respecting their authority rather than mocking or challenging it.

Whether or not this official Elvis is a contrivance, it fit perfectly Tom Parker's plans for the star. As various accounts of Elvis's career assert, Parker's goal was to make him a pop singer. It would, after all, have been impossible in 1955 for him to want to make Elvis a rock & roll star, since such a career path did not yet exist. Thus if the teen audience was to be Elvis's base, the peak he would try to reach would be a mass audience of the white middle class of all ages. His early, unsuccessful appearance in Las Vegas is a testimony to that plan, as is the mixture of material Elvis recorded, including an album of Christmas songs. Such a career plan precluded Elvis from producing a persona to match his R&B performance style, and may have contributed to perceptions of his feminization.

Elvis's performance style must be understood in terms of the social and cultural environment that would produce such a career plan. The mass audience had a very narrow range of expectations about male sexuality, and it did not include any overt form of self-display; that mode was reserved for women. But television would also change the perception of the sort of performances a Wynonie Harris or a T-Bone Walker might perform in a nightclub. In a club setting, there is more interaction between the audience and the performer, and the performer is less the center of attention. The patrons may be more engaged in other activities than they are in watching the musicians, and their own dancing especially would render the performer more a part of an event than the event itself. Even in a concert setting—which was relatively rare for blues or R&B performances—a singer or bandleader is no more than the most important point of attention, and he or she never consumes the entire visual field. On television, however, the performer becomes not merely the center of attention but often its sole object. In other words, as a television performer, Elvis was the object of a much more focused and intense gaze than his predecessors had been. Elvis was not merely introducing a style with which whites were unfamiliar, he was using that style under conditions that transformed its cultural significance.

Contemporary commentators revealed by their descriptions of Elvis that they were aware that this display violated gender codes. The terms in which Elvis's performance was discussed are ones usually applied to striptease: for example, "bumping and grinding." By the middle of 1956, the time of the *Milton Berle Show* performance, he had already been given the nickname "the pelvis," a name that of course means what it doesn't say. What is it that is not being said? The standard answer is "the phallus," but unlike performances by some later male stars, in these TV performances at least the penis itself is not emphasized. Elvis's costume, which includes a jacket, hides, rather than displays, his genitals, and while there are stories about Elvis stuffing his pants to make himself look well endowed, the television performances reveal none of this. Rock critics in the late 1960s often celebrated what they saw as his prodigious endowment, and these claims at best reflect the way adolescent male fans of the 1950s might have interpreted Elvis. What contemporary adult audiences saw in Elvis's performance was not his parts but the whole. His motions suggested intercourse, and his performance was read as a public display of "sex." Elvis thus put the "sex" that the name "rock & roll" described explicitly into his performance. But in presenting himself as an object of sexual incitement or excitation, he violated not just Victorian morality—which was no longer hegemonic—but more importantly the taboo against male sexual display. In violating this taboo, Elvis became, like most women but unlike most men, sexualized. Women are routinely sexualized. Various parts of women's bodies—for example, hair, legs, breasts—become loci of sexualization; women's fashion always calls attention to these features, which are presented for the male gaze and thus mark the woman as a sexual object. While women are the most sexually marked group, some men are marked in different, lesser degrees. Gay men are perhaps the most marked, but black men are more sexually marked than white men. This last point suggests that if a black man had performed on television in the same way as Elvis, it might not have been met with the same response.

There is, however, one aspect of these early television performances that might have caused the largely white audience to be even more outraged had the performer been black: the pictures of white teenage girls losing control under the influence of the performer. Elvis's "effect" on young girls threatened those men who assumed that young girls needed to be protected, both from sex in general and from its expression in questionable characters like Elvis in particular. According to one narrative, Elvis made his "pelvic gyrations" a regular part of his act after female members of his audiences screamed and applauded at them.[46] Photos of one of these early performances already show young women in various states of rapture while watching Elvis perform. When Elvis is featured on major national TV programs, the audience becomes part of the show. In the *Milton Berle Show* performance, the film cuts between the stage and the audience, the latter presented not as a large mass of indistinguishable faces but of particular faces whose response tells us of the excitement the performer is generating. This editing also reinforces Elvis as the object of a specifically sexual gaze. It is not just an audience, of which each viewer is a member, that is watching Elvis. Rather, television or newsreel viewers experience Elvis as the object of the gaze of the (almost exclusively female) individuals who scream, faint, and otherwise enact ecstasy. This representation of Elvis is formally equivalent to the shot/reverse shot editing that structures the gaze in narrative cinema. It becomes a standard trope of the representation of rock and will be repeated numerous times during the British invasion of the '60s.

Now it may seem that the logic of my argument would lead inevitably to the claim that these girls who watch Elvis are masculinized by their place in the visual hierarchy, but the pictures themselves prohibit one from following this line of reasoning. The point is made clearer if we compare these screaming, ecstatic teenage girls to the familiar representations of male audiences watching striptease. The latter enact voyeurism; rather than expressing their desire, and thus their lack of control, these men sit impassively or they make jokes to relieve the embarrassment of experiencing sexual excitement in the company of other men. Thus the very expressiveness of these rock fans defines them as female, whatever they are read to be expressing. Often it was that most "female" of all emotions, hysteria.

The visual relation between fan and star under these conditions is ambiguous. The star remains an object of the fan's gaze and thus vulnerable to her, but the fan's visible response is

Figure 2.3 Elvis was the object of the gaze of ecstatic female fans, 1956. (courtesy Photofest)

apparently produced by the star and thus in his control. This ambiguity made Elvis all the more threatening, for he seemed, like alcohol, to cause girls to lose their proper inhibitions. This reading of Elvis and his fans can only come from the outside, for the fans themselves do not feel driven. But one might also argue that the girls who watched Elvis or the Beatles and screamed out their adoration were exercising agency, both in their choice of object and in their insistence on making themselves seen and heard. Sue Wise describes her Elvis as a "Teddy Bear" for whom she felt affection rather than desire.[47] She argues that Elvis was "an *object* of his fans," rather than the all-powerful subject that both adult opponents and male adolescent fans assumed him to be.[48] In fact, fans do behave as if Elvis and other rock stars are objects over which they exercise some control. Simon Frith argues that "the power struggle between stars and fans is what gives concerts their sexual charge."[49] The rock star becomes a fetish, not in the psychoanalytic sense, but in the root sense of an object believed to have magical power. To the fan, the star as fetish has power for her, not over her. How else do we explain the enormous market for trinkets carrying names or likenesses of Elvis or other stars? In Elvis's case, the process has gone so far that he now seems quite literally to be deified.

Elvis was not the only rock star to violate gender codes in the 1950s. Little Richard emerged from gay subculture to be billed as the "queen of rock & roll," but Richard's race made him less threatening, not only because black men were already more sexualized, but also because the color line kept him out of the center of public attention. Furthermore, consciousness of Richard's sexual orientation was low among the white teen audience for his work. The gay themes of his lyrics were either expunged ("Tutti Frutti") or lost ("Long Tall Sally") on the straight audience.[50] Elvis's example created new possibilities for male performers, but it took a few years for these possibilities to be realized. Perhaps the first expressions were the teen idols, which the entertainment industry marketed as "safe Elvises." Performers such as Frankie Avalon, Bobby Rydell, and Fabian were essentially male pinups, that is, objects to be gazed at, but little in their behavior or appearance—except their passivity—realized the feminine position this placed them in. They were safe because their sexualization was relatively minor, and their appeal was explicitly likened to the "matinee idols" of the cinema. Yet this comparison does not adequately reflect the passivity that the role of teen idol entailed. Without fictional roles with which they could be identified, and even without great success making or selling records, the teen idols were little more than objects to be gazed at.

The Elvis Generation

If adults felt that Elvis threatened a social order built on racial, class, and gender hierarchies, Elvis's teenage fans were attracted to him both because they were less invested in them and because they liked the idea of upsetting their parents. Of course, they found Elvis appealing for other reasons as well. They certainly liked the music and the way he performed it. But Elvis also served as a symbol of what might be termed a new or newly significant social division, the generational one. The invention of the category "teenager" corresponded to a growing sense of age-group identity among those it named. While "youth" had first been named an identity group in the 1920s, it referred to an older group who belonged to a much narrower socioeconomic stratum. The typical twenties youth was a college student or recent graduate, and the image was defined by F. Scott Fitzgerald, both personally and in his novel about Princeton, *This Side of Paradise*. This group rejected some of the manners and morals of their parents, but they did not otherwise have a politics. Moreover, the "flaming youth" of the twenties burned out by the end of the decade, and the Depression and World War II would inhibit the formation of a significant new youth identity until the late 1940s.

Unlike the 1920s youth, the postwar teenager was invented for political reasons, and the concept had a political edge from the start. The term was first used in 1945 by Eliot Cohen in an article called "A Teen-Age Bill of Rights."[51] It was a response to the greater independence that the war had thrust upon teens, who, with dad off at war and mom working outside the home, had less parental supervision and who themselves joined the workforce in large numbers. The response of Cohen and other experts of the era was to urge parental and societal recognition of "the growing capacity for autonomy in the teen years." Leerom Medovoi argues that "the 'Teen-Age Bill of Rights' ... petitions its readers to honor and respect youth as *the embodiment of emergent identity*," and he argues that the meaning of "teenager" was tied up with American ideology articulated against both fascism and communism.[52] The category of teenager then involved an identity politics right from the start.

It must be stipulated, however, that teenagers in the 1950s were unlikely to have been conscious of having a generational politics. The idea that the 1950s was a period of quietude and conformity is not without foundation. The Cold War, McCarthyism, and the ideology of domesticity all restricted the range of overt political activities among all age groups, but especially among the young. However, the cohort most aptly described as conformist were those who would have entered college in the 1950s, while younger teens—those whose identity would have been most strongly shaped by the idea of the teenager—went on to become the campus rebels of the 1960s. It is these younger teens who were Elvis's most devoted fans, and what they developed could be said to be an identity in search of a politics. This identity was shaped as much by the experience of being part of new consumer group, the target of specialized products and advertising aimed at attracting a new source of disposable income. It was in the 1950s that teenagers became the most reliable movie audience, and as media historian Thomas Doherty has shown, the industry responded to this change by producing teenpics, films designed to appeal especially to it. Such specialized marketing strengthened teenage identity.[53]

Elvis was arguably the single most important product marketed to 1950s teenagers, but he was also their most important figure of group identification. James Dean had preceded Elvis and had influenced him, but his brief career as a movie star meant that Dean would reach a much smaller audience. Moreover, since his character was mediated through film narrative, he would never have the immediate rapport with his fans that Elvis did when he performed. The adult reaction against Elvis meant that identifying with him was a marker of generational difference.

Television brought Elvis into the living room and created immediate generational conflict where previously there had been agreement. In his history of the New Left, Todd Gitlin explains:

> For those of us who were ten or twelve when Elvis Presley came along, it was rock 'n' roll that named us a generation. The shift was abrupt and amazing. One moment parents and children were listening together to the easygoing likes of Dean Martin's "Memories Are Made of This," of Rosemary Clooney's "Hey There" ("you with the stars in your eyes"), and gathering together on Saturday night to watch the regulars of *Your Hit Parade* cover the week's hits; the next, the spectacle of crooners trying to simulate Elvis Presley and straddle the widening cultural chasm was too laughable to behold. … Popular music often serves to insulate young people against the authority of the previous generation, and the commercial search for the Latest makes generation tension over music virtually automatic. But in rock's heyday there was a special intensity on both sides. On one side, generational defiance: "Hail hail rock 'n' roll / Deliver me from days of old" (Chuck Berry); "Rock and Roll is here to stay" (Danny and the Juniors). On the other: Perry Como, Patti Page, Tony Bennett, adult fear and loathing.[54]

Elvis was the most important symbol of this divide, and one could argue that he was awarded the title "King of Rock & Roll" for that reason. In challenging the old social divisions, Elvis became the central figure in a newly important one. The generational chasm would only widen in the 1960s, as generational identity became the basis for a political movement. The iconicity of the other stars in this book is dependent on youth as a political and cultural identity.

Notes

1 Gary R. Edgerton, *The Columbia History of American Television* (New York: Columbia University Press, 2007), 103, 107.

2 Lynn Spigel, *Make Room for TV: Television and the Family Ideal in Postwar America* (Chicago: University of Chicago Press, 1992), 101.

3 Robert Lowell, "Memories of West Street and Lepke," in *Life Studies* (New York: Farrar, Straus, 1956).

4 Thomas Doherty, *Cold War, Cool Medium: Television, McCarthyism, and American Culture* (New York: Columbia University Press, 2003).

5 Brian Ward, *Just My Soul Responding: Rhythm and Blues, Black Consciousness, and Race Relations* (Berkeley: University of California Press, 1998), 2.

6 Ibid., 19.

7 Ibid., 105.

8 Ibid., 109.

9 Eric Lott, *Love and Theft: Blackface Minstrelsy and the American Working Class* (New York: Oxford University Press, 1993), 103.

10 James Gilbert, *A Cycle of Outrage: America's Reaction to the Juvenile Delinquent in the 1950s* (New York: Oxford University Press, 1986).

11 Leerom Medovoi, *Rebels: Youth and the Cold War Origins of Identity* (Durham, NC: Duke University Press, 2005), 29.

12 Barbara Ehrenreich, Elizabeth Hess, and Gloria Jacobs, *Re-Making Love: The Feminization of Sex* (Garden City, NY: Doubleday, 1986), 11.

13 Beth L. Bailey, *From Front Porch to Back Seat: Courtship in Twentieth-Century America* (Baltimore: Johns Hopkins University Press, 1988), 98.

14 Ibid., 104.

15 On the postwar ideological effort to return women to traditional roles, see Betty Friedan, *The Feminine Mystique* (New York: Dell, 1963).

16 Bailey, *From Front Porch to Back Seat,* 105.

17 Marjorie Garber, *Vested Interests: Cross-Dressing and Cultural Anxiety* (New York: Rout-ledge, 1992).

18 Ibid., 368.

19 Ibid., paraphrasing Albert Goldman, *Elvis* (New York: McGraw-Hill, 1981).

20 Garber, *Vested Interests,* 368, quoting Goldman, *Elvis.* Garber doesn't seem to understand the cultural significance of the insults Goldman directs at Elvis's masculinity. Such insults are a staple of working-class-male culture and an expression of homophobia. She writes as if Goldman were also celebrating transvestism, when his goal is in fact to castrate Elvis, to deprive him of his cultural power.

21 Nancy Henley, *Body Politics: Power, Sex, and Nonverbal Communication* (Englewood Cliffs, N J: Prentice-Hall, 1977), 160–66.

22 Laura Mulvey, "Visual Plea sure and Narrative Cinema," in *Feminism and Film Theory,* ed. Constance Penley (New York: Routledge, 1988), 57–68. In "Afterthoughts on 'Visual Plea sure and Narrative Cinema' Inspired by King Vidor's Duel in the Sun (1946)," in *Feminist Film Theory: A Reader,* ed. Sue Thornham (New York: New York University Press, 1999), 122–30, Mulvey discusses how female spectators respond to being positioned to identify with male protagonists, but she does not discuss

the female gaze. While the "female gaze" has been the topic of numerous scholarly articles, it has not been discussed with regard to rock performers. As might be obvious, my citation of Mulvey is not meant to invoke the details of her larger argument rooted in Lacanian psychoanalysis.

23 John Berger et al., *Ways of Seeing* (London and Middlesex: BBC and Penguin, 1972), 47. But see Richard Leppert, *The Nude: The Cultural Rhetoric of the Body in the Art of Western Modernity* (Boulder, CO: Westview, 2007), 8–15, for some important qualifications to Berger and Mulvey.

24 Steve Neale, "Masculinity as Spectacle: Reflections on Men and Mainstream Cinema," *Screen* 24, no. 6 (1983): 15. See Jackie Byars, *All that Hollywood Allows: Re-reading Gender in 1950s Melodrama* (Chapel Hill: University of North Carolina Press, 1991), for an extended discussion of gender in 1950s melodramas that supports Neale's position.

25 Mulvey, "Visual Plea sure and Narrative Cinema."

26 Miriam Hansen, "Plea sure, Ambivalence, Identification: Valentino and Female Spectatorship," *Cinema Journal* 25, no. 4 (1986): 12–13.

27 Gaylyn Studlar, "Valentino, 'Optic Intoxication,' and Dance Madness," in *Screening the Male: Exploring Masculinities in Hollywood Cinema,* ed. Steven Cohan and Ina Rae Hark (London: Routledge, 1993), 23–45.

28 Jon Savage, "The Enemy Within: Sex, Rock, and Identity," in *Facing the Music,* ed. Simon Frith (New York: Pantheon, 1988), 144.

29 Ibid.

30 Sue Wise, "Sexing Elvis," in *On Record: Rock, Pop, and the Written Word,* ed. Simon Frith and Andrew Goodwin (New York: Pantheon, 1988), 395, 397.

31 Henley, *Body Politics,* 167.

32 Peter Guralnick, *Last Train to Memphis: The Rise of Elvis Presley* (Boston: Little, Brown, 1994), 284.

33 Jack Gould, "TV: New Phenomenon," *New York Times,* June 6, 1956, 67.

34 Quoted in Ward, *Just My Soul Responding,* 110.

35 Ibid., 107.

36 Marc Weingarten, *Station to Station: The History of Rock 'n' Roll on Television* (New York: Simon & Schuster, 2000), 29.

37 Steven Cohan, "'Feminizing' the Song-and-Dance Man: Fred Astaire and the Spectacle of Masculinity in the Hollywood Musical," in *Screening the Male,* 46–69.

38 This is not to say that athletes cannot present themselves as objects of the sexual gaze, as tennis stars Andre Agassi or Anna Kournikova have done. Moreover, as male bodies have become more often the object of the sexual look in the culture at large, male athletes have increasingly been understood as such objects.

39 Henry Glover quoted in Nick Tosches, *Unsung Heroes of Rock 'n' Roll* (New York: Scribner's, 1984), 37.

40 Robert Henry quoted by Margaret McKee and Fred Chisenall, *Beale Black & Blue,* quoted in Greil Marcus, *Dead Elvis: A Chronicle of a Cultural Obsession* (New York: Doubleday, 1991), 57.

41 Wynonie Harris quoted in Tosches, *Unsung Heroes of Rock 'n' Roll,* 40.

42 Charlie Gillett, *The Sound of the City: The Rise of Rock and Roll* (New York: Dell, 1972), 139.

43 Peter Guralnick, "Elvis Presley," in *The Rolling Stone Illustrated History of Rock & Roll,* 3rd ed., ed. Anthony DeCurtis, James Henke, and Holly George-Warren (New York: Random House, 1992), 26.

44 Greil Marcus, *Mystery Train: Images of America in Rock 'n' Roll Music* (New York: Dutton, 1976), 204.

45 Guralnick, "Elvis Presley," 21.

46 *Elvis '56,* prod. Alan Raymond and Susan Raymond (Media Home Entertainment, 1987), videocassette (VHS).

47 Wise, "Sexing Elvis," 395.

48 Ibid., 397.

49 Simon Frith, *Music for Plea sure: Essays in the Sociology of Pop* (New York: Routledge, 1988), 167.

50 T. H. Lhamon, *Deliberate Speed: The Origins of Cultural Style in the American 1950s* (Washington: Smithsonian Institution Press, 1990), 92–96.

51 Eliot Cohen quoted in Medovoi, *Rebels,* 27.

52 Ibid.

53 Thomas Doherty, *Teenagers and Teenpics: The Juvenilization of American Movies in the 1950s* (Boston: Unwin Hyman, 1988).

54 Todd Gitlin, *The Sixties: Years of Hope, Days of Rage* (New York: Bantam, 1987), 43.

Elvis from the Waist Up and Other Myths

1950s Music Television and the Gendering of Rock Discourse

Norma Coates

Elvis Presley's third appearance on *The Ed Sullivan Show* on January 6, 1957, is commonly accepted as the birth—and the death—of rock and roll on network television. Rock and roll mythology de-emphasizes Presley's many other appearances on television variety programs in 1956. Presley's national television exposure began with multiweek appearances on the Dorsey Brothers' *Stage Show* in January and continued with appearances on *The Milton Berle Show* and *The Steve Allen Show*. Sullivan finally consented to book Presley after losing to Allen the weekly ratings battle in his time slot in the week of Presley's appearance. The fact that Presley's whole body graced his first two Sullivan appearances—or cultural critic Gilbert B. Rodman's well-supported contention that Presley's most risqué 1956 appearance occurred on Milton Berle's show—is minimized, despite the easy availability of visible evidence.[1] Instead, Presley's third Sullivan appearance is invoked to immediately position rock and roll music and culture in opposition to conservative and feminized mass culture, represented in this case by television. Even respected chroniclers of rock and roll history fall into this trap. For example, Charlie Gillett, in *The Sound of the City: The Rise of Rock and Roll*, originally published in 1970 and still one of the best accounts of rock and roll history, avers that "Sullivan allowed Presley on his show provided he wore a dinner suit and the camera was kept above waist level."[2] Again, visual evidence that refutes this is easily available on video anthologies and on cable channels.

Because rock criticism and even rock scholarship exist in something of a vacuum, little has been written about the impact of television, or any other media besides FM radio, on the transformation of gender- and race-inclusive "rock and roll" to white masculine "rock." The cultural critic David Shumway is one of the only scholars to recognize the importance of the visual aspect of Elvis Presley's appearances on television in defining rock and roll.[3] With this essay, I continue to fill the critical void about the important relationship between television and rock and roll long before the advent of MTV. In particular, I focus upon the impact of television rock and roll in the 1950s on later discourses that inscribed normative masculinity into rock and roll culture.

The selective historiography about Elvis on television in 1956 symbolizes the active exclusion of the feminine from rock and roll discourse, especially as discursive formations emerged around rock and roll in the mid-1960s. This is not a literal exclusion, of course, as women have played significant roles (in one way or another) throughout rock and roll history. The mechanics of this exclusion can be observed in the inaugural issue of *Crawdaddy* magazine in February, 1966. *Crawdaddy* was the first magazine devoted to the critical analysis of rock and roll. Its editor, a Swarthmore undergraduate named Paul Williams, was very clear that his magazine was for those who took rock and roll "very seriously indeed," not the fans who "would debate over who was greater, Elvis or Fabian."[4] Williams's references to two of the major targets of teenage female adulation in the late 1950s, as well as his choice to ignore the enormous appeal to male as well as female audiences of Elvis in 1956, clearly identifies those who would take rock and roll seriously as male, with the implication being that teenage girls did not embrace rock and roll for its aesthetic merits.[5] Williams's 1966 broadsides in the hand-typed pages of his dorm-room magazine marked the beginning of the discourses of rock and roll exceptionalism and authenticity that continue to be reiterated and thus retain their abjecting power.

Given the obvious entry, or at least belated recognition, of women as active participants in most aspects of rock and roll music and its industry, why do the masculinized mythologies of rock and roll remain so active and potent? In this essay I posit one possible answer to this not-so-simple question by focusing on the relationship between the television and music industries in the pre-rock and roll and post-rock and roll 1950s. My primary argument is that the gender roles within rock and roll and, indeed, its masculinization were heavily influenced by prevailing social norms as reiterated and reinforced through television programs and representational, industrial, and economic practices in the 1950s. This influence was especially potent at the point where television intersected with rock and roll, beginning, for this argument as for so many others, in 1956 and continuing through the end of the 1950s. I examine several programs, notably *The Ed Sullivan Show*, *The Big Beat*, and *American Bandstand*, in terms of their reception in the trade press at the time, their fit with the industrial imperatives and conventions of American television in the 1950s, and their later insertion into developing discourses that naturalized a particular inflection of heterosexual masculinity in rock and roll culture. I assert that in critical hindsight these programs, especially *American Bandstand*, caused considerable damage both to the reputation of rock and roll on television and to the primary audience for these programs, teenage-girl music fans. Later rock critics blamed the female fans as much as the performers and the music industry itself for encouraging the musical blandness of the late 1950s.[6]

Rock and roll mythology (along with its implicit demonization of television) remains influential, as indicated by the treatment of the conjunction of the two forms of media in the book

Station to Station: The History of Rock and Roll on Television (2000), written by the rock critic Marc Weingarten. In light of this point, I offer from Weingarten's book an extended quote about rock and roll on television in the 1950s:

> TV's ultimate mission—to sell things—essentially hasn't changed over the last half century, which makes it the most culturally intransigent electronic medium ever created. We need only track the programming history of the big three networks—CBS, NBC, and ABC—against the cultural and social currents that have roiled America over the past four decades to discover how out of touch TV has been in reflecting the other cultural impulses taking place "outside the box." Rock and roll, on the other hand, was created to provide the insurgent teen culture with a voice and an attitude at variance with mainstream values. It was supposed to stir things up and rage against the decade's complacent, smug ethos, not propagate the status quo. Rock and roll was loud, brash, and impudent; TV was soothing and polite. Rock and roll was sex; TV was violins. Rock and roll was Elvis Presley; TV was Robert Young. TV was black and white; rock and roll was Technicolor—it was black *and* white only in the sense that it accommodated the miscegenation of pop and R&B. If kids wanted to see youth run wild, they had to go to the movies.[7]

Weingarten's analysis speaks to an image of 1950s television that ignores its historical and other contexts, as well as its ongoing relationship with popular music, including the rock and roll genre. To address this issue, I discuss in this essay the industrial, social, and economic contexts in which the television industry launched these and other music programs of the 1950s in order to complicate the notion that television watered down and thereby "feminized" rock and roll in order to exploit and contain it. An understanding of the context in which these programs and presentations of rock and roll were created and launched is less a narrative of co-optation and containment than it is a story of a new medium trying to negotiate between numerous economic, social, cultural, moral, and industrial imperatives.

The television networks, sponsors, and variety-show hosts of the 1950s needed the audience drawn by Elvis Presley and, subsequently, by rock and roll artists, but they did not need the controversy generated by Presley's unbridled performances. I turn now to a discussion of *The Ed Sullivan Show* in the 1950s and how it and other programs, particularly *American Bandstand*, came to represent the feminizing impact of television on rock and roll. I examine *The Ed Sullivan Show* because of its enduring link and importance to the spread and popularity of rock and roll music in the 1950s and 1960s. For example, Elvis Presley appeared on many other programs in 1956 before he was finally invited onto *The Ed Sullivan Show*. His performances on the Dorsey Brothers' *Stage Show*, starting in January 1956, are arguably the most radical and sexualized of Presley's 1956 performances. These performances capture Presley while he was still identified as a rockabilly artist on the Sun Records label, just before he signed with RCA. After his move to RCA, Presley's music acquired a more polished, popular sound. His *Stage Show* appearances also capture his rawness and vitality, which would soon become more of an act as he gained awareness of his power. But Presley's signing by Sullivan meant that he—and rock and roll—had become commercial forces to be reckoned with. Moreover, it is *The Ed Sullivan Show*, not the others, that has become a part of popular memory and consciousness, in large part because of its association with rock and roll.

By 1956 *The Ed Sullivan Show* was an institution. It had no "brow" as it breeched promiscuously the boundaries of high-, low-, and middle-brow culture. For most Americans, the Sullivan show represented the best of culture from both the U.S. and abroad. It drew a huge audience every Sunday night. For performers, an appearance on the program guaranteed mass popularity; for the sponsor, it guaranteed great profit. It was incumbent upon Sullivan, then, to deliver an inoffensive program that would meet the needs of his entire constituency. Presley, and rock and roll, disturbed the equilibrium that Sullivan had coaxed out of television's inherent conflict between the public good and private profit.

The Ed Sullivan Show, originally titled *The Toast of the Town*, premiered in 1948, the same year as the *Texaco Star Theater*. Sullivan's program outlasted all of the other "great" variety shows of the era, and it remained on the air virtually unchanged in format until 1971, when it was canceled by CBS along with other programs lacking so-called urban appeal. Sullivan was hardly an avuncular figure. He was an ungainly, tongue-tied, nationally syndicated New York gossip columnist. Oddly, this persona contributed to his appeal. That a gossip columnist could become television's most successful variety program host is not surprising. Sullivan may have succeeded where arguably more talented individuals did not because of his particular inflection of the variety program. In many ways, Sullivan's program was closer to the spirit of traditional vaudeville than were the more well-known, arguably better, variety shows of television's early years. *Your Show of Shows* and *Texaco Star Theater* focused on sketch comedy, which was only a part of a typical vaudeville show. Each weekly edition of *The Ed Sullivan Show* contained the same main components as a basic vaudeville show, as well as "something for the youngsters." As the vaudeville historian Albert F. McLean Jr. asserts, "At one time or another vaudeville brought just about every form of entertainment known to man under its umbrella, but its main components were those drawn from early variety shows—skits, songs, dances, and comic monologues—together with some of the minstrel show's humor and the staples of circus programs—acrobats and animals."[8] Here McLean could have been describing a typical Sullivan hour, minus the overt minstrel routine.

The Ed Sullivan Show and Ed Sullivan the persona epitomized the dual nature of 1950s culture. The program's elevation, in nostalgic hindsight, to the position of sacred text, as well as exemplar of a kinder, gentler time in American culture, is evidence of Sullivan's skill in submerging the contradictions covered over by the veneer of benign pluralism.[9] *The Ed Sullivan Show* helped to ease the introduction of television into the American home with its (and Sullivan's) particular vision of "something for everyone." Every Sunday night, viewers would be treated to acts as disparate as opera and rock and roll, serious dramatic readings and children's puppets.

Sullivan also brought his audience overseas to Europe in an effort to showcase acts that he considered the best that the "high-culture" continent had to offer to American families. Sullivan's archived papers indicate that he was passionate about his vision and thus took the lead role in finding and booking acts for his show.

As much as Sullivan avowed to focus on pleasing the American people, he was most motivated by the weekly Trendex ratings detailing the number of viewers tuned into messages for his sponsors. Numbers and dollars thus dictated Sullivan's vision of "family entertainment" or "cultural enlightenment." For example, Sullivan canceled a contract for a multiweek series of vignettes by the Metropolitan Opera after the ratings proved to be abominable. Sullivan could rail against certain acts or individual performers as being in bad taste or inappropriate for his core family audience, but he would do a quick reversal whenever he lost the ratings race in his time slot. The paramount example of Sullivan's fluctuating definition of good taste was his very public refusal to book Elvis Presley on the show in 1956. Sullivan had been quoted as saying that Presley "would never go on our show. Ours is a family show. If I were selling cigarets, maybe I'd book him, but how many Elvis Presley fans are going to buy new cars?" (a direct reference to his sponsor, the Lincoln-Mercury division of Ford Motor Company).[10] Elvis, apparently, went from being in bad taste to being in good taste, as well as a great car salesman, as soon as his appearance on *The Steve Allen Show* helped that program beat Sullivan in the ratings one Sunday night. Sullivan soon booked Presley for three appearances, paying him an unprecedented fee of $50,000.[11] By the mid-1960s, Sullivan was taking credit for discovering Presley.[12] His later published comments about this and other "discoveries" reveal an artificiality and duplicity that later rock critics would attribute to television as they constructed it, its programs, and even its performers as inauthentic compared to "real" rock and roll.

Nevertheless, Ed Sullivan and his eponymous program have stuck in American cultural memory for a role that Sullivan played inadvertently, that of rock and roll impresario. An appearance on the Sullivan show in the 1960s catapulted bands into public consciousness, and in the case of the first U.S. appearance of the Beatles on February 9, 1964, it fueled a cultural revolution. But rock and roll's association, indeed need for, Sullivan and his program was fraught with tension, a tension central to the relationship between the television and music industries over the presentation of rock and roll. By the 1960s, Sullivan's program was a necessary evil for rock artists seeking to find an audience or to promote their latest release. Sullivan's concerns for propriety would translate into a further revilement of television by counterculture critics, especially rock journalists. Their contempt would feed into their ongoing scorn for television as a feminine and feminizing medium.

Rock and roll was a necessary evil for Sullivan, too. Throughout his television career he frequently found himself caught between a vision of his moral mission to maintain an archaic conception of cultural propriety and his overwhelming need to win each week's ratings race in his Sunday-night time slot. *The Ed Sullivan Show* embodies tensions between the public and private inherent in commercial television from the 1950s to the present time. Rock and roll, particularly in the 1950s, posed thorny problems for program hosts like Sullivan, along with his sponsors, and the network and stations that distributed his program, in that it was discursively constructed as an outlaw form of entertainment. It was therefore consistent with the public-interest responsibilities granted to television stations to withhold rock and roll from America's television screens. At the same time, television's sponsors sought to make the most money they could from the medium, and it was the responsibility of figures like Sullivan to make it for them. Rock and roll attracted the lucrative teenage audience to the screen in an unprecedented manner, and thus profit-making trumped public interest—to an extent. By the mid-1950s, Ed Sullivan had established himself as America's paternalistic arbiter of family entertainment. His "blessing" of Presley as "a real fine boy" after an appearance on his program helped to establish a place for rock and roll on television. It also helped later rock critics to blast television as a corrupter of authentic rock and roll.

As noted above, Sullivan's ability to manage the inherent contradiction between television's public and private imperative was ultimately tested, and compromised, by the advent of rock and roll music in the form of Elvis Presley. Presley was more than a performer—he was representative of an increasingly powerful social group, the teenager, and their economic power. Sullivan, along with other television variety-show hosts, were thus forced to choose between social propriety and winning ratings. Ever the scoop-loving newspaperman, he chose ratings. In the meantime, his program, and the errant nostalgia that figured it as a symbol of tradition and ultimately an enemy of progress, inadvertently set the stage for the gendering of rock and roll as a white heterosexual male form. This process would be greatly assisted by other rock and roll music programs of the late 1950s.

Before addressing these other programs, I first want to note that it is important to understand the various contexts in which rock and roll on television was situated. Televised rock and roll highlighted points of friction between two media that were at the same time complementary and often incompatible. Popular music was an integral part of television from the dawn of network programming, but it was difficult for television programmers to provide an effective visual treatment of music on television outside of variety-show appearances or the insertion of songs into dramatic programs. Rock and roll exacerbated this problem, because its performance was almost too visual: rock and roll artists wiggled the wrong way, or were the "wrong" color and threatened to wiggle the wrong way, for family television. Performances of rock and roll thus challenged the television industry and its sponsors' avowed desired to deliver "appropriate" entertainment into the sanctity of the (white) American home, and in so doing opened the medium to popular, critical, and political attack.

But rock and roll drew teenagers, an important "market in training," to the television set in an unprecedented manner. Rock and roll was therefore an economic godsend for the television industry and its sponsors; indeed, its money-making ability could not be denied or ignored. Ed Sullivan and others who lived and died by the Trendex ratings found themselves in the midst of a Hobson's choice: feature rock and roll performers and risk a degree of public disapproval, or ignore rock and roll and lose money. Needless to say, they chose the former. The trade press of the mid-1950s documents that it was widely supposed that rock and roll was a fad that would quickly die out. Therefore, why not make the money and run? The "solution" to the challenge posed by rock and roll on television was to water it down—that is, to make it more acceptable for mass consumption while the fad was at its peak, then wait for the fad to die out on its own. There was no reason to suppose that rock and roll would not do so, as music fads such as the popularity of crooners in the 1930s and the bobbysoxer mania for Frank Sinatra in the 1940s were contained and faded away. The fact that this move was "contextually consistent" given the era's social and cultural mores, as well as its audience expectations and interests, was ignored by later rock critics who mapped the countercultural values of the 1960s that they espoused onto the very different public values of the 1950s. Thus the rock and roll television of the late 1950s, beginning with the treatment of Elvis on both the Ed Sullivan and Steve Allen variety shows, and the representative youth music program of the era, *American Bandstand*, was to shoulder the blame for the near-death of rock and roll.

As noted above, the critical hindsight about 1950s music programs espoused by 1960s and 1970s rock criticism was complicit in naturalizing rock and roll music as a white, male, and heterosexual cultural form. As I will demonstrate, much of this programming was targeted to prepubescent females (the much-maligned "teenyboppers"), their older teenage sisters, and young housewives. Because masculinity was not immanent in rock and roll in this (and any other) period, it was constructed into the form as discourses about "authenticity" were created, circulated, and reiterated in the 1960s. As part of these discourses, television came to symbolize the artificial and, in a critical schema ruled by binary thinking, the feminine. Televised rock and roll became representative of the inauthentic, and its feminine, or more accurately feminized, audience was placed in a marginal position in rock and roll culture and discourse.

Rock and roll discourse, emanating as it does from a link to and concern with the industrial, social, and cultural dynamics of popular music in the 1960s, does not take into account the parallel dynamics of the television industry in the 1950s. Television in the mid-1950s was well on its way to becoming a truly mass medium, but utopian hopes and visions for its future still remained. This period has since been constructed as television's "golden age" of anthology drama, strong writing, and the hallowed virtue of "liveness" that provided it with a degree of cultural legitimacy that it has not been able to obtain since.[13] A decision to "water down" rock and roll, if it were a conscious decision at all, was not made in a vacuum. Rather, social, cultural, economic, and audience expectations all came to bear upon programming decisions and conventions.

Rock and roll was a programming challenge on many levels. It was connected to two important changes that would have an enormous impact on all aspects of American life: the economic birth of the teenager, and the civil rights movement. Rock and roll was a musical form that appealed to the new white, suburban, affluent teenager, and it was directly descended from the rhythm and blues music that had been popular in African American communities for a decade. If that weren't problematic enough, the music also had strong roots in the "hillbilly" music of the American South and the folk music popularized by the left-leaning intelligentsia (who were not the most popular people in the mid-1950s). Through its lineage alone, rock and roll threatened the cozy picture of American political and social life as comfortably pluralistic yet oddly homogeneous, thus espousing a key contradiction at the core of American civic life. As the music historian Trent Hill observes, rock and roll provided a means by which "subterranean social forces" could assert themselves. While rock and roll, he argues, "may have been fine for the kids, for their parents and the other authorities rock & roll was a threatening reminder of the existence of others and otherness that set a dangerous precedent that had to be examined, understood, criticized and controlled."[14]

Perhaps the biggest threat of rock and roll was its overt recognition of the plausibility of racial miscegenation. Musical miscegenation could to some extent be contained, as it had in jazz, but rock and roll had a much wider appeal. It was a short step from the fear of musical miscegenation, the primary effects of which were between the ears, to the fear of racial miscegenation, concerned with feelings lower down the body. Rock and roll thus challenged and put into crisis the prevailing racial and sexual mores of the day.

Indeed, rock and roll gave rise to a "dangerous" mixing of the races, physically through the mixed-race revues popularized by leading disk jockeys, and aurally through the widespread broadcast of rhythm and blues music on the radio. Such mixing threatened to upset the prevailing racial norms of the 1950s, in the North as well as in the South.[15] Rock and roll was also, and often incorrectly, articulated to juvenile delinquency, in part because of the visual iconography of black leather jackets, black or blue jeans, and outlaw hairstyles circulated by the spate of movies produced in the mid-1950s to capitalize on rock and roll's appeal to youth.[16]

The problem for television programmers and variety-show hosts like Ed Sullivan was that rock and roll's white teen audience was too large and too wealthy for them to ignore. This was compounded, if not confounded, by the fact that the teen audience was hard to reach as well as hard for television sponsors to rationalize. Articles from various industry and business magazines of the era indicate that although there was much eagerness to capture the teen audience, there was great uncertainty as to why. That this was a market with great potential spending power was clear: a 1956 article in *Sponsor* quoted a study by the Gilbert Youth Research Organization, the leading market research firm specializing in teen tastes and trends in the 1950s, which estimated that year's teenage buying market to be between nine and ten billion dollars.[17]

This article, published at the height of Elvis Presley's popularity in 1956, grappled with whether or not Presley and other rock and roll artists could sell basic consumer goods. Rock and roll could do so, the article concluded, but only for a while. As a trend, it would soon die out. In the meantime, rock and roll could "plant for the harvest," that is, condition youth to brand names as they prepared to become adult consumers. Radio was deemed to be the best medium for reaching teens with product messages, particularly about items such as shaving products, cosmetics, personal hygiene products, milk, ice cream, and soda, which were perceived to be staples of teenage life that would carry over into adulthood.[18]

The article also claimed that teenage girls spent more time than their male counterparts listening to rock and roll on the radio. Girls were also responsible for a slim majority of record purchases. Radio and television sponsors, the article implied, would be well served by targeting the teenage girl audience. Given the young average age of marriage in the 1950s, these girls would soon be nineteen-year-old homemakers and mothers. Or, if they chose to go to college instead, they would spend an average of $456.22 as a college freshman to outfit themselves and their dorm rooms.[19] But teenage girls, according to a 1955 Ohio State University study quoted in the article, lost their taste for "hot" music once they assumed adult responsibilities and purchasing power. By their late teens, "their taste veers to the sweet and 'schmaltzy' (*viz.* Lawrence Welk, Liberace)."[20]

The teen audience, especially teenage girls, was well worth capturing, but rock and roll was a potentially dangerous lure, the use of which could backfire on sponsors and stations. Radio play was bad enough, but teens would shortly outgrow rock and roll and move on to more appropriate music, or so it was thought. Rock and roll radio could, therefore, be tolerated in the short term in order to make money for sponsors and radio stations. Presenting rock and roll on television in a noncontroversial manner was much more problematic, for economic as well as social reasons. That television was seen as well as heard opened the medium, the networks, and its sponsors to greater scrutiny and criticism. Rock and roll was more potent, and thus more dangerous, on television. The potential sales impact of Elvis Presley's 1956 television appearances was clear early on. Rock and roll, particularly in the person of Presley, drew the teen audience to the television screen. It also drew great criticism, which was aimed more at the television industry than at Presley himself.

Jack Gould, the influential television critic for the *New York Times* in the 1950s, fired a damaging broadside at the television industry in an article written for the widely read Sunday edition, published September 9, 1956, after Presley's first appearance on the *Ed Sullivan Show*. Presley had been appearing on national television since January of that year. Gould wrote a short article about Presley on June 6, 1956, describing the performer "as a rock-and-roll variation on one of the most standard acts in show business: the virtuoso of the hootchy-kootchy."[21] In this second article Gould, whose *New York Times* pulpit made him perhaps the most influential critic of the era, placed the blame for rock and roll and its attendant evils on the television industry's pursuit of profit at any moral cost. The headline said it all: "Elvis Presley—Lack of Responsibility Is Shown by TV in Exploiting Teen-Agers." The full brunt of Gould's wrath fell on Presley's performance on the previous week's *Ed Sullivan Show*. Gould grudgingly acknowledged that television was not alone and that the magazine and recording industries shared the blame for casting rock and roll upon the national scene, as well as white teenage affluence, mobility, and hormones. But in his analysis, television, as a medium created and programmed by adults who should know better, had the most opportunity—and necessity—to act responsibly to stem the spread of rock and roll and its attendant social maladies. Television was free, providing easy access to its wares. Therefore, young children as well as teens could be "overstimulated" by Presley's bump and grind. Gould was especially critical of a "perennial weakness in the executive echelons of the networks ... their opportunistic rationalization of television's function." He characterized the industry's code as giving the public what they want, and he condemned them for abrogating their social responsibility to that end, fulminating that "when this code is applied to teen-agers just becoming conscious of life's processes, not only is it manifestly without validity but it, alas, is perilous.

Catering to the interests of the younger generation is one of television's main jobs; because those interests do not always coincide with parental tastes should not deter the broadcasters. But selfish exploitation and commercialized overstimulation of youth's physical impulses is certainly a gross national disservice."[22]

Whether Gould's condemnation inspired Sullivan and his producers to present Presley from the waist up in a subsequent appearance is unclear.[23] Gould's implicit condemnation of network executives and his reminder of their social responsibilities likely influenced the subsequent presentation of rock and roll on network television. They could not stop showing rock and roll, as it drew a desired audience for potential sponsors, but neither could they continue to take the blame for disseminating and furthering the cause of a perceived social ill. In turn, making rock and roll acceptable for network television meant moving it further away from its roots in rhythm and blues—thus literally whitening both the composition of its groups and its sound, regardless of the race of its performers.

Moreover, by 1957 it was clear that rock and roll would be more than a fleeting fad, thus making it in the television establishment's best interest to exploit it for profit while they could. Accordingly, the ABC television network—still in the shadows of the giant networks of CBS and NBC and trying to establish a niche for itself—decided to experiment with rock and roll program-ming in a stand-alone format. Their first attempt involved signing Alan Freed (the Cleveland disk jockey who popularized the term "rock and roll" to make rhythm and blues more palatable to the white audience) for a thirteen-week stint as the host of *Alan Freed's Big Beat*. The program premiered on Friday, July 12, at 10:30 PM eastern time. Freed was signed by ABC after a rock and roll program hosted by the disk jockey scored a solid 13.3 rating earlier that year. The network took special care, according to its programming chief Ted Fetter, to ensure that "the show was acceptable as family fare—screening lyrics and inviting a selected studio audience, culled from Freed's own fan club." Fetter also mentioned that the network had not received any viewer complaints about the racially mixed talent lineup.[24]

Nevertheless, the program's late prime-time slot owes as much to the fear of televising rock and roll as to ABC's hunting for an available slot. *Billboard*'s review of the initial program of the thirteen-week series states that there were no commercials, thus indicating that ABC had not yet found a sponsor brave enough to bankroll a rock and roll program. The reviewer, Charlie Sinclair, opened his critique by gently but decidedly castigating both rock and roll and ABC for the program's mediocrity: "The Big Beat" is hygienic rock and roll. Under the watchful eye of ABC's network censors, the show's cameras view the acts from the waist up. Forced thus to stand or fall primarily on its minor musical merits, this Alan Freed package frequently stands around with egg on its electronic face." Sinclair continued in this vein, criticizing the program's flaccid presentation of rock and roll while also criticizing the music itself and its audience. Sinclair also questioned ABC's wisdom in presenting a program with little adult appeal that was instead "slanted toward teenagers—who seldom watch TV anyway." Sinclair's pen threw acid on the host itself, too, describing Freed as combining "the unctuous charm of Ralph Edwards with the manic gymnastics of Jerry Lewis."[25] A bad audience combined with bad music made for, in Sinclair's view, bad television.

Freed's program did not stay on the air long. This was not due to its quality or the lack of an audience, but because it transgressed television's—and 1950's society's—racial boundaries. Freed had long flirted with trouble by staging gala rhythm and blues and later rock and roll revues that drew racially mixed audiences. Often, the races were physically separated within the host auditoriums to prevent contact, especially mixed dancing. Although it was especially important to maintain this division on television, doing so did not seem difficult because the programs were open to white audiences only. African American performers were not excluded, and indeed they comprised many of the popular bands. According to Freed's biographer John Jackson, the program was after the third week immediately canceled by ABC because of the public uproar caused when its cameras caught the African American performer and show guest Frankie Lymon dancing with a white teenage girl.[26] As I discuss below, ABC's timidity and subsequent treatment of Freed would add fuel to the critical condemnation of the payola scandal that ruined Freed's career in the early 1960s, and from which another television disk jockey, Dick Clark, escaped with his reputation even enhanced.

Despite this setback, ABC went ahead with its plans to introduce an afternoon rock and roll dance program. Dance programs targeted to teenagers were a staple of early local and network programming. The renowned bandleader Paul Whiteman was ABC's music director in its early days, and he hosted its TV-*Teen Club* dance program for years. Local stations in big cities throughout the country, including Chicago, Detroit, and Minneapolis, presented afternoon dance parties for teenagers.[27] As reported in *Billboard* late in 1956, "Altho record shows have yet to gain general acceptance at the network level, the TV disk jockey format has become increasingly important in the local station market in the last year."[28] The foray by ABC into the world of dance programs launched a television institution—and gave rock and roll on television a bad reputation among the rock cognoscenti until the dawning of the cable era.

Of the many stations that produced local disk jockey programs, none was more successful than WFIL in Philadelphia, home of *American Bandstand*—an afternoon "dance party" featuring local teens dancing to the lip-synched beat of their favorite rock and roll bands. *American Bandstand* premiered as *Bandstand* on October 6, 1952, and it "was a sensation from the start."[29] From the start, *Bandstand* was little more than visual radio, fitting into the early television category of "disk jockey program." It drew high ratings, as local teens did not seem to tire of watching other local teens dancing. Moreover, dances seen on the program would soon spawn local dance fads. Although primarily a venue for the saccharine white pop music of the day, *Bandstand*, encouraged by some of its teenage regulars, occasionally experimented with African American rhythm and blues music and artists—a trendsetting and taboo move for television in the pre-rock and roll era.

Much of *Bandstand*'s early energy and success came from its host, the experienced Philadelphia disk jockey Bob Horn. A sex scandal involving a teenage girl ended Horn's career in 1956, just as rock and roll was beginning to make its impact. A young and ambitious WFIL disk jockey, Dick Clark, was tapped to take Horn's place. Clark's tenure with *American Bandstand* began on July 9,

1956, and did not end until March 1989. The show itself ended six months later. Clark's public persona was squeaky clean, as was his vision of the show. When the sex scandal involving Horn broke open in 1956, Clark used his "choir-boy" image to disassociate his program from it. This effort also entailed keeping the show clean and free of any untoward physicality. John Jackson quotes a 1990 interview in which Clark claimed that had Bandstand been "a snake pit of writhing bodies," it would have been "off the air in a week."[30]

American Bandstand premiered on ABC as an afternoon program just as *The Big Beat* was imploding. According to a recollection printed in Leonard Goldenson's autobiography (Goldenson was ABC's chairman in this period and was instrumental in its establishment as the third major network), his president, Ollie Treyz, was responsible for bringing *American Bandstand* to network television. Treyz, an advertising industry veteran, enjoyed poring through ratings books. On one of his forays into audience numbers, he was struck by the consistently high ratings garnered by a local afternoon entry on Philadelphia's WFIL television station. He contacted an associate in Philadelphia and requested a kinescope of *American Bandstand*. As Treyz recounts: "I saw the Kine, and I thought, I can see why. I had a 16 mm Kine projector at home, so I showed it to my kids, and they liked it. I told them, Bring in all your school friends, the girls, get them to come over. I was interested in the girls' reaction, because I saw girls dancing with girls. And they loved it. They asked to see it again. They loved that kind of music and the dancing, the Twist and all that. 'Would you come home and watch that right after school?' Oh, yes, they would."[31] If this recollection is correct, it is notable because Treyz's children, both boys, were nine and five at the time.[32] Their "school friends" would have been prepubescent junior high and elementary school students, or "teenyboppers," not teenage rock and roll fans. *American Bandstand* and, by association, music on television would suffer at the hands of later rock critics and aficionados for being aimed at teenyboppers, preteens who had not yet developed "good" musical taste.

In its network incarnation, *American Bandstand* helped ABC—and local stations—solve a number of problems. *American Bandstand* and local dance programs reached the elusive teenage audience in unprecedented numbers.[33] On October 7, 1957, *Billboard* reported that *American Bandstand* was the number one program in its time period (3:00–4:30 PM eastern time) according to the September, 1957, Trendex report. According to Trendex, the program's 5.7 rating and 35.6 audience share were 62 percent higher than CBS's numbers and 35 percent higher than NBC's during those time slots.[34] Regionally broadcast and syndicated dance programs were also doing well.[35]

Indeed, *American Bandstand* drew the teen audience. The program highlighted performances (usually lip-synched) of hit songs by the original artists, white or African American.[36] A set of regular dancers soon developed, and the romances and friendships between them became as much of the program's appeal to teen viewers as the music. *American Bandstand* also drew an unexpected bonanza to the screen—homemakers who were not interested in game shows or soap operas, the other afternoon fare.[37] The younger average age of marriage in the 1950s meant that many homemakers were barely out of their teens, if they were out of them at all.

American Bandstand's success in pulling this audience also disproved the idea that women turned to Lawrence Welk for musical pleasure upon marriage.

American Bandstand's best asset, in terms of its appeal to television executives, was Dick Clark. A 1958 *Variety* article attributed Clark's success to his "underemotional, relaxed 'all-American boy' personality."[38] These same qualities would later be used in rock culture to diminish Clark and his program's achievements. Even more heinous in the eyes of rock critics, Clark was a one-man record promotion giant. A representative of the Dealers of Greater St. Louis, a trade organization of music store owners, called Clark "the greatest stimulant to the record business we as dealers have ever known."[39] *American Bandstand*'s Trendex rating of 5.6 topped both NBC and CBS in the 4:00–4:30 PM time slot just two months after its national introduction on ABC.[40]

Sponsors were eager to jump on the Dick Clark bandwagon, too. Although the half-hour version of *American Bandstand*, presented on Monday nights at 7:30 PM from October 7, 1957, to December 30, 1957, failed miserably, ABC created a new vehicle for Clark.[41] *The Dick Clark Show* was essentially a half-hour version of *American Bandstand* combined with a liberal sprinkling of *Your Hit Parade*. One of the program's attractions was the weekly "*American Bandstand* Top Ten," a preview of the songs that would be featured on the afternoon program during the following week. Unlike *Your Hit Parade*, only the hit performances of featured songs were offered, and they were performed, or more often lip-synched, by the original artists.[42] *Variety*, normally no friend to rock and roll television, published a glowing review of the program's premiere. The review was particularly sanguine about Clark, whom it called "a young wholesome type who makes with hip chatter," and his ability to "gain a hefty adult quotient" for the program.[43] Accordingly, the audience for the Saturday night *Dick Clark Show* was estimated to be over half adult. The other half, teenagers, comprised 40 percent of the market for chewing gum, thereby leading Beech-Nut Gum to sign on as its sponsor two weeks into the program's run. An early 1959 article in *Printer's Ink* forecast that the company would soon announce a sizable gain over the previous year's sales. The article quoted a company spokesman as declaring, "I can tell you quite frankly, we hope we'll be associated with Dick Clark for a long time. He's an outstanding salesman, the kind that a company like Beech-Nut welcomes."[44]

This very attractiveness to sponsors, and what was later perceived as the program's, and Clark's, championing of the prefabricated "teen idols" of the late 1950s, particularly Fabian and Bobby Rydell from Philadelphia, caused the program's contributions to the spread and legitimization of rock and roll to be obscured and ignored. That is not to say that *American Bandstand* did not "sanitize" rock and roll to some extent. Indeed, the program was complicit in the relegation of most African American artists, except those who could emulate a white pop sound, to the newly reghettoized rhythm and blues category. *American Bandstand* cemented rock and roll as a white musical form. The racial implications of this move on what would become rock and rock culture were skirted over later by white rock critics who turned rock into a signifier of white masculinity and authenticity and denied the implications of its African American roots as much as did Clark's programs.

Dick Clark and *American Bandstand* cannot shoulder all of the blame for the whitening and mainstreaming of rock and roll. Certainly, the program circulated wholesome images of rock and roll and popularized artists who were more congruent with the conservative sexual and social mores of the late 1950s than were rhythm and blues artists and first-wave rock and rollers like Elvis Presley. The cultural historian Brian Ward's observation that the program "stood both as a testament to rock and roll's rapprochement with white middle-class values, and as an example of the dominant culture's capacity to absorb, transform and ultimately commodify 'threatening' sub-cultural styles in accordance with its own core values" exemplifies the usual critical assessment of the program.[45]

Ward's point is accurate but incomplete. The mainstreaming of a cultural form is neither complete nor irreversible. Mainstreaming will always create insiders and outsiders, and not necessarily those that are obvious. For example, the mainstreaming of rock and roll turned it into a predominantly white form of popular culture. This point is generally acknowledged. At the same time, this operation turned rock and roll into a predominantly male and heterosexual preserve of "authenticity" and resistant culture, positioned against the feminized "other" of "inauthentic" and commercialized popular culture—and music—promoted on television. That is, the same white middle-class values cited by Ward as an inauthentic and feminizing influence on rock and roll drew on the middle-class gender politics of the 1950s to do so. Rock's "counterculture" may have run counter to mainstream middle-class values in some ways, but it depended upon and reinforced them in others.

It was, and remains, easier to place the blame on television, teenyboppers, and teen idols for rock and roll's "mainstreaming" in the late 1950s than to scrutinize the internalized value systems of those who defined the discursive boundaries of "rock culture" in the 1960s. This is not to claim that there were no efforts to contain rock and roll. For example, it may be compellingly argued that it was the payola scandal of 1959 and 1960, coming on the heels of the television quiz show scandals, that forced some of the pioneering rock and roll deejays, most notably Alan Freed, off the air. Payola, a practice in which disk jockeys received money from record companies to play new songs, was a long-standing practice that preceded rock and roll by almost a century. The music historian John Jackson, for example, traces payola back to 1863. According to Jackson, representatives of ASCAP, the composer and publisher's organization associated with the pre-rock and roll music industry, took advantage of the political and popular outrage engendered by the quiz show scandals in an attempt to shut down rock and roll and its primary publisher, rival BMI.[46] The only notable rock and roll disk jockey to survive the payola scandals with his reputation—and job—intact was Dick Clark. It is well documented that Clark's business interests were very much entwined with the recordings of many performers featured on *American Bandstand*.[47] That Clark came out of the payola hearings unscathed while others suffered grave consequences is marshaled as evidence of his fiscal importance to big broadcasting, notably ABC. Jackson reports Alan Freed's opinion that "because Dick Clark grossed about $12 million a year for the ABC network, compared to Freed's $250,000 yearly figure for the local WABC radio, there was no doubt in his mind that ABC had a double standard for him and for Clark."[48]

I have no doubt that Clark's utility to ABC, and the television magnetism and savvy that each day attracted teenage and adult female audiences to *American Bandstand*, influenced more than a little the outcome of the payola hearings. I argue, however, that rock and other cultural critics overemphasize *how* hegemonic tactics contained rock and roll in the late 1950s. A more interesting area to explore is *why* it was so easy to do so.

Blaming the mainstreaming of rock and roll on television genres, conventions, and programs and foisting prefabricated teen idols onto unsophisticated female audiences solves but a part of the puzzle. I suggest that the culture was not ready for the generational rebellion and massive social changes that pushed rock and roll firmly onto the scene in the 1960s. Programs such as *American Bandstand*, *The Ed Sullivan Show*, and *Ozzie and Harriet* may be perceived as mainstreaming rock and roll, but they can also be seen as paving the way for the cultural importance of 1960s rock and roll. Mainstreaming, particularly of cultural forms, is a much more contradictory process than generally is considered. I suggest that the answer has as much to do with cultural receptiveness as with a program, organized or otherwise, of cultural repression. Hegemonic forces can always be marshaled to wipe out or decrease the power of an oppositional cultural form, but, as in the 1960s, they do not always succeed in full. Why did this work, to some extent, in the late 1950s?

Articles in the music trade, business, and "lifestyle" magazines and newspapers of the late 1950s confirm that rock and roll was very popular among teenagers, generally defined as belonging to the 12–18 age cohort. But while we can comfortably assert that rock and roll was the primary form of popular music embraced by teenagers in the 1960s, their counterparts in the 1950s were not as parochial in their listening habits. Mitch Miller, the artists and repertoire head of Columbia records, noted in 1956 that teens still had a fondness for conventional pop music, for which he cites the enduring popularity with that audience of more mainstream artists such as Johnny Ray and the vocal group the Four Lads. Miller, portrayed in the trade press as an outspoken critic of rock and roll, sought to disavow or at least temper that image by stating, "What is necessary is a balanced viewpoint and a long range view." Miller also noted that rock and roll's popularity "reminded us [the mainstream music industry] of the necessity of stressing the element of rhythm in our pop recordings."[49] Miller is often pointed to as the exemplar of industry opposition to rock and roll in the 1950s. These observations indicate much more of a rapprochement with rock and roll, not on substantive or creative grounds but on economic ones. Contrary to rock and roll mythology, the music industry did not try to kill rock and roll on moral or economic grounds. They were justifiably uncertain about its "staying power" and its ability to retain the interest of the teen audience as it aged. Given that rock and roll remains discursively constructed as youth music, and that the social pressure, from both sides, is to grow away from it as one ages, Miller's concern is not an idle one. The incorporation of a "heavy beat" into standard pop songs may be viewed as mainstreaming rock and roll, but it may also be viewed as a capitulation to popular tastes.

By the end of the decade rock and roll's circulation via television and radio helped to loosen the grip held on it by censors. June Bundy, in a January 1959 *Billboard* article, asserted that a survey of network continuity-acceptance heads and recording librarians showed that the "public is becoming more broadminded and censors are becoming more lenient about the lyric content of songs aired over both radio and TV (both local and network) every year."[50] Such leniency may be interpreted as a result of the success of a concentrated effort to mainstream rock and roll, but it is equally valid to surmise that rock and roll was becoming accepted as a valid form of popular culture.

An obvious point that is apparently lost on those who criticize the teenybopper audience for Fabian and his ilk in the late 1950s is that these same prepubescent girls would form the core of the audience for the British invasion and other rock and roll bands of the 1960s. More was done, then, to "prep" the audience for rock culture than is generally acknowledged. Indeed, in the 1960s rock culture was created and promoted by college students. In the 1950s, this same age cohort, according to studies and surveys, had little use for rock and roll.[51] Girls have always bought more records than boys; without this audience, rock and roll may never have achieved the power it held for some time.[52] Men were responsible for the discursive gendering of rock and roll in the 1960s, but in the 1950s girls and women drove it economically with their purchases as well as their influence as consumers.

The critical narrative that blames rock and roll programming targeted to teenyboppers, teenage girls, and young adult women for the decline of rock and roll in the late 1950s ignores the salient facts that do not support such a claim. For example, Ed Sullivan is not the only person who "neutered" Elvis Presley. Sullivan, by ordering that cameras be trained on the upper half of Presley's body, provided the crucial visible evidence that is privileged as "truth" of the operation. Little if any blame is placed on Elvis's manager, Colonel Tom Parker, who engineered Elvis's every professional, and occasionally personal, move. In volume two of his painstakingly researched definitive biography of Presley, the cultural historian Peter Guralnick claims that during Presley's stint in the army (1958–1960), Parker undertook a "campaign of scarcity" by withholding new releases to provide the impression that Presley was busy serving his country. The savvy Parker also believed that he was protecting Presley's reputation in the wake of a general slump in the recording industry.[53] Guralnick also chronicles Parker's plan to move Presley to the middle of the road through a series of B-movie vehicles and Parker's choice of mediocre pop songs as Presley's post-army recordings. Parker's impact on Presley's post-army decline has been eschewed by critics who favor a narrative that constructs a dictatorial teenybopper and teenage audience that demanded pop rather than rock and roll.

Many factors contributed to the mainstreaming of rock and roll in the late 1950s, but these have been selectively recalled in order to support the naturalization of the masculinity in rock and roll in the service of myths about the popular form's authenticity and exceptionalism. Rock and roll is no longer the leading music genre favored by or representing youth; in fact, many claim that it no longer exists. If it does exist, it does so in its most extreme forms, championing hyperbolic masculinity and sexuality while reaching out to a small audience of teenage boys. Youth music is fragmented, and if any form now unifies youth as rock and roll did in the 1950s and 1960s, it is rap music, which also is constructed as a masculine preserve. Although rock has fragmented into hundreds of subgenres that often barely resemble the original, it is still regarded as a male form. The male gender of "rock" is no longer as blatant as it was from the 1950s through the 1970s, but the dynamics of its naturalization are still at work in, for example, the use of the term "women in rock" when discussing female rock musicians. The logical semantic mate, "men in rock," is not used when discussing male rock musicians. As I write this essay, the best-selling youth music in the United States falls into the rap and the teenybopper categories. Teenybopper artists such as Britney Spears and the "boy bands" N'Sync and the Backstreet Boys, primarily appeal to prepubescent and teenage girls. Accordingly, these groups, on cable as well as on network television, are the butt of critical and cultural jokes and even some moral panic. Their female fans are as often as vilified as their grandmothers were in the late 1950s. Rock and roll may have fragmented, but its myths, and its constructions of insiders and outsiders, remain curiously potent.

Notes

1 Gilbert B. Rodman, *Elvis after Elvis: The Posthumous Career of a Living Legend* (New York: Routledge, 1996), 153.

2 Charlie Gillett, *The Sound of the City: The Rise of Rock and Roll* (New York: Pantheon, 1970), 207.

3 David Shumway, "Rock and Roll as a Cultural Practice," in *Present Tense: Rock & Roll and Culture*, ed. Anthony DeCurtis (Durham, N.C.: Duke University Press, 1992), 125.

4 Paul Williams, "Along Comes Maybe," *Crawdaddy*, August 1966, 22.

5 By 1966, Elvis had not appeared publicly for nine years, and his music had moved in the direction of Vegas pop. His touted "comeback" (via television, ironically) was still two years away.

6 For example, the critic Greg Shaw, writing in *The Rolling Stone Illustrated History of Rock & Roll*, the first attempt to create a canon of rock and roll performers, blamed this music on "the teenage girls, the ones in the suburbs who wanted big fluffy candy-colored images of male niceness on which to focus their pubescent dreams." "Teenyboppers" thus remain a convenient villain for critics decrying the sorry state of popular music. See Greg Shaw, "The Teen Idols," in *The Rolling Stone Illustrated History of Rock & Roll* (New York: Rolling Stone Press, 1980), 96–100.

7 Marc Weingarten, *Station to Station: The History of Rock and Roll on Television* (New York: Pocket Books, 2000), 3.

8 Albert F. McLean Jr., *American Vaudeville as Ritual* (Lexington: University of Kentucky Press, 1965), 21–22.

9 See, for example, John Leonard, "Ed Sullivan Died for Our Sins," in *Smoke and Mirrors: Violence, Television, and Other American Cultures* (New York: New Press, 1997).

10 *New York Post*, July 13, 1956.

11 Sullivan's dismissal then embrace of Elvis Presley in 1956 is well documented in many journalistic accounts of the time as well as in recent cultural history and criticism. See, for example, David Halberstam, *The Fifties* (New York: Fawcett Columbine, 1993), 476–79; Peter Guralnick, *Last Train to Memphis: The Rise of Elvis Presley* (Boston: Little, Brown, 1994), 301, 351–53, 378–79; and Gilbert B. Rodman, *Elvis after Elvis: The Posthumous Career of a Living Legend* (New York: Routledge, 1996), 146–54.

12 In a letter to Sir Lew Grade, the talent manager of a number of "British invasion" rock and roll groups, Sullivan claimed to "discover" Presley's drawing power "in a 1956 incident [during] my public appearances throughout the United States for Lincoln-Mercury, in the South. I read newspaper headlines in Southern papers about the then unknown Elvis Presley who was drawing record crowds to Fairgrounds. Because I am a newspaperman, whenever a Page 1 phenomenon occurs—whether it involves and [*sic*] unknown Presley—or the unknown Beatles ... my newspaper training instinctively translates a Page 1 story into a Page 1 showbiz attraction." Sullivan spun quite the yarn to Grade, given that his initial opposition to Presley was well documented, as was Presley's previous appearances on network television in 1956 prior to his relatively late-in-the-year initial appearance on the Sullivan program.

13 William Boddy's *Fifties Television: The Industry and Its Critics* (Urbana: University of Illinois Press, 1993) provides an insightful account of the critical and industrial tensions as television grew into a mass medium in the 1950s.

14 Trent Hill, "The Enemy Within: Censorship in Rock Music in the 1950s," in *Present Tense: Rock & Roll and Culture*, ed. Anthony DeCurtis (Durham, N.C.: Duke University Press, 1992), 45–46.

15 This is not to claim that rock and roll had any direct effect on the civil rights movement or in changing the minds of young white Americans regarding racial equality. In fact, Brian Ward, in *Just My Soul Responding: Rhythm and Blues, Black Consciousness, and Race Relations* details a number of incidents of battles between African American and white fans after rock and roll concerts in the mid-1950s, not in the South but in Newport, Rhode Island, and Boston, Massachusetts.

16 See, for example, Thomas Doherty, *Teenagers and Teenpics: The Juvenalization of American Movies in the 1950s* (Boston: Unwin Hyman, 1988); and John A. Jackson, *Big Beat Heat: Alan Freed and the Early Years of Rock & Roll* (New York: Schirmer Books, 1991).

17 "Can Elvis Sell Soap?" *Sponsor* 10.21 (October 15, 1956): 33.

18 Ibid., 106–8.

19 Ibid., 96.

20 Ibid., 108.

21 Gould's identification of Presley with a traditionally female role indicates anxiety at Presley's displacement of traditional 1950s gender roles, subverting the norms of heterosexual masculinity, while at the same time representing sexual potency on the television screen. See Jack Gould, "TV: New Phenomenon—Elvis Presley Rises to Fame as Vocalist Who Is Virtuoso of Hootchy-Kootchy," *New York Times*, June 6, 1956, 67. The cultural critic David R. Shumway characterizes the reaction to Presley's "hootchy-kootchy" as "feminization," arguing that Presley "became feminized because he displayed his body as a sexual object," thus violating gender boundaries. For Shumway, Elvis's self-feminization is transgressive. Rock critics of the 1960s and beyond, I suggest, did not acknowledge the transgressiveness of Presley's gender performance because it did not fit their model of rock and roll as heterosexually masculine, modernist, and out of the mainstream. Instead, their reading of Presley in the 1950s privileged Presley's sexual and racial transgressions as the major points of conflict with mainstream culture. It was also easier for rock critics to displace part of the blame for television's neutering of Presley and rock and roll onto over half of the audience, teenage girls, who were pathologized even by supporters of rock and roll. Those who privileged Presley's sexual threat found it easy to blame those who most needed to be "protected" from it for television's subsequent turn to bland rock and roll programming and performers, most notably characterized by *American Bandstand*. See David R. Shumway, "Watching Elvis: The Male Rock Star as Object of the Gaze," in *The Other Fifties: Interrogating Midcentury American Icons*, ed. Joel Foreman (Urbana: University of Illinois Press, 1997), p. 127.

22 Jack Gould, "Elvis Presley: Lack of Responsibility Is Shown by TV in Exploiting Teen-Agers," *New York Times*, September 16, 1956, part 2, p. 13.

23 Ed Sullivan's coproducer Marlo Lewis claims that the controversial choice to film Presley from the waist up was due to a circulating rumor, allegedly confirmed by an eyewitness. The rumor had it that "Elvis has been hanging a small soft-drink bottle from his groin underneath his pants, and when he wiggles his leg it looks as though his pecker reaches down to his knee!" Presley was therefore shot from the waist up to ensure that his prosthetic self-endowment would not grace America's living rooms. I question the veracity of this account, in that Lewis and Lewis place Presley's first televised appearance on the Sullivan show as occurring in 1955. Presley did not appear on national television until January 1956. Lewis and Lewis also place that appearance as Presley's second on the show; many other sources assert that it was his third appearance. See Marlo Lewis and Mina Beth Lewis, *Prime Time* (Los Angeles: J. P. Tarcher, 1979), 146.

24 "Web Reports Solid Rating for First ABC-TV R&R Show," *Billboard*, May 13, 1957, 34.

25 Charlie Sinclair, "'The Big Beat' Rocks, Rolls—and Stumbles," *Billboard*, July 22, 1957, 20.

26 Jackson, *Big Beat Heat*, 55–56.

27 John A. Jackson, *American Bandstand: Dick Clark and the Making of a Rock and Roll Empire* (New York: Oxford University Press, 1997), 18–21.

28 June Bundy, "TV-DJ.s' Status Up at Local Level," *Billboard*, Novermber 10, 1956, 62.

29 Jackson, *American Bandstand*, 19. I am indebted to the Jackson book for much of my descriptive account of *American Bandstand*.

30 Ibid., 37.

31 Oliver Treyz, quoted in Leonard H. Goldenson (with Marvin J. Wolf), *Beating the Odds: The Untold Story behind the Rise of ABC: The Stars, Struggles, and Egos that Transformed Network Television by the Man Who Made It Happen* (New York: Charles Scribner's Sons, 1991), 162.

32 "ABC-TV's Oliver Treyz: Daring Young Man with a Mission," *Printer's Ink*, June 20, 1958, 56.

33 Technically a local program, *American Bandstand* in this period was a two-hour broadcast on WFIL in Philadelphia. It was transmitted daily by ABC for an hour and a half, leaving the remaining time to local sponsors.

34 "TV Jock Finally Comes into Own," *Billboard*, October 7, 1957, 28.

35 Ibid., p. 32.

36 This was not unproblematic, as we will see, and it may have led, in part, to the reghettoization of rock and roll performed by African American artists to the post–rock and roll rhythm and blues category.

37 Jackson, *American Bandstand*, 75.

38 Bob Rolontz, "From Radio Jock to Nat'l Name—How Clark Does It," *Variety*, Mach, 24, 1958, 4.

39 "TV Jock Finally Comes Into Own," 28.

40 Rolontz, "From Radio Jock to Nat'l Name—How Clark Does It," 4.

41 John Jackson theorizes that *American Bandstand* failed as a weeknight prime-time offering for two reasons. First, the teens and housewives drawn to the afternoon version of the program were otherwise occupied at that time. Second, male breadwinners had control of the television dial by 7:30 in the evening, and they were not interested in watching the program.

42 Jackson, *American Bandstand*, 105.

43 Review, "The Dick Clark Show," *Variety*, February 19, 1958, 31.

44 "Beech-Nut Hitches Its Sales to TV Star," *Printer's Ink*, January 30, 1959, 72.

45 Brian Ward, *Just My Soul Responding: Rhythm and Blues, Black Consciousness, and Race Relations* (Berkeley: University of California Press, 1998), 168.

46 Jackson, *Big Beat Heat*, 244.

47 See, for example, Jackson, *American Bandstand*, chapters 5 and 9.

48 Jackson, *Big Beat Heat*, 280.

49 "'Teen Buyers Grow Up,' Warns Miller," *Billboard*, September 8, 1956, 17, 22.

50 June Bundy, "Censorship Eases on Aired Lyrics as Acceptance Grows," *Billboard*, January 19, 1959, 2.

51 "Can Elvis Sell Soap?" 108.

52 According to a 1956 survey of 4,000 teens (12–18) conducted by Scholastic Magazines, 73 percent of boys and 79 percent of girls owned radios, and 60 percent of girls owned phonographs. In addition, 61.7 percent of girls in junior high and 48 percent of girls in senior high purchased records on a monthly basis, compared to 46.6 percent and 41.9 percent, respectively, of their male counterparts. See June Bundy, "Gals Best Disk and Phono Buyers in Teen-Age Bracket," *Billboard*, August 25, 1956, 15, 20.

53 Peter Guralnick, *Careless Love: The Unmaking of Elvis Presley* (Boston: Little, Brown, 1999), 29.

Girl Groups

Gillian Gaar

> "Nobody in the business really took female performers too seriously back then. The system just wasn't open to women. If a man's career wasn't successful anymore, he could move into A&R or production, or into the company hierarchy—but we couldn't do that."
>
> —Lesley Gore, in *Girl Groups: The Story of a Sound*

In early 1961, the Shirelles became the first all-female group to top the singles charts with "Will You Love Me Tomorrow." In the next two years they would have ten more hits in the Top 40, including five in the Top 10. But more important than their string of hits was their role in popularizing the "girl group" sound, the first major rock style associated explicitly with women. Its roots lay in the '50s, in the music of groups like the Bobbettes and the Chantels, but where those groups had been rarities in the male-dominated landscape of vocal groups, by the early '60s there was a veritable explosion of all-female groups on the music scene.

The girl groups provided a voice for a generation of adolescents, female and male, in literally thousands of songs that addressed the issues of romance, heartbreak, and the endless search for true love. The appealing honesty and sincerity of the genre was underscored by the fact that the girls in the groups were primarily in their teens themselves, and many of the best songwriters of the era were also in their early twenties. Though the groups occasionally wrote their own material, it was their image that made the greatest impact with audiences, especially the female audiences that comprised most of the record-buying public at the time. Suddenly, aspiring female performers didn't have to look to the likes of a Frankie Lymon to provide inspiration, as the Chantels had—they could now find ready role models in girls their own age.

The importance of the girl group image and its effect on the female rock audience has traditionally been overlooked by rock historians, who tend to regard girl groups as interchangeable, easily manipulated puppets, while the ones with the "real" talent were the managers, songwriters, publishers, and producers who worked behind the groups. And because the life expectancy of the groups was usually brief, and because their successors appeared in a seemingly never-ending stream, the role of the "girls" in the girl group equation has been diminished. An equally persistent stereotype has been the assumption that any group of girls with the ability to carry a tune could have a hit—as long as they remained malleable to the whims of the male Svengalis who really called the shots.

Unfortunately for the groups, their dependence on the manager/songwriter/producer teams around them did put them at a disadvantage as far as maintaining their careers after the initial flush of success. Once a winning formula for a group had been identified, it was repeated in subsequent singles until the group stopped having hits. The group was then left to return to obscurity, while the production teams moved on to the next formula and the next group. It was a scenario that would be repeated innumerable times during the girl group era. Because of their age and lack of experience, the groups were unsure how to go about voicing their own concerns, leaving them at a further disadvantage. In later interviews with these performers, a recurring complaint is the complete lack of involvement, let alone control, they were allowed in decisions affecting their careers. With the focus on getting hits the primary goal, it was all too easy to overlook the feelings of, again, the most expendable element in the unit: the performers.

Ultimately, trying to single out who played the most "important" role in the creation of a girl group hit record is an exercise in futility. A poor vocal has the capability of ruining the best written, best produced song; among the girl groups, the whole was certainly greater than the sum of its parts. There was also the fact that the "man behind the scenes," whether producer, songwriter, or manager, was sometimes a woman—so much for the "male Svengali" theories. To the public, it was the overall sound—the vocal harmonizing of doo-wop with a bright, uptempo backbeat—that was important, not the offstage machinations. And unlike the male "teen idols," with their placid musings on eternal devotion, the material performed by the girl groups often went beyond one-dimensional Moon-and-June sentimentality in its examination of adolescent emotions, creating engaging, well-crafted, and impassioned songs that changed the simple scenario of boy-meets-girl into something far more complex.

After the success of previous hits like the Bobbettes' "Mr. Lee" and the Chantels' "Maybe," the Shirelles' "Will You Love Me Tomorrow" heralded the true start of the girl group era. It was the first major hit for the group (and the first major success for the songwriters, Carole King and Gerry Goffin), who had been performing together since the late '50s. Shirley Owens, Beverly Lee, Doris Coley, and Addie "Micki" Harris, who attended the same high school in Passaic, New Jersey, had been inspired by groups like the Chantels to form their own group, originally called the Poquellos. After making their debut at a school show, a classmate introduced the group to her mother, Florence Greenberg, who ran her own record label, Tiara. Greenberg signed the group, now called the Shirelles, and released their first single, "I Met Him on a Sunday," in the spring of 1958. A group composition, "Sunday" was the story of a weeklong romance, set against a backdrop of the Shirelles' vocal harmonies with handclaps and fingersnapping providing a smooth, steady beat. After being leased to Decca Records, the single eventually reached number 49 on the charts.

Further singles followed, but none were able to match the mild success of "Sunday." In 1959, Greenberg started a new label, Scepter, and brought in a new producer to work with the Shirelles, Luther Dixon, a former member of the Four Buddies and a songwriter for such artists as Pat Boone, Perry Como, and Nat "King" Cole. Dixon's first collaboration with the Shirelles was producing and arranging "Tonight's the Night," a song written by Shirley Owens. Released in 1960, "Tonight" offered a personal perspective of teenage romance, with Owens (who sang the lead vocal) preparing for her big date in a mood of nervous anticipation, vacillating between the doubts and excitement of beginning "a great romance." The single cracked the Top 40, reaching number 39, and set the stage perfectly for "Will You Love Me Tomorrow," a song Dixon brought to the group.

Dixon had heard "Tomorrow" while visiting the offices of Aldon Music, the publishing company where Carole King and Gerry Goffin worked. King and Goffin had originally offered "Tomorrow" to Johnny Mathis, but when it was turned down, Dixon was able to persuade the songwriting team to give it to the Shirelles, in addition to having them shorten the song, which was originally over four minutes long. The Shirelles had their own reservations about recording "Tomorrow," feeling the song sounded "too white." But "Tomorrow" was a logical follow-up to "Tonight's the Night," taking the teenage drama to the next level. If Owens had pondered, somewhat obliquely, the dangers of going "too far" with her boyfriend in "Tonight's the Night," she had now clearly decided to give in to his demands, but wondered about the consequences of her actions by asking, "Will you still love me tomorrow?" The directness of the question was a startling one from a teenage girl, and unusual in a genre that generally assumed a lifetime of happiness would follow once you'd attained the boy of your dreams. In "Tomorrow" Owens had attained the boy, but her feelings about the permanence of love appeared to be more uncertain than ever.

Released in late 1960, "Tomorrow" (which also featured Carole King on kettle drums) hit the top of the charts in early 1961, and the hits continued for the next two years. "Soldier Boy," released in 1962, became the Shirelles' second number 1 hit, and they had further Top 10 successes with "Baby It's You," "Mama Said," and "Dedicated to the One I Love," a song which only reached number 83 on its original release in 1959, but which climbed up to number 3 after the success of "Tomorrow." But the Shirelles' dependence on Dixon as their producer, arranger, and song provider meant that the foundation of their success was shaky, as they discovered when Dixon quit working with the group at the end of 1962. The group managed another Top 10 hit with "Foolish Little Girl," but by the end of 1963 they'd made their last appearance in the Top 40.

Nor was there any financial compensation to enjoy now that their run on the charts was over, for on turning twenty-one the group members found that the money they had earned, supposedly held in trust for them by Greenberg, had been spent in the usual manner—for recording costs, promotion, touring, and so on. The fact that they were also legally forced to remain with Scepter did nothing for the Shirelles' quickly disintegrating morale, though they continued recording for the label until 1968. Afterwards, Shirley Owens—now Shirley Alston—formed her own group called Shirley and the Shirelles, and later recorded two solo albums as "Lady Rose"; the other group members formed their own "Shirelles" combinations and found work on the "oldies" circuit.

In contrast to the performers, the women songwriters of the early '60s were in a better position to both exert control over their careers and make the kind of money the girl groups themselves rarely saw. Three of the main female/male songwriting teams of the time were also husband and wife: Carole King and Gerry Goffin, Ellie Greenwich and Jeff Barry, and Cynthia Weil and Barry Mann. King and Goffin and Weil and Mann worked for Aldon Music, which was formed by Al Nevins and Don Kirshner in 1958. The company had their first hit that same year with Connie Francis's "Stupid Cupid," which was also the first hit for the songwriters, Neil Sedaka and Howard Greenfield. Sedaka, a solo performer as well as a songwriter, had grown up in the same Brooklyn neighborhood as Carole King and had a number 9 hit in 1959 with a song written for her, "Oh Carol" (King later answered Sedaka with "Oh Neil").

Born Carole Klein in 1942, King began playing the piano at age four and was writing songs and performing in vocal groups by her teens, recording some unsuccessful singles for ABC-Paramount and singing on demo records with another neighborhood friend, Paul Simon. While attending Queens College she met aspiring songwriter Gerry Goffin, whom she married when she was eighteen. The two quit college to see if they could make their mark in music, and were hired by Aldon in 1959. King also continued her recording career and had a Top 40 hit in 1962 with "It Might as Well Rain Until September," originally written for Bobby Vee. But she quickly abandoned performing for the work she really preferred: writing, arranging, and producing.

As songwriters, it was relatively easy for women to get involved in the different aspects of record production, especially in the whirl of activity surrounding the Brill Building. Located at 1619 Broadway in Manhattan, the building was seen as the home of the hits, though in fact all manner of music industry offices were located in surrounding buildings as well (Aldon, for example, was located across the street at 1650 Broadway). Still, the Brill Building became synonymous with hit records, and the area was full of hopeful singers, songwriters, and producers, all looking for that one deal that would lead to a hit. Songwriter Ellie Greenwich's reflections on the girl group era in Charlotte Greig's *Will You Still Love Me Tomorrow?* demonstrate the energized atmosphere of the times: "There were many small labels in the Brill Building ... If you played a song and they liked it, they'd say, 'Let's think. Do we know anyone who can do this? Do you?' So then you could go out and look for an artist, and a record label would give you a shot to produce a single. If it did well, great, you started getting a name for yourself. If it didn't, so what, no big deal."

After their success with the Shirelles, Goffin and King went on to work with a wide range of female vocalists in the early '60s, maintaining a longer presence in the Top 40 charts than the performers they wrote for were able to match. Little Eva was one such performer, who became virtually an overnight star when she recorded the team's "The Loco-Motion" but who disappeared from the charts completely in less than a year. Born Eva Narcissus Boyd in Belhaven, North Carolina, in 1943, Boyd had moved to New York in 1960, where she met Earl-Jean McCrea, a singer with the Cookies, Boyd then decided to try singing herself and auditioned for Goffin and King, not only winning a place as an alternate Cookie, but also netting a job as the songwriters' live-in babysitter. At the time, Goffin and King were working on a follow-up for Dee Dee Sharp, who'd had a number 2 hit with "Mashed Potato Time" in March 1962. Inspired by Boyd's dancing while listening to the radio, the team wrote "The Loco-Motion" and also had Boyd sing on the demo of the song.

There are differing accounts as to whether "Loco-Motion" was ever actually offered to Sharp at all, but the end result was the same: Sharp did not record it, and it was Boyd's demo that was released as the first single on the new Dimension record label, credited to "Little Eva." Released in June 1962, the song's pulsing, driving rhythms took "Loco-Motion" to number 1 by August, and "Little Eva" was a star at age nineteen; in the wake of her success, even Boyd's sister, Idalia, was brought in to release her own single, "Hula Hoppin'" / "Some Kind of Wonderful" in early 1963. By that time, Boyd's own career was in descent. Her second single, "Keep Your Hands Off My Baby," was released in November 1962 and reached a respectable number 12, but her next single, another "dance" song called "Let's Turkey Trot," was her last Top 40 entry. Boyd retired from the music business in the 1970s, but returned in 1989 with the album *Back on Track,* and performed on the oldies circuit.

The Cookies, who had provided backup vocals on "Loco-Motion," also had their own string of Top 40 hits by Goffin and King. The group, Ethel "Earl-Jean" McCrea, Dorothy Jones, and Margaret Ross, had started in Brooklyn, and after winning an Apollo Theatre Amateur Night contest, had become backup vocalists; in addition to Boyd's records, they also sang on records for Tony Orlando, Ben E. King, Neil Sedaka, Carole King, and on Eydie Gorme's hit "Blame It on the Bossa Nova" (written by Barry Mann and Cynthia Weil). Their first Top 40 entry as the Cookies came in 1962 with "Chains," followed by "Don't Say Nothin' Bad (About My Baby)" in 1963 (both written by Goffin and King) and their final Top 40 hit, "Girls Grow Up Faster Than Boys," came in 1964. McCrea also pursued a solo career as "Earl-Jean," and had a minor hit with Goffin and King's "I'm Into Something Good," which reached number 38 in 1964, three months before Herman's Hermits would take their version of the song into the Top 20. In the late '60s, the Cookies broke up; some of the members later reformed the group in the late '90s.

The Chiffons were another group that found success with Goffin and King songs. Hailing from the Bronx, Judy Craig, Barbara Lee, Patricia Bennett, and Sylvia Peterson attended high school together and, in the expected fashion, had put together a group. Their first record, released on the Big Deal label in 1960, was a cover of the Shirelles' "Tonight's the Night," after which the group recorded for a number of other small labels. The Chiffons were then signed to Laurie Records on the strength of a demo tape they recorded for their friend Ronnie Mack, an aspiring songwriter who also became the Chiffons' manager.

"He's So Fine," one of the songs on the demo the Chiffons recorded for Mack, became their first single for Laurie, released in early 1963. The song's opening "doo-lang doo-lang" phrase proved to be an irresistibly catchy hook, and "He's So Fine" spent five weeks at number 1. The follow-up, "One Fine Day," was written by Goffin and King and had originally been intended for Little Eva but was given instead to the Chiffons to tie in with the "fine" theme of their first hit. Little Eva had already recorded her version of the song, but her vocals were erased from the master recording (which also featured a vibrant piano part from Carole King) and new vocals by the Chiffons were dubbed in. "One Fine Day," released within a few months of "He's So Fine," became a number 5 hit for the Chiffons—while Little Eva was stuck with releasing a "Loco-Motion" tie-in called "Old Smokey Locomotion," which didn't even crack the Top 40. The Chiffons had a final "fine" hit at the end of the year with "A Love So Fine," which reached number 40. The group also recorded under the name the Four Pennies and attempted to move beyond the girl group genre, recording the psychedelic-flavored "Nobody Knows What's Going On (In My Mind But Me)" in 1965 (the Shirelles had tried a similar ploy with "One of the Flower People"). When this proved to be unsuccessful, the group reverted to their earlier style and had a final Top 40 hit in 1966 with "Sweet Talkin' Guy." Bennett and Craig continue to perform as the Chiffons on the oldies circuit.

Ellie Greenwich's work as a songwriter soon rivaled Carole King's in the girl group sweep-stakes. Born in Brooklyn in 1940, Greenwich moved to Levittown, Long Island, in 1951, picking up the accordion as her first instrument before moving to piano. Like King, she recorded a number of singles beginning in the late '50s, under a variety of names (Ellie Gaye, Ellie Gree, Kellie Douglas) with little success. After graduating from college in 1961, she taught high school for three and a half weeks, but quit to pursue a career in music, which ensured her arrival at the Brill Building soon after. Initially mistaken for Carole King when she visited the offices of Jerry Leiber and Mike Stoller, who were now running their own publishing company, Trio Music, Greenwich was hired as a staff writer at one hundred dollars a week.

The Exciters were one of the first groups Greenwich worked with. The group, based in Jamaica, Queens, was originally an all-female quartet (Brenda Reid, Lillian Walker, Carol Johnson, and Sylvia Wilbur) called the Masterettes who sang with a male vocal group called the Masters. After recording the single "Follow the Leader" / "Never Never" for a local label, the group auditioned for Leiber and Stoller, who suggested a name change and gave them a record by Gil Hamilton, "Tell Her," to learn. Herb Rooney, a singer with the Masters, helped the group arrange the song (he added the "doop-dee-doop" background phrase), and ended up becoming a member of the newly named Exciters.

Released in 1962 (by which time Wilbur had quit the group), "Tell Him" raced up the charts to number 4, powered by Reid's energetic lead vocal, Leiber and Stoller's bright production, and, of course, the "doop-dee-doops." Unfortunately, "Tell Him" proved to be the high point in the Exciters' career, for none of their subsequent singles reached the Top 40. Their second single, "He's Got the Power," written by Greenwich and Tony Powers and released in 1963, featured another gutsy vocal from Reid, but failed to crack the Top 40. The Exciters' original version of

"Do-Wah-Diddy," written by Greenwich and her new collaborator (and husband) Jeff Barry, and also released in 1963, again fared poorly, peaking at number 78; the following year the song would become a number 1 hit for the British group Manfred Mann as "Do-Wah-Diddy-Diddy." The group broke up in 1974, but a revamped line up was formed in the late '80s.

In 1963, Greenwich began working with record producer Phil Spector, who used her material for the roster of girl groups he was producing; Greenwich and Tony Powers wrote for Darlene Love ("(Today I Met) The Boy I'm Gonna Marry"), and Greenwich and Jeff Barry wrote for such groups as the Crystals ("Da Doo Ron Ron" and "Then He Kissed Me") and the Ronettes ("Be My Baby"). Greenwich also inadvertently found herself back in the performing arena briefly in 1962 via a song written with Barry, "What a Guy." The two recorded the song as a demo for the Sensations, overdubbing all the voices themselves, but when their publishers decided to release the demo itself as the single, it was credited to a nonexistent "group" called the Raindrops. When "What a Guy" reached number 41, and a second record by the two, the lively "The Kind of Boy You Can't Forget," was a Top 40 hit the following year, a real group was needed for live work, and Greenwich, her sister, and Bobby Bosco (who replaced Barry) were assembled to lip-synch songs for the Raindrops' "live" performances.

Greenwich and Barry also became the primary songwriting team for Red Bird, a label Leiber and Stoller started in 1964. Leiber and Stoller had also brought in George Goldner, who'd previously released the Chantels' records, to help with promotion, promising him a partnership in the company if the first record was a hit. While listening to an assortment of demos at home, Goldner's wife suggested choosing a Greenwich/Barry/Spector song, "Chapel of Love," an ode to everlasting marital bliss previously recorded, though not released, by the Ronettes and the Crystals. A New Orleans trio called the Dixie Cups ultimately released the song, giving Red Bird their first number 1 record. In addition to the Dixie Cups, Barry and Greenwich provided songs for a number of Red Bird acts, including the Jelly Beans, the Butterflies, and, most notably, the Shangri-Las.

The records of the Shangri-Las plumbed the depths of teenage angst with a high sense of melodrama that had been completely absent from other girl group records. The group, twins Mary Ann and Margie Ganser, and sisters Betty and Mary Weiss, grew up in Queens, and began singing together in high school, performing at local sock hops and talent shows. They eventually found a manager/producer/songwriter in George "Shadow" Morton, and recorded two singles for Smash and Spokane Records before Morton, who had met Greenwich in high school, brought a demo of the Shangri-Las singing his own "Remember (Walkin' in the Sand)" to Red Bird. Initially over seven minutes long (complete with a spoken intro from Morton), Greenwich and Barry tightened up the song and created a lament to lost love that was an epic on a grand scale, from the opening piano chords relentlessly banged out on the keyboard to the fade-out that mixed seagull cries with the Shangri-Las' own finger-snapping chorus.

"Remember," released in 1964, reached number 5 in the charts, but the Shangri-Las' next record created even more of a sensation. "Leader of the Pack," a Morton-Barry-Greenwich collaboration, was another melodramatic epic, a Romeo and Juliet teenage tragedy with all the contemporary trappings—a leather jacketed rebel without a cause, a good girl whose love will save him, and (via the appropriate sound effects), a motorcycle. Released in the fall of 1964, the record's focus on death (after the singer's parents forbid her to date the rebellious "Leader," he dies in a motorcycle accident) kicked off considerable controversy, resulting in the song's being banned in Britain. But in the U.S. (where the record was "unofficially" banned at some stations), it went to number 1, and paved the way for a further two years of hits from the group.

Barry and Greenwich wrote much of the Shangri-Las' subsequent material, including "Out in the Streets," "He Cried," "The Train from Kansas City," and "Give Us Your Blessings," another "death disc" where both the young lovers die in a car accident. "Blessings," which only reached the Top 30, was a genteel rewrite of "Leader" minus the allure of a "bad" boy; "I Can Never Go Home Anymore," written by Morton and released in 1965, was a far more effective tale of untimely death, and the Shangri-Las' final Top 10 hit. In this story, it is the singer's mother who dies as the result of the loneliness brought on by the selfishness of the daughter, who has left home to be with her boyfriend. As the thoughtless daughter, Mary Weiss sang the lead with a tortured intensity, her heartrending cries of "Mama!" ringing out like a primal scream.

The Shangri-Las' image was as striking as their music. Unlike most of the girl groups, who wore matching frilly dresses and heels, the Shangri-Las projected a more streetwise look in their hipster trousers, ruffled shirts, and go-go boots. The girl groups were usually promoted more as "groups" than as individuals, and the substitution of one girl for another in the studio and on the road was rarely noticed, much less commented on; and though the Shangri-Las were no exception in this regard (the group's four members rarely appeared together), their "tough" look gave them a greater individuality than most other girl groups of the time.

But the circumstances of the group's demise were painfully familiar. Despite their hits and frequent tours, the Shangri-Las saw little of the generated profits, which were eaten up in the black hole of management and studio costs. The group had a Top 40 hit in 1966 with "Long Live Our Love," an uncharacteristically chipper song of support for a boy no longer a rebel but a patriot serving his country overseas, but two subsequent singles, "Dressed in Black" and the haunting "Past, Present, and Future" (based on Beethoven's "Moonlight Sonata") failed to chart. The Shangri-Las moved on to Mercury Records, but never regained their previous momentum, and after a brief turn on the oldies circuit in the '70s, monumentally dropped out of sight. Mary Ann Ganser died of encephalitis in 1971, and the remaining Shangri-Las reunited in 1980, but the group broke up for good when Marge Ganser died of breast cancer in 1996.

In spite of the contributions to the girl group genre made by Florence Greenberg, Carole King, and Ellie Greenwich—or, for that matter, Don Kirshner and Shadow Morton—when rock historians write about the "male Svengalis" who called the shots behind the girl group scene, they are usually referring to one man in particular: Phil Spector. The creator of the glorious "wall of sound" is revered in countless rock histories which gloss over the price Spector exacted in creating that sound. Born in New York City, Phil Spector moved to Los Angeles with his family when his father died, and while in high school wrote a song taken from a line on his father's tombstone, "To Know Him Is to Love Him." The song was his first number 1 hit as a songwriter, producer, and performer, having been recorded by his own group, the Teddy Bears (which included Spector, Marshall Leib, and lead singer Annette Kleinbard) in 1958. When the group found themselves short-changed as far as their royalties were concerned, they wasted no time in confronting the matter head-on, declaring the contract with their record company (Dore) void because they weren't twenty-one when they signed. But a move to Imperial Records resulted in no further hits, and additional tensions within the group led to their breakup.

Spector had by this time made the acquaintance of Lester Sill, a music industry figure and, later, Spector's partner in his record company Philles Records. Sill set him up with Leiber and Stoller, then working for Atlantic Records in New York, where Spector moved in 1960. He quickly gained experience working with such performers as Arlene Smith (who was trying for a solo career after leaving the Chantels), Ruth Brown, LaVern Baker, and the Paris Sisters, producing the latter group's Top 5 hit "I Love How You Love Me." In 1961, Spector started Philles Records, and latched on to the growing girl group boom by signing the Crystals. The Crystals, who consisted of Barbara Alston, Dolores "La La" Brooks, Dee Dee Kennibrew, Mary Thomas, and Patricia Wright, were from Brooklyn and had been brought together by their manager (and Alston's uncle) Benny Wells. After meeting them, Spector produced the group's (and Philles') first record, "Oh Yeah Maybe Baby"—though it was the B-side, the doo-wop flavored "There's No Other (Like My Baby)," that became the hit, reaching number 20 in early 1962.

Though a dispute over money made the Crystals hesitant about working with Spector again, the group relented and recorded Barry Mann and Cynthia Weil's "Uptown" (originally intended for Tony Orlando) for Philles, and the song hit the Top 20 in the spring of 1962. But the group's suspicions about Spector's treatment of them were hardly assuaged when he then had them record Goffin and King's stark "He Hit Me (And It Felt Like a Kiss)." Goffin later claimed that he and King were "inspired" by Little Eva's explanation that the black eye her boyfriend had given her was proof that "he really loves me," though he did admit the song's blatant masochism was "a little radical for those times." Lester Sill was more critical in his assessment, calling the tune a "terrible fucking song." Nor were the Crystals happy with the number. "We didn't like that one," Alston told writer Alan Betrock. "We absolutely hated it. Still do."

But the feelings of the Crystals were hardly uppermost in Spector's mind. Hearing a demo of a new Gene Pitney song, "He's a Rebel," while visiting the offices of Liberty Records (who were planning to have Vikki Carr record it), Spector managed to acquire a copy of the demo from Pitney and flew to Los Angeles, where he decided to record the song as the next Crystals record—without the Crystals, since they were proving so troublesome. A group of L.A. backup singers, the Blossoms, were pulled in to provide the vocals (with Darlene Love on lead), though the song was released as a "Crystals" record, which Spector was able to do since his contract with the group gave him ownership of their name. "He's a Rebel," like "Leader of the Pack," explored the redemptive power of a "good" girl's love for a "bad" boy, but where "Leader" was darkly melo-dramatic, "Rebel" was bright and optimistic. Released in the fall of 1962, "Rebel" went straight to number 1, neatly beating out Carr's version.

The real Crystals were on tour in Ohio when they learned, to their surprise, that they had recorded the number 1 song in the country—and now had to learn it so they could include it in their live act. The Blossoms also recorded the next "Crystals" hit, Mann and Weil's "He's Sure the Boy I Love," which went to number 11; meanwhile, the real Crystals found themselves recording "(Lets Dance) The Screw," another ploy of Spector's to fulfill a royalty obligation. Their next two hits, Greenwich and Barry's infectiously happy "Da Doo Ron Ron" and "Then He Kissed Me," were the first Crystals records to reach the Top 10 that featured their own voices and not those of the Blossoms, but they were also the last records by the group to make the Top 40. By the end of 1963, Spector was involved with a new group, the Ronettes, and the Crystals were no longer of any interest to him. In an effort to try and salvage something from their career, the Crystals actually sued Spector for unpaid royalties, a move rarely undertaken by any girl group. The Crystals lost their suit, but they did manage to secure the rights to their name again, enabling them to continue performing.

If his eye (or ear) for detail, as well as his relentless drive for perfection had resulted in a string of hits readily identifiable as "Phil Spector records," Spector's obsessiveness was also about to manifest itself in a particularly unpleasant fashion in the case of the Ronettes. The Ronettes were two sisters, Veronica (Ronnie) and Estelle Bennett, and their cousin Nedra Talley, who grew up in New York's Spanish Harlem. Ronnie was already a budding performer when she found further inspiration from Frankie Lymon; as she quite candidly says in her autobiography *Be My Baby*, "If he hadn't made a record called 'Why Do Fools Fall in Love,' I wouldn't be sitting here writing this today." It wasn't long before Ronnie and a variety of other relatives became a group, making their debut at Amateur Night at the Apollo. After that performance, the group slimmed down to Ronnie, Estelle, and Nedra, and billed themselves as Ronnie and the Relatives. The group then began building their career by taking singing lessons and next found a manager who got them live work at neighborhood bar mitzvahs.

Their manager also got them a deal with Colpix Records, who released the Relatives' first single, "I Want a Boyfriend" / "Sweet Sixteen," in August 1961. The group continued recording for Colpix until 1963—with little to show for it except a name change to the Ronettes, which they'd adopted in 1962—in addition to working as backup singers on records for Del Shannon and *Gidget* star James Darren. But as a live act, the Ronettes were moving up with greater results, graduating from the bar mitzvah circuit to neighborhood sock hops and, shortly after the release of their first single, to the Peppermint Lounge, one of New York's hot spots. The three had dressed up for a night on the town in form-fitting gowns and beehive hairdos ("stacked up to the ceiling," in Ronnie's words) and while waiting in line to get into the Lounge were mistaken for the girl group hired to dance at the club and told to come in. Their dancing skills won them a regular gig at ten dollars each per night, as well as the chance to occasionally sing with the house band, Joey Dee and the Starlighters (who had a number 1 hit with "Peppermint Twist" in 1962). Their stint at the Peppermint brought them to the attention of WINS DJ Murray "The K" Kaufman, who hosted his own rock shows at Brooklyn's Fox Theater and booked the Ronettes as his "dancing girls." Their Peppermint connection also got them hired as extras in the Starlighters' film *Hey, Let's Twist*.

Though some accounts relate that the Ronettes connected with Phil Spector via a misdialed phone call, Ronnie's book maintains the call was no "accident"; Estelle had simply worked up the courage to dial Spector at his office, and her courage was rewarded with a chance to audition. Spector was immediately taken with Ronnie and tried to sign her as a solo act, but when the Bennetts' mother refused to let him break up the group, Spector signed all three Ronettes. Nonetheless, he set about dividing the group internally anyway, singling out Ronnie for preferential treatment from the start. When the group recorded their first material for Spector in Los Angeles, Ronnie was allowed to fly out, while Estelle and Nedra had to drive cross-country in the company of Bobby Sheen (from Bob B. Soxx and the Blue Jeans, another Spector group). Ronnie and Phil also began what would end up being a very tumultuous affair.

After recording a number of tracks during 1963 that were initially unreleased (including versions of "The Twist," "Mashed Potato Time," and "Hot Pastrami" that later turned up as "Crystals" songs when they appeared on the album *The Crystals Sing Their Greatest Hits*), the Ronettes made their official Philles debut with a bang: "Be My Baby," co-written by Spector, Greenwich, and Barry. It was a tune that couldn't miss, an evocative ode to love dripping with Spector's extravagant production and Ronnie's sultry voice coming out on top. Released in September 1963, the song quickly reached number 2 in the charts. But what should have been a spectacular beginning for the group turned out in retrospect to be the high point, for by the end of 1964 the Ronettes had their last Top 40 hit, and two years later they disbanded.

Spector's increasing possessiveness of Ronnie helped to accelerate the group's decline. When the group toured England with the Rolling Stones in early 1964, Spector sent the Stones a telegram forbidding them to speak with "his" Ronettes. When the group was scheduled to tour with Dick Clark's Caravan of Stars in 1963, and on the Beatles' final U.S. tour in 1966, Spector kept Ronnie in the studio and had her replaced in the Ronettes' road lineup by another cousin of the Bennetts', Elaine. Spector continued recording Ronettes material, but little of it was released. He began not only separating Ronnie from the group on the road and in the studio, but also keeping her away from anyone on hand while she was recording, bringing her into the production booth with him and then refusing to let her leave.

Yet even after learning from Darlene Love that Spector was married, Ronnie was reluctant to end the relationship, since the Ronettes were so dependent on him for providing their material and producing their records. But after having one of his biggest hits with the Righteous Brothers' "You've Lost That Lovin' Feeling" (written by Mann and Weil), the U.S. failure of Ike and Tina Turner's "River Deep, Mountain High" in 1966 (which Spector co-wrote with Greenwich and Barry) was partially responsible for Spector's temporary withdrawal from recording, effectively ending the Ronettes' career. During this sabbatical, Spector divorced his first wife and married Ronnie, who then became a virtual prisoner in their Los Angeles mansion. Though Ronnie maintains Spector was never physically abusive, his psychological torture proved to be sufficiently demoralizing. Ronnie was allowed to roam the estate—now surrounded by an electrified gate—during the day, but was locked up in the house at night, when the servants' entrance in the kitchen was closed. Her only chance of gaining access to the outside world was if one of the servants unlocked the gates for her—but only with Spector's permission. Spector also provided Ronnie with her own car, complete with inflatable male "decoy," for those times when she was allowed to venture beyond the gates.

Ronnie eventually escaped from Spector, with help from her mother, in 1972, though she'd developed a drinking problem she wouldn't kick for another decade; in *Be My Baby* Ronnie relates that toward the end of her time with Spector she deliberately went on drinking binges in order to get sent to the local rehab center, finding it a pleasant alternative to her life at home. But the years she'd spent with Spector had left their mark. "Darlene and I saw Ronnie after the divorce and we were shocked at how she looked." Blossom Gloria Jones said in a later interview. "She was not the same person … Ronnie was like the cheerleader in the old days, happy-go-lucky. Phil took that away from her."

For his part, Spector did resurface to produce the occasional record (most notably for the Beatles and solo LPs for George Harrison and John Lennon), but eventually became as well known for his eccentricities as for his production skills. In the British television documentary *Rockin' and Rollin' with Phil Spector,* Ronnie charitably attributed Spector's behavior to the intense media scrutinization he received as the "Tycoon of Teen," a title Tom Wolfe had bestowed on him in an article which had originally appeared in the *New York Herald Tribune.* "I think Phil was a very normal person at the very beginning of his career," Ronnie said, "but as time went on, they started writing about him being a genius, and then he'd say, 'Yeah, I am a genius.' Then they say he's the mad genius, so he became the mad genius." She quoted a line from the song "When I Saw You" ("I knew I would lose my mind") to further illustrate her point. "It kinda happened to him," she said. "Not meaning losing his mind over me, but just losing his mind!"

Dee Dee Kennibrew of the Crystals, while calling Spector "obnoxious," also shared some of Ronnie's perceptions: "He was a normal enough person," she told *Rolling Stone.* "But after he began to be successful, I think he tried to be more of a star than his groups—you know, 'Without me, there would be nothing.'" But others who worked with Spector have been more critical in their assessment of his behavior. Miriam Abramson, the business manager at Atlantic Records, recalling Spector's time at the label in the book *Music Man,* stated, "I thought he was insane. I think now, in some sense, you would excuse it as … 'star quality.' But at the time he did it he was no star—he was a pain in the neck."

Ronnie, like many performers who worked with him, had feared that breaking with Spector would cause irreparable damage to her career. But as the later career of Annette Kleinbard, the lead singer in Spector's first group, the Teddy Bears, demonstrates, breaking with Spector might have been the one thing that could have saved the Ronettes' career from being relegated to the oldies circuit. After the Teddy Bears' split, Kleinbard changed her name to Carol Connors and became one of the few women to write and record songs in the hot-rod/surf music genre of the '60s (including "Little Red Cobra" and "Go Go G.T.O."), having later successes as co-author of "The

Night the Lights Went Out in Georgia," "Gonna Fly Now (Theme from *Rocky*)," and "With You I'm Born Again," as well as serving on the Academy Awards music nomination committee.

Darlene Love was another "Spector Survivor," managing to work for him yet not wind up completely under his thumb (though she did change her last name from Wright to Love at his suggestion). Love, the daughter of a Pentecostal minister, had been asked to join the Blossoms by Fanita James, who heard Love singing in church. The group, which also included Gloria Jones and Bobby Sheen, was initially managed by Johnny Otis; they also recorded for a variety of labels in the late '50s and by the early '60s had become well-respected backup singers. The group enjoyed the stability studio work offered, which could also be more lucrative than live work. By the time the Blossoms recorded "He's a Rebel" for Spector, Love had enough financial savvy to ask to be paid triple scale for her work, though she received no royalties. When Spector next approached her to record "He's Sure the Boy I Love," she pressed for better financial compensation, and recorded the song, thinking it would be released under her own name—only to see it released as another Crystals record. Leery about the same thing happening again, she never recorded a final version of "Da Doo Ron Ron" for Spector, who ended up having an actual Crystal, La La Brooks, provide the lead vocal.

Love eventually got her contract and was able to release other singles under her own name in addition to recording as a member of Bob B. Soxx and the Blue Jeans. But the contract made little difference when it came to being paid; Love later claimed to have received only one royalty statement for three thousand dollars during the years she worked with Spector. "That's when we started not really getting along," she said in *Rockin' and Rollin' with Phil Spector.* "It didn't bother me as much then because I was young, inexperienced, and never thought at the time that I was being used. It wasn't till years later that I started feeling like that. Because the records were still being produced and still being put out ... and nobody was getting paid." Love and the Blossoms went on to appear as regulars on the TV rock series *Shindig,* and Love continued doing session work, singing for performers as varied as the Mamas and the Papas, the Beach Boys, Luther Vandross, U2, Dionne Warwick, and Whitney Houston. She also branched out into acting in the '80s, most notably as Danny Glover's wife in *Lethal Weapon* and *Lethal Weapon 2.*

Love sang lead vocals on some of the most memorable records in rock history—and yet, ironically, her face would probably be unfamiliar to many of the people who have bought her records over the years. The same was true for a number of acts in the girl group era, regardless of the fact that the groups, unlike Love, toured regularly and were also having substantial hits. The attacks that branded rock as "nigger music" may have faded, but racism was still very much a part of American society, and despite the beginnings of a civil rights movement, the black girl groups were rarely given the exposure their white counterparts received. As Ruth Brown had found in the '50s, radio may have been colorblind, but television was not: none of the black girl groups of the early '60s appeared on *The Ed Sullivan Show* no matter how many hits they had, whereas a minor contender like Britain's Cliff Richard, who had only two U.S. Top 40 hits at the time, appeared three times. This attitude was common throughout the industry. When producer Jack Good first enlisted Love and the Blossoms to appear as regulars on the TV rock show *Shindig,* he faced opposition from the ABC network because the group was black; only after threatening to take the show elsewhere did the network concede. Love wryly remarked that the Blossoms had been a successful studio act "because nobody knew whether we were black or white." The racial mix in the Ronettes' heritage (the Bennetts' mother was black and Cherokee, their father was white) presented further confusion: initially considered to play the Starlighters' girlfriends in *Hey, Let's Twist,* the group was rejected by the casting director, who found them "too light to play black girls and too dark to play white girls." Fan magazines, primarily catering to a female audience, tended to cover male stars over women, and white performers over black ones.

The denial of such mainstream exposure also eroded the groups' slim grasp on their careers; if the audiences had never seen them, it was easy enough for them to be replaced on the road by other performers—and hard to establish their own image if they did manage to break away from management with the right to use the group's name. Both black and white groups were likely to face monetary disputes, but white acts still had greater opportunities as far as film and television work—though sexism in these fields was powerful enough to undercut women of any race. It was an assessment of the entertainment industry that singer Lesley Gore readily agreed with. Gore might have made it to *The Ed Sullivan Show,* and sung "Sunshine, Lollipops and Rainbows" in the film *Ski Party,* but when remembering the era in *Girl Groups: The Story of a Sound* she stated: "Even though I was a big seller, they only cared about males. That was always clear to me. They just thought it was easier to sell males. It really got to me after a while."

Born in 1946 in Tenafly, New Jersey, Gore was readily accepted as the all-American girl-next-door from the moment she burst onto the music scene in 1963 with "It's My Party." After spending her childhood years practicing songs in front of her bedroom mirror ("Behind that closed door, I slicked my hair back in a fairly credible Elvis imitation," she later told *Ms.*), Gore decided to try for a larger audience, and recorded a demo tape after her sixteenth birthday. The tape got her a contract with Mercury Records, and Gore worked with her producer, Quincy Jones, in choosing her debut single, going through a box of 250 demo tapes. "It's My Party" was eventually selected, partially because Gore liked its "rebellious attitude," and she recorded it on March 30, 1963. The single was released within a week, and shortly afterwards shot to number 1. "It's My Party" had Gore lamenting the loss of her steady boyfriend to an unprincipled rival, and its good-girl-done-wrong theme firmly established Gore as a Nice Girl (who was nonetheless able to exact her revenge in the follow-up single, "Judy's Turn to Cry," which went to number 5).

But though Gore's songs by and large focused on girl group scenarios of love lost and found, she threw a curve ball at her audience with the song "You Don't Own Me," a feisty statement of independence released in 1963, the same year that Betty Friedan's groundbreaking feminist work, *The Feminine Mystique,* was published. In a radical departure from the norm, Gore, in the song, refuses to be seen as the "possession" of a boy, not because she prefers the company of a different boy, but out of a desire for establishing her own autonomy and making her own decisions, whether deciding what to wear or whom to date. This was a defiant attitude at a time when having a boy who hit you instead of kissing you was preferable to having no boy at all, but it was evidently one Gore's audience was more than pleased to hear—the song (written by John Maera and Dave White) went to number 2 and became Gore's second-biggest single.

Gore's subsequent material returned to more conventional ground, and she continued having Top 40 hits through 1967, among them Greenwich and Barry's "Maybe I Know" and "Look of Love." Though her run on the charts gave Gore little in the way of financial reward ("I saw one check and then I didn't see any money until two years ago," she told *Ms.* in 1990), she continued working in the music business, eventually moving into songwriting, co-writing Irene Cara's hit singles for the film *Fame,* and continuing to perform live.

Nona Hendryx is another performer who managed to persevere after the monetarily dry girl group period despite the hardships. "We got ripped off really badly over the years, especially from the Bluebelles era," she says. "We ended up with nothing but our name—I don't know who had the brains enough to ask for that at the time, but somehow we ended up with the name so we could work without any limitations. But we lost a lot of the money that we were entitled to." Born in Trenton, New Jersey, in 1944, Hendryx's career as a performer developed almost by default, for despite growing up in a household where "there was always music around ... it was very much a part of everyday existence," she had little desire to pursue a musical career herself. That began to change in her teens when her friend Sarah Dash invited Hendryx to sing in a local group, the Del Capris. "So I said sure," Hendryx says. "It sounded like fun to me. It wasn't something that I considered as a living, as a vocation. It was just something that was fun to do; it was not something that I felt I was going to be doing for the rest of my life."

Hendryx and Dash eventually met the manager of a Philadelphia group called the Ordettes, who joined them with Ordettes singers Patti LaBelle and Cindy Birdsong to form the Bluebelles in the early '60s. "He put us together initially because a man in Philadelphia was looking for girls to be a group," Hendryx says. "But I wasn't seeking anyone to make me a star at that time because it just did not enter my mind. I didn't want to be a recording artist, I didn't want to be a songwriter, I didn't want to be any of those things! I was just sort of going along with friends." But the Bluebelles became recording artists nonetheless, making records for Newtown Records. Typically, the group had little input regarding the songs they recorded. "The managers pretty much chose material," Hendryx says. "We did very standard material—'Somewhere Over the Rainbow' or 'You'll Never Walk Alone.' We would rework the standard songs into gospel renditions or more soulful renditions. And then we would do our songs about teenage angst, our hearts being broken—you know the stuff!"

It turned out to be the standards that provided the group (now billed as Patti LaBelle and the Bluebelles) with their other Top 40 hits, including "Down the Aisle (Wedding Song)" in 1963 and "You'll Never Walk Alone" in 1964 (they also recorded the original version of "Groovy Kind of Love," later a number 2 hit for the Mindbenders). And despite their forays into "teenage angst," the group gave little thought to being part of the girl group scene at the time. "I don't really look back on it at all to tell you the truth!" says Hendryx now. "When I do, I see that we were a part of the history, but you never know that you're making history when you're doing it. You just don't.

And certainly when you're a teenager you really don't know anything. You're just doing stuff and hoping you get good grades and graduate."

But if the Bluebelles were unaware of making history as a girl group, they soon became well aware of the financial hazards of being a girl group, eventually taking their record company to court for lack of financial compensation. The group had already observed standard music industry swindles: "We would record songs, and listed on there as the writer would be his eight-month-old grandchild!" says Hendryx of their record company's owner. "It was just ridiculous. He owned the recording studio, he owned our contracts, he had his lawyers ... I mean, talk about conflict of interest! But I didn't know anything about conflict of interest. I was fifteen years old. What do I know about conflict of interest, and making a recording contract deal?"

Problems with their label led to the Bluebelles' departure in 1964, by which time the music scene was beginning to change drastically. In February of that year, the Beatles arrived in America, an event that launched the "British Invasion." The Beatles' U.S. success opened the doors for a wide range of British acts, who were no longer dismissed as second-rate imitations of American performers. British beat groups had found their own voice, creating an innovative sound that was now making a sizeable impression on the American charts. The irony was that many of the British groups had been raised on a diet of American rock & roll and rhythm & blues, and were merely reintroducing U.S. audiences to their own musical heritage. The Beatles themselves started out playing songs by Little Richard, Chuck Berry, Buddy Holly, and Elvis Presley, and were now recording Motown and girl group covers (the Shirelles' "Baby It's You" and "Boys," the Marvelettes' "Please Mr. Postman," and the Cookies' "Chains," among others), and as songwriters, John Lennon and Paul McCartney aspired to be the new Goffin and King.

More importantly, the Beatles are credited with re-establishing the idea of a performer's self-sufficiency; they played their own instruments and wrote much of their own material, as the early rock & rollers had. This made the assembly-line techniques of the Brill Building seem obsolete, and as the Beatles and the ensuing wave of cute boy bands in neat suits began to dominate the charts, the girl group production teams seemed all too willing to concede defeat. As a result, the groups that depended on the production teams for their material naturally began to disappear from the charts.

In the changing climate, even the women who had previously been seen as integral to the hit-making process found their power eroded. Ellie Greenwich ultimately lost her production credit on the "Barry and Greenwich" records due to her husband's argument that it was more important for him to establish his name as sole producer; according to him, she'd be having children one day and would be staying home to take care of them. As a result, when the marriage and songwriting partnership crumbled, Greenwich had a hard time re-establishing her own credentials as a producer. The Goffin and King songwriting team and marriage also split (though King remarried soon after her divorce), and after the girl group era had ended, King curtailed her production work to concentrate on developing her skills as a musician and songwriter.

King's career as a performer was revived with great success in the early '70s after the release of the album *Tapestry,* and her records regularly featured covers of the songs she'd written during her girl group days. Greenwich also recorded albums with covers of her girl group hits (1968's *Ellie Greenwich Composes, Produces and Sings* and 1973's *Let It Be Written, Let It Be Sung*). Her songs also provided the basis for the musical *Leader of the Pack,* which opened on Broadway in 1985. Loosely based on Greenwich's life story, *Leader of the Pack* featured Darlene Love in a starring role and also closed with a solo spot from Greenwich. Three years earlier, in a more tongue-in-cheek homage to the era, the musical *Little Shop of Horrors* opened Off-Broadway, featuring a sassy, black, girl group—styled trio of backup singers—named Ronnette, Chiffon, and Crystal.

But if the death knell had been sounded in the Brill Building by the mid-'60s, the Beatles' example of self-sufficiency gave inspiration to rock's next generation of artists, and young men began grabbing guitars and rushing to their parents' garages to practice—an idea which seemed to bypass young women of the time completely. Women folk singers were able to hold acoustic guitars, since the emphasis in folk music was on the song rather than the singer's instrumental skills, but in general women instrumentalists were still too rare in the music community to provide much of an example to budding female musicians. "I really think that had to do with the roles that were put forward of what girls do and what boys do," says singer Holly Near, who was a high school student at the time when the British Invasion was inspiring the birth of hundreds of groups in America and Britain. "All the kids started putting together bands," she remembers. "Everybody wanted to be in a band, everybody wanted to play guitar. Well, the 'everybody' were boys. And I played the acoustic guitar, probably knew more chords and more about music than any of the guys who were diving in and plugging in their guitars. And it never even occurred to me to plug in. It's not even that I was told not to, it just didn't even cross my mind. 'Louie Louie'—how many chords does it have, right? But it just wasn't something girls did. So I put the guitar away and became a girl singer."

In fact, "girl singers," or solo vocalists, were beginning to replace the girl groups in the charts by the mid-'60s, and again, the lead came from England, though America was not quite as receptive to Britain's female solo artists as it was to the cute boy bands. Singers like Petula Clark and Dusty Springfield enjoyed the greatest success, while the response to others, such as Marianne Faithfull, Lulu, Cilla Black, and Sandie Shaw, varied greatly. And while these singers didn't cover the girl group songs with the regularity that the boy bands did, Lulu, Black, and Springfield still reflected a brassy, soulful delivery that owed an obvious debt to the girl group era and especially the high energy sounds that were now coming out of Detroit (Springfield in particular was an unabashed fan of Motown artists). The new singers also presented a more sophisticated image to their audience—grown-up, yet hip, giving the impression of independence, unlike the "little girl" dependence of the girl groups. Most significant, despite slack periods, each singer was able to maintain a long-term career, instead of sinking into obscurity like the U.S. girl groups, who, if they did survive, found themselves with few options other than toiling on the oldies circuit.

Petula Clark was the oldest of Britain's new "girl singers," in her thirties at the time she broke through in the American market with "Downtown" in 1965, after several years of chart success in Britain and Europe. In contrast, most other female soloists were in their teens or early twenties. Lulu, born Marie McDonald McLaughin Lawrie, was discovered in Glasgow as the lead singer of the Luvvers (formerly the Gleneagles) at age fifteen, and with the renamed Lulu and the Luvvers began her career in 1964 with a cover of the Isley Brother's "Shout." Lulu was immediately dubbed "the Scottish Brenda Lee" and her first American hit came in 1967 with the theme song of the film *To Sir With Love*. "Swingin'" Cilla Black, who released her first record at age twenty, was the only female artist handled by Brian Epstein, manager of the Beatles. Just as the Beatles had been tidied up by Epstein, forsaking their leather gear for suits and ties, Black's act was toned down, and the former nightclub coat-check girl who sang rock songs with the band on her break was put in a dress to sing Burt Bacharach—Hal David ballads. Black enjoyed far greater success in the U.K., where she had a total of eleven Top 10 hits (including two number 1's), as opposed to the U.S., where her sole Top 40 hit was "You're My World," which went to number 26 in 1964. The same was true of Sandie Shaw (Sandra Goodrich), who launched her singing career at age seventeen and whose trademark was performing in her bare feet. Shaw had three number 1 hits in the U.K. and became the first British artist to win the Eurovision Song Contest (an annual song competition among European countries) with "Puppet on a String," but she couldn't even crack the U.S. Top 40. Lulu and Shaw also had female managers, Marion Massey and Eve Taylor respectively.

Marianne Faithfull was the odd-woman-out in this crowd, at least musically, for her clear voice and folk-tinged material had more in common with the work of folk singers like Joan Baez than with the realm of pop music. Faithfull was, in fact, a reluctant pop star who preferred the music of Baez and Bob Dylan to pop music, and had arrived in the music business almost by accident. Born in 1946 to a university professor and an Austrian baroness, Faithfull had grown up in Reading, England, where she attended a convent school and played folk music in local coffeehouses in her teens. In 1964, her boyfriend John Dunbar (later her first husband) brought her to a party Paul McCartney was giving in London, where she met Andrew Loog Oldham, the manager of the current "bad boys" of rock, the Rolling Stones. Upon learning Faithfull was a singer, Oldham offered her a record contract and co-wrote her first single, the melancholy "As Tears Go By," with the Stones' Mick Jagger and Keith Richards (the song which finally got the Jagger-Richards songwriting partnership off the ground).

At the time, Faithfull was not especially concerned about the record's success. "I didn't think anything would come of it," she said later. "It came out in the summer, I did a few TV shows, and that was all very boring, and I thought 'Oh God, this is a big fuss about nothing.' And I just went back to school in the fall." But when the song went to number 9 in the British charts (number 22 in the U.S.), she left school and began pursuing a singing career in earnest. Though she continued having pop hits, Faithfull was also able to record folk albums (only released in the U.K.): *North Country Maid* featured highly effective renditions of "She Moved Through the Fair," "Scarborough Fair" (recorded two years before Simon and Garfunkel would have a Top 20 hit with the song), and the title track. Another folk album, *Come My Way*, had Faithfull performing traditional songs like "Fare Thee Well" and "Once I Had a Sweetheart," and reading Lewis Carroll's poem "Jabberwocky" from his book *Through the Looking Glass*. Yet despite her success, Faithfull still felt some uncertainty about her career in music. "The only thing that was—that *is*—difficult, is I wonder why I ever did it," she said in 1990. "I wonder if it was a good idea; maybe I should have just not done it and stayed at school. Now I love it and I'm glad it all happened, but I have thought that sometimes, I'm enjoying it … but it took a long time to get there."

Dusty Springfield was a more familiar face to American audiences. Born Mary Isabel Catherine Bernadette O'Brien in 1939 in London, Springfield first sang in a group called the Lana Sisters in the late '50s; after their breakup in 1960, she formed the Springfields, a folk trio that also included her brother Tom and their friend Tim Field (later replaced by Mike Hurst). The Springfields had a few British hits—and a Top 20 hit in the U.S. with the song "Silver Threads and Golden Needles"—before disbanding in 1963. Springfield wasted no time in starting a solo career and had an immediate hit with "I Only Want to Be With You," which captured the spirited, danceable fun inherent in her favorite Motown dance hits. Released in December 1963, "I Only Want to Be With You" reached the Top 10 in England and went to number 12 in the U.S., the first in a string of ten Top 40 hits in the '60s.

With her dramatic use of black eyeliner and her elaborate hairdo, Springfield reflected the cool of "Swinging London," as the British capital was now dubbed; by the mid-'60s London was the center of the pop universe, home to everything that was with-it and hip in music and fashion. But while America was won over by such exports as the British Invasion bands, Mary Quant mini-skirts, and Diana Rigg's "Emma Peel" character (the stylish, leather jumpsuit-clad heroine of the British TV spy series *The Avengers*), Britain's musical in-crowd championed black American soul music (as R&B was beginning to be called). Springfield's love of black music led to her hosting the British television special *The Sounds of Motown* when the "Motown Revue" package tour arrived in England in 1965, and in 1968 she traveled to the States to record *Dusty in Memphis,* produced by Jerry Wexler, who had revitalized Aretha Franklin's career by bringing her to Atlantic Records (unsuccessful at the time of its release, *Dusty in Memphis* is now considered a classic album). When Franklin turned down the opportunity to record "Son of a Preacher Man," Springfield (who was occasionally referred to as "the white Aretha Franklin") recorded it for *Dusty in Memphis* and also had a Top 10 hit with the song. Vicki Wickham, producer of the British television rock show *Ready, Steady, Go! (RSG),* credits Springfield with introducing her—and *RSG*—to a variety of black performers, many of whom ended up receiving greater television exposure in Britain than in the U.S. "We did specials with Otis Redding and James Brown and it was great because nobody in England had ever seen these people," says Wickham. "Only people like Dusty or the Beatles or the Rolling Stones, who were going to America and buying their records. England was still a very virgin country when it came to that music, so we made a big impact."

Ready, Steady, Go! debuted in 1963 to capitalize on the British beat group explosion (which took off in the U.K. a year earlier than in the States), and bubbled with freshness. In some ways a U.K. equivalent to *American Bandstand, RSG* traded in Dick Clark's paternalistic image for youthful hosts whose age matched the show's audience. "There just hadn't been anything like it," says Wickham. "People, the same as myself, were sitting at home and didn't realize that there was fashion out there, that there was art, that the music was very much a part of what was going on, that really the focal point of everything creative or artistic was coming from the music." Wickham had left her previous job as a production assistant at BBC Radio with the hopes of landing a job in television; she was taken on as a secretary by the independent station then planning *RSG* with a promise for advancement within a year. She ended up becoming the show's producer—at age twenty-one. "I was lucky because in every situation I always ended up being the only person there," she says. "I'm naturally pushy, so I always was doing the next thing because there was nobody else to do it, and then it was always much easier to find a new secretary than it was to get somebody who should have been doing my job. So there was never a real promotion; it was just because I was doing it—booking it, writing it, producing it, everything. By the time we'd done the pilot, I was the producer. There wasn't anybody else."

RSG quickly established itself as *the* music show to appear on in Britain, with a healthy roster of current stars and new acts, chosen by Wickham, Michael Lindsay-Hogg, the show's director, and the show's presenters, Michael Aldred and Cathy McGowan. "We were conscious of the charts and what was happening," Wickham says. "You have to be. And you had to be slightly visual, otherwise it just wasn't going to work. We really stayed away from what I would call the more middle-of-the-road people even if they were number 1 in the charts. And, honestly, it was who we liked. Luckily, we liked a lot of different things, and the four of us truly depended on somebody telling us about somebody we'd go see, and if we liked them, they were on. So we were mixing between the Kinks and the Swinging Blue Jeans, then we would have John Lee Hooker."

Patti LaBelle and the Bluebelles were among the black groups that appeared on the show, and after striking up a friendship with Patti, Wickham later became the group's manager. "Not many acts were on two weeks running, but the Bluebelles were because they were just phenomenal," she says. "They sang 'Groovy Kind of Love,' which was brilliant." For their part, the Bluebelles enjoyed the less racially charged atmosphere of Britain as compared to what Nona Hendryx describes as "the usual prejudice" they'd faced in the U.S.—"traveling and not being able to go in certain restaurants, and actually having someone point a gun at us to get out of his restaurant, not being able to stay in certain hotels. Whereas when you'd go to England, yes, there are less black people there, and if prejudice was in somebody's heart, in their mind, I don't know, but there were not black and white water fountains. It just did not exist."

Another American group that made a strong impression on *RSG* was Goldie and the Gingerbreads, one of the few all-female bands of the time who did play instruments. "I think they were the only girl group that played live that we ever had on," Wickham says. "I don't think there was anybody else in those days, so it was perfect for us. They had quite a good following at one point." It was a following the group hadn't been able to find in the U.S., where the Gingerbreads had been working since the early '60s, defying convention by trying to make it as an all-female rock band. But despite their success in England, the group was unable to make a dent in the American market, and today there are few rock histories that make even a passing reference to the band. Yet the Gingerbreads should certainly stand out to historians if for no other reason than the fact that they were one of the few female rock bands playing their own instruments at a time when the very idea was still seen as a contradiction in terms.

Carol MacDonald, the Gingerbreads' guitarist, had been playing guitar for many years before meeting up with the rest of the group, who had been busy perfecting their skills on their instruments too. Born in Wilmington, Delaware, MacDonald started out on ukulele at age nine and graduated to guitar at ten; by high school she was performing in a doo-wop group called the Tranells and with a rock band from Maryland that played the Bainbridge Naval Base on weekends. After graduating in 1960, an illicit trip to a local nightclub led to her first offer to record. "This guy gave me his card and said, 'We want to record you,' so I said okay," she recalls. "I was really torn because I wasn't supposed to be in this place. But then I had to tell my mother and father because the record company was in Philadelphia! So I had to end up telling them the truth because I really wanted to do this."

Armed with her parents' permission, MacDonald traveled to Philadelphia and made her first record, "I'm in Love" / "Sam, Sam, Sam, My Rock and Roll Man," for a local label before starting college. After two years, MacDonald quit college and moved in with an aunt in Trenton, New Jersey. In 1963, having tried to figure out a way to get back into music, an invitation MacDonald accepted for a night out provided the answer. "I met this guy who said to me, 'You want to go to New York? I gotta take you to this club in the Village, you won't believe it,'" she remembers. "I was so naive, I didn't even know what 'the Village' was. This is at twelve o'clock at night, and I said, 'Isn't everything closed?' He said, 'No, they stay open until four in the morning!' So he takes me to this place and it was the hippest jazz club, the Page Three. I go in with him, and we sit down and I looked at the hippest jazz trio I'd ever heard in my life, and I just flipped out. I said, 'Oh my God, this place is fantastic!'"

A few drinks later, MacDonald was ready to ascend the stage herself. "I said to the MC, 'I want to sing,' and he said, 'Oh, do you?' like who-the-hell-are-you type of thing," she says. "And I said, 'Yeah, I'd really like to get up.' I had all the nerve in the world. I had no idea what I was doing, I just said, 'Let me get up and sing.'" Her nerve won her a weekend spot at the club, making ten dollars a night, sharing the billing with Tiny Tim. "He was making eight dollars, so I was really highly paid!" MacDonald says. "And we had to sit there all night long; little did I know I was like a B-girl. They'd tell you who you could go sit with and have a drink with—I thought it was great, I'm getting free drinks! Little did I know I'm selling the drinks for them! I was very, very naive."

A short time later she met Goldie and the Gingerbreads, who paid a special visit to the Page Three to ask her to join them. "The MC said, 'There's this girls' group that just came off the road; they're in the back, and they want to talk to you.' And I thought, 'Girls' band? This is interesting, let me go check this out!'" she says. "So I go in the back, and here is this ragged bunch of women, because they had really, literally, just come off the road. They had heard about me and they asked if I wanted to play guitar in their band, and I said, 'No, no, no, I don't think so; I'm really happy with this job.' They looked ragged and scary to me ... this turned out to be so funny later on."

If the Gingerbreads had appeared "ragged and scary," MacDonald's introduction to the realities of the music industry were more unpleasant, as she found when she acquired her first manager, Milton Ross. "He was one of the most obnoxious men I'd ever met in my life when I first met him," she remembers. "Really, he was disgusting. Every other word out of his mouth was 'fuck.'

I couldn't believe this mouth. This was just the way he was, your typical New York manager—at that time! They're a lot different now. I will say that because I'm one now! He was into showing me the sleazier side of the industry. Now they put record deals together with drugs ... in those days it was sex, and they'd set the executives up with girls. It was really weird—this was how they used to make record deals, I swear to God. In the '60s you got your money stolen because you were naive. In the '70s it got stolen because you were stoned. But you still got your money stolen! It's the truth! And I just kept singing. My whole thing was, I don't want to know about that, I just wanted to write."

A recording contract with Atlantic didn't make MacDonald much happier, as she bristled against the company's intended manipulation of her. "They wanted me to be Lesley Gore," she says. "My first record, 'Jimmy Boy,' was that type of thing. So they give me this image, and I'm not happy. I'm not playing guitar, number one, and I'm not doing my own music. They changed my name, too—they didn't like MacDonald, so it was Carol Shaw." The fact that her record was starting to sell offered little consolation, but shortly after getting her record deal, she encountered Goldie and the Gingerbreads again—and this time she liked what she saw. "We went up to 45th Street, to the Wagon Wheel," she remembers. "And I see on the thing 'All Female Band, Goldie and the Gingerbreads.' So I walk in and these girls are up on stage, and my socks are knocked off. I just stood there with my mouth hanging open. They go on break, and I run up and say, 'Listen, remember me? You asked me to play—you don't have a guitar, do you still need a guitarist?' They said, 'Yeah, you want to get up and sit in?' So we picked a song, and I fit in like I had been there forever. I was like the missing piece of that puzzle. And then Goldie looked at Margo, and Margo looked at Ginger, and they were looking at me, and I'm smiling. I'd never felt so good on stage. I had to be there, and that was it. I started working with them."

When manager Ross was unable to persuade MacDonald to not join the band, he relented and got the group—Goldie Zelkowitz (later Genya Ravan), Margo Lewis, Ginger Bianco, and, now, MacDonald—a deal with Atlantic (the group had previously recorded for Scepter before MacDonald joined). And though MacDonald admits the group was perceived as a "novelty" by the industry, the members themselves remained nonplussed. "We didn't think anything of it," she says. "We got more jobs because they were exploiting the hell out of us. All Girl Band! They'd do the whole thing, tits and ass. And we didn't care. We were happy because we knew we could play, and we were knocking the socks off of most of the male bands. And the guys couldn't believe it. They'd start off laughing, and then they'd walk out crying." As a joke, the group would also deliberately play up to the expectations club owners had about "girl bands" in order to turn the tables later, as Genya Ravan later recalled on a panel at the New Music Seminar in New York in 1990: "We'd walk into a club with all our instruments and you could see the owner going 'Oh my God, these broads? They know how to play? They really know how to play?' We'd set up and have a sound check and play totally out of tune, and I would sing the wrong lyrics. And the guy'd be chewing on his cigar going 'Oh my God! Oh my God! Oh my God!' And by the time we went on and counted off the song, we were cookin'. You could see the cigar drop and the guy had a heart attack ... We had fun with this."

As "the darlings of the New York scene" the Gingerbreads met many of the visiting musicians when the British Invasion began, usually while playing society parties and debutante balls. They also met the Rolling Stones when they played at the band's U.S. welcoming party, but were unimpressed. "We all went in their dressing room and we were thinking, 'My God, they're such pigs!'" MacDonald remembers. "They were so dirty. They really were—but that was their image." When the British band the Animals arrived, the band's manager, Michael Jeffery, was impressed by the Gingerbreads' and extended an offer to bring them to England, which the group accepted. On their arrival in Britain the band was put in the studio to record the song that became the Gingerbreads' first hit, "Cant You Hear My Heartbeat." "I hated the song," says MacDonald. "We're doing stuff like 'Harlem Shuffle,' and then they give us this 'Every time I see you ... dee de dee de dee.' Eeeow! I said, 'Goldie! What are we doing?' She said, 'We gotta do what they say!' It's like we had to do everything they said or we were not going to be successful. So we record this stupid song, and then they shove us off to the Star Club in [Hamburg] Germany because we don't have our working visas yet."

While playing in Hamburg's notorious red-light Reeperbahn district (where the Beatles also received an education—musical and otherwise), "Can't You Hear My Heartbeat" landed in the British Top 10, and the Gingerbreads were called back to England to appear on the comedy program *Not Only, But Also*. The Gingerbreads were now on a roll and were soon touring England in the company of the Yardbirds, the Hollies, the Kinks, and the Rolling Stones, though the group's negative impression of the Stones was reconfirmed in an unwanted "groping" incident between Mick Jagger and Margo Lewis. "Margo almost punched his head off his neck," remembers MacDonald. "She came around and slapped his head off his shoulders and said, 'Who do you think you are? How dare you!' Because he thought he could do that! He's the star so he could do that. That's the kind of shit we'd have to put up with."

As always, live performance gave the band greater satisfaction. "They put us in what they called the 'hot seat,' which was right before the main act," MacDonald says. "Because we could hold their attention. By that time, these kids have sat through nine million groups—they want to see the Stones already! The kids would jump out of the balconies and break their teeth, bleeding, they didn't care. They'd dive under the fire curtain after these guys, almost get chopped in half—I never saw anything like it. And now they're screaming and yelling for us too. They would try to jump on our van while we were going out. It was unbelievable. We couldn't even go to the post office without getting bombarded by kids, little girls coming and falling asleep on our doorsteps, finding out where we lived, camping out, wanting to go with us and live with us—oh, forget it! We were very big stars over there."

Unfortunately for the Gingerbreads, Atlantic only released three singles by the group, on their subsidiary label Atco. The group's launching in the States was further botched by Michael Jeffery's eagerness to have the group record "Heartbeat," when his partner, Mickie Most, who managed Herman's Hermits, felt he had first rights to the song. "That little song was on Mickie's desk," MacDonald explains. "So when Michael took the song and gave it to us, Mickie got pissed off with him and said, 'All right, I have Herman's Hermits, I'm gonna record it with Herman, and

I'm gonna release it in the States.' And he released it two weeks before ours." The Hermits' version went all the way to number 2. "That blew our hit," says MacDonald. "It really ruined it for us because they were already known. Talk about bad timing! And that was our bad luck. We never got a hit."

Nor did the Gingerbreads end up making any money. After three years of continual touring in Germany and England and three British Top 10 singles, the group learned their finances had been misappropriated by their management. In the wake of this dispiriting blow, the group returned to the U.S., where they remained relatively unknown and soon broke up. (They would play a reunion show in New York in 1997.) It was not the first time an American group found a larger audience overseas than it would at home, nor would it be the last, though later bands would be able to build on their success overseas to win equal recognition at home. In 1980, an all-female band called the Go-Go's, who released their first single in England, would be able to maintain the momentum and eventually become the first all-female band to reach number 1 in the album charts. The Gingerbreads, while receiving little recognition themselves, helped to lay the groundwork that enabled other female performers to break out of the conventional roles women were still expected to play in the music industry.

The girl group era as a whole had brought an unprecedented number of female artists to the charts, and more women were able to develop their roles in offstage positions during the era as well. The years between the first wave of rock & roll in the '50s and the arrival of the British Invasion in the '60s have generally been regarded as a musically barren period, save for the bland offerings of the male teen idols. But songs like "Will You Love Me Tomorrow," "Be My Baby," "I Can Never Go Home Anymore," and "You Don't Own Me" were bold statements of desire, anguish, and independence that could hardly be considered bland or tame. Some performers, like Carole King, Lesley Gore, and Nona Hendryx were able to use the momentum of the period to generate substantial careers for themselves. Others, like Goldie and the Gingerbreads pushed beyond the stereotypes for female performers to forge a path for later groups to follow. And as the decade progressed, women would find the atmosphere of social change providing them with further opportunities they were now in a better position to take full advantage of.

Post-Reading Questions for Part I

1 Was there anything distinctive about the personal backgrounds of the early rock and roll artists? Did they have anything significant in common or does the diversity of their backgrounds seem more important? What separated Elvis Presley and Little Richard from the first rock and roll artists such as Fats Domino and Bill Haley?

2 How did rock and roll challenge traditional gender stereotypes in the 1950s? Why did so many people feel so threatened by this challenge? What did girl groups contribute to the popular culture and rock and roll landscapes? Did they challenge gender stereotypes or merely serve to conserve or reinforce them?

3 In what ways did rock and roll foster "the separation of youth from parental control"? Did rock and roll cause or contribute to a generation gap, or was a generation gap inevitable during the years in which rock and roll became popular?

4 Why do you think American popular culture appealed so much to British teenagers such as the Beatles? What about American rock and roll in particular appealed to them?

PART II

AMERICAN POPULAR CULTURE IN BRITAIN AND EUROPE IN THE EARLY YEARS OF THE BEATLES

Introduction

The musical heritage of American popular culture exported to Britain during the 1950s had its share of controversial racial overtones because of the growing popularity of black rhythm and blues music among white audiences in the states. Teenagers in Britain and the United States wanted to dance and found rhythm and blues and its derivative, rock and roll, more conducive to movement than the pop hits performed by the likes of middle-aged pop singers like Frank Sinatra and Perry Como. As we saw in the previous section, Elvis Presley became such a big star because of his crossover appeal to young white audiences clamoring for the new beat of rock and roll. However, Elvis differed from other popular singers not just because of the music he sang; his poor southern roots contributed to the disapproval he received among middle-class Americans. The elevation of hillbilly or "rockabilly" music to pop status gave it a special appeal in Britain, where many performers began to affect southern accents that made them virtually indistinguishable from their American counterparts. Part II of this volume deals with the reception of the American music discussed in Part I in Britain during the 1950s and early 1960s. The authors of the three selections in this section all raise important questions about the appropriation of American music by British artists during this period, a topic of special relevance for understanding the Beatles.

Brian Ward argues that rock and roll did not cause the British to be interested in the American south, but rather reflected an interest that already existed. Ward points out, for example, that the British viewed Southern culture as having a strong connection with their own cultural heritage, even as he illustrates some of the stereotypical, distorted, and sometimes contradictory ways in which they viewed the American South. Even more importantly, he demonstrates the ways in which images in Britain of the American South changed in the second half of the 1950s because of the rise of rock and roll, the incipient civil rights movement, and the resistance toward it by many white southerners. The civil rights movement raised awareness in Britain of the implications of appropriating a culture with a long history of problematic race relations that the fans and practitioners of Dixieland jazz and skiffle music had previously ignored. In fact, Ward argues that critics of rock and roll in Britain who feared its influence on the youth began to use its southern roots as a weapon in their arguments for the new genre's immorality. These critics gained more ammunition when the American southern rocker Jerry Lee Lewis embarked on a tour of Britain, bringing along his recently wed thirteen-year-old bride. Ward expertly recounts the British reaction to this scandal and places it within the context of their evolving attitudes toward the American South.

In the next selection, Bob Groom explores more deeply the relationship of the music of the American South and British performers, particularly through the lens of Lonnie Donegan's popular skiffle number, "Rock Island Line." The origins of the term "skiffle" are uncertain, though some music historians have suggested it derives from "skiffle parties," a term used for fundraising gatherings for rent payments in the American South. Skiffle music was a style of folk or country music that mainly employed homemade instruments such as jugs or washboards, though skiffle bands, which numbered in the hundreds in the 1950s, generally employed guitars and sometimes drums as well. The Beatles may have drawn their inspiration from Elvis and early rock and roll, but John Lennon's first group, the Quarrymen, focused on joining the skiffle craze inspired by Donegan's smash hit. Groom shows how complicated issues of authorship could be when it came to re-recordings of popular songs based on old blues or folk standards in the 1950s. In the process, he also sheds light on additional aspects of the relationship between American popular culture and British skiffle artists and, by extension, British rock and roll and the music of the Beatles. For around this time, the Quarrymen were beginning to discover music dating back to early twentieth-century America, including a song discussed by Groom called "Freight Train" by Elizabeth Cotten, which the group performed regularly from 1957 to 1959. Finally, Groom explains why the popularity of skiffle died out relatively quickly while rock and roll retained and increased its appeal. Readers who fall into the trap of thinking the triumph of rock preordained would underestimate the extent of skiffle's appeal at the time, which Groom does much to elucidate.

In the third and final selection in this section, Andre Millard demonstrates that the triumph of American rock and roll in Britain was far from a foregone conclusion. Yet he also shows how the absence of a major recording label interested in promoting rock and roll did not prevent young aspiring British artists from not only hearing the music but also recording early cover versions of popular American rock and roll songs. It did not take long before British record companies were releasing American originals on their labels, giving British teenagers even greater access to the American sound. Millard dismisses the myth, perpetuated by John Lennon himself, that Liverpool had a geographical advantage based on its location as the first destination for American ships that allowed its young people early access to American rock and roll and R & B records. Millard's other contribution to this chapter is in providing some of the history of *British* rock and roll before the Beatles emerged from among the pack. Millard makes it clear that these early British rock and rollers owed everything to American popular culture and frequently went so far as to imitate American artists as closely as possible. Still, their success was important and helped to prepare the way for the Beatles and the phenomenon of Beatlemania.

Pre-Reading Questions for Part II

1   Are there instances when it is inappropriate for individuals to borrow or imitate the musical heritage of another culture? Alternatively, is any preexisting musical tradition fair game for any artist?

2   Does a cover song have any claim to originality? When and under what circumstances?

3   Does an artist need to have a historical awareness of the cultural baggage of the musical tradition in which she operates? For example, can a singer perform songs such as "Dixie," which celebrated the American South, without implicitly endorsing the history of slavery and racial segregation associated with the region?

4   How has the history of the American South been presented in previous classes you have taken? Has the region's rich musical heritage been included in that treatment?

'By Elvis and All the Saints'

Images of the American South in the World of 1950s British Popular Music

Brian Ward

> "The South appears in British culture through a number of stereotypes: there is the simple South of comical accents and mountain people or small-town folk asleep on front porches; the romantic antebellum South of courtly beaux and beauteous belles; and most familiar in recent years, the violent or gothic South of evil stirrings behind the magnolia in moonlight, usually some terrible racial or sexual sin or secret."
>
> –Helen Taylor, *Circling Dixie*

In September 1956, Betty Hurstfield began her teaching career in a large comprehensive school in northwest London. Years later she recalled how rock and roll from the American South had first intruded upon her working day: "I shall never forget the elderly senior mistress coming into the staff room one morning and saying sternly, 'I must speak to a boy called Elvis Presley because he has carved his name on every desk in the school.'"[1] While Hurstfield's senior colleague may have been oblivious to Presley's impact, his early popularity among British youths could be measured not only by the countless times his name was scratched lovingly into wood but also by the more prosaic evidence of enormous record sales and huge box office receipts. By the end of 1956, British branches of Woolworths already stocked Selcol's four-string plastic "Elvis Presley Guitar"—complete with auto-chord device, naturally, and available for a mere 79 shillings.[2] Two years later, Presley ranked behind only Winston Churchill as the best-known public figure among Scottish schoolchildren.[3] And lest Grady McWhiney should try to claim this as evidence of some kind of special

Caledonian link to the South, a similar poll of thirty fourteen-year-olds in Bridgewater, Somerset, revealed that while only twelve students knew the name of Eisenhower, seven of Khrushchev, and four of Nehru, "everyone was on Christian name terms with a Mr. Presley."[4]

British youths' enthusiasm for Presley and for rock and roll more generally was but one example of a longstanding interest in the music of the American South—a musical culture which, of course, had its own historic indebtedness to British, as well as other European and African, influences. Indeed, rock and roll was not the only British musical vogue of the decade with close musical and emotional ties to the region. Before Elvis's first chart hit in the spring of 1956, the British traditional ("trad" or Dixieland) jazz revival and the skiffle craze which grew out of it had also betrayed a deep fascination with the real and imagined South.

Rather than simply cataloguing the enormous stylistic debts that British artists in each of these idioms owed to southern music, the focus here is more on how British fans, practitioners, and critics of first trad, then skiffle, and finally rock and roll harbored a set of preconceived, often highly romanticized and stereotypical, ideas about the region. The most important of these images was the perception of southerners, black and white, as, well frankly, rebels. In one corner of the British popular imagination, southerners always existed as outsiders, free spirits engaged in some kind of perpetual hedonistic struggle with restrictive codes of behavior and against the bonds of suffocating authority. It was certainly no coincidence that future Beatle George Harrison should call his first skiffle group the Rebels—a band that, in keeping with the do-it-yourself ethic of the skiffle craze, initially dedicated itself to recreating the sounds of southern country, blues, and rockabilly music on cheap guitars and sundry kitchen utensils.[5]

If at one level the South and its music were permanently available to British fans and per-formers as symbols of counter-cultural defiance, independence, and nonconformity, at another level they also conjured up images of solidity, stability, and rootedness. Sometimes these images of continuity and heritage merged with notions of southern reactionary conservatism, backward-ness, intolerance, and insularity. More positively, however, they promoted a sense that southern music was literally well grounded, that it was linked to a particular place—often expressed in terms of a passionate veneration of the land itself—and that it exhibited a laudable respect for its own traditions. Thus, although rock and roll was sometimes dismissed as simply the latest frothy and disposable product of an avaricious American mass culture industry, relatively few critics leveled the same accusations against either trad or skiffle, both of which were preoc-cupied with ideas of authenticity and imbued with a deep reverence for their versions of the South's musical past.

The second major theme of the essay concerns how during the second half of the 1950s stock British ideas about the South underwent something of a transformation, becoming more complex, ambiguous, and ultimately less unequivocally positive toward the region. From the mid-1950s, extensive news coverage of the emerging southern civil rights movement and of the desperate white resistance that often greeted it forced British fans of southern-derived music to reexamine their attitudes about the South. It was a contradictory period during which the South was largely defined in the British media in terms of racial intolerance and a predilection for sudden violence and lawlessness and yet remained for many the source of a vibrant and utterly beguiling popular culture.

The trad jazz revival first stirred in Britain during the Second World War and flourished during the subsequent decade before reaching its commercial peak between the mid-1950s and early 1960s. Initially spearheaded by a coterie of enthusiastic amateurs who were variously bored by what remained of swing, bewildered by the esoteric experiments of bebop, and indifferent to the cool cerebral sounds of Miles Davis and his West Coast disciples, the revivalists attempted to turn back the clock and revisit the music of the New Orleans jazz pioneers of the early twentieth century. Part of an international phenomenon, the British trad boom was encouraged by the rediscovery in wartime America of one of those Crescent City veterans, Bunk Johnson, who had begun performing and recording again with much fanfare. Even more significant for the British Dixieland revival was a November 1949 appearance in London by the great Creole saxophonist and clarinetist Sidney Bechet. Making his first appearance in the country since 1920, Bechet performed with Humphrey Lyttleton's band, defying a musicians' union ban on foreign acts playing in Britain.[6]

The British jazz revivalists wore their admiration for the American South literally on their sleeves. Bobby Mickelburgh's combo took to the stage in the garb of Confederate troops, while Dave Hunt led a London group called the Confederate Jazz Band. Presumably both men saw the roots of the music as much in the grays as in the blues. Bob Wallis and his band routinely dressed as Mississippi gamblers, while George Webb succinctly dubbed his group the Dixielanders.[7] By 1956, even Luton could boast its own Delta Jazz Club at the Cresta Ballroom featuring trumpeter Steve Mason's Delta Jazz Band—this despite there being no obvious sign of a river, let alone a delta in that Bedfordshire town.[8] By the end of the decade Liverpool, which could at least claim a river—the Mersey—also boasted the services of its own Merseyssippi Jazz Band.[9]

Ken Colyer and his onetime trombonist Chris Barber were the two most influential figures in establishing trad as a significant force in British popular music. Both exhibited a deep fascination with the American South. Colyer was a genuinely gifted trumpeter and an evangelical enthusiast for early jazz. Too poor to pay for his own pilgrimage to New Orleans, he had joined the merchant navy hoping to make land there at some point. A docking at Mobile, Alabama, proved close enough, and Colyer hitched his way to New Orleans, where he effectively replaced the recently deceased Bunk Johnson in the group taken over by George Lewis. After a spell with Kid Ory's legendary band, Colyer was deported. In England, he formed his seminal Dixieland band, whose hit single "Isle of Capri" began to transform trad from an underground cult to a mass phenomenon. Chris Barber, who left Colyer in the early 1950s, completed that process. Barber played a smoother, somewhat less frenetic and collectively improvised style of Dixieland that he hoped would have even more popular appeal. By 1956, the proprietor of the Winchester Lido Ballroom was able to report that, with the new rock and roll craze still gathering momentum and of uncertain longevity, "traditional jazz is the established 'order of the day.'"[10]

Chris Barber also mentored the trad revival's single most successful artist: the clarinetist Acker Bilk, a man who almost single-handedly inspired a resurgence of interest in goatees, bowler hats, and waistcoats as fashion accessories for British men. In many ways Bilk personified trad's awkward synthesis of southern antiquarian chic and British music hall kitsch. As George Melly, himself a flamboyant jazz vocalist as well as a shrewd observer of British pop culture, noted, there was something faintly ridiculous about Bilk and the whole British impulse to revive—as opposed to revere—the music of turn-of-the-century New Orleans. As Melly put it, "In effect then the public was asked to accept a cider-drinking, belching, West Country contemporary dressed as an Edwardian music hall *lion comique*, and playing the music of an oppressed racial minority as it had evolved in an American city some fifty years before. More surprisingly, they did accept it. Acker was soon a national idol."[11]

Melly was amused and intrigued, rather than appalled and offended, by the dislocated southern nostalgia at the heart of the trad revival. Some critics, however, had always been uncomfortable with trad's tendency to romanticize a bygone South. A report of Sidney Bechet's 1949 breakthrough concert with Humphrey Lyttleton's band, for example, had praised Bechet's performance but expressed deep misgivings about the way that the show traded on old southern stereotypes. The presence of a rustically attired banjo player in Lyttleton's band was an especially unwelcome throwback. "If it is necessary to employ that anachronism, the banjo, is it necessary to expose the wretched exponent [Buddy Vallis] dressed as a hill-billy, right in front of the stage?" asked the reviewer.[12]

Other British jazz buffs, including many of those associated with *Melody Maker*, where the vogue was for bebop or cool jazz, also objected to Dixieland on aesthetic grounds that were often explicitly linked to the regional source of the music. While trad's devotees warmed to the sense of roots and tradition they found in Dixieland, its detractors often deemed this a reactionary development, founded upon a dangerously romantic attachment to a crude and unsophisticated form of music emanating from a crude and unsophisticated part of the world. "Dixieland jazz was born in the streets and riverboats of the Southern States of America; it was played by people who didn't want to be burdened by music stands, even if they'd known what they were for," carped one *Melody Maker* columnist. "The Dixielanders," he maintained, "were primitives, and they played the Dixieland style because they didn't know of any other." Moreover, he insisted that the trad craze was fundamentally inauthentic, a commercially driven fabrication—this despite trad's deep sense of its own musical and commercial integrity. It had "nothing to do with streets, riverboats or the South, it is played by musicians in dinner jackets who are trying to convince us that they are recreating the spirit of jazz as it was played before some of them were born."[13]

The internecine strife that trad provoked within the British jazz fraternity was a serious business. In his 1959 novel *Absolute Beginners*, Colin MacInnes brilliantly evoked the bitter musical rivalries between London's young jazz modernists and those who were drawn to both trad and the skiffle movement that eventually evolved from it. MacInnes's anonymous narrator describes the differences between two young habitués of the Chez Nobody coffee bar, Dean Swift and the Misery Kid. "These two don't mix in public, on account of the Dean being a sharp modern jazz creation, and the Kid just a skiffle survival, with horrible leanings to the trad thing. That is to say, the Kid admires the groups that play what is supposed to be the authentic music of old New Orleans, i.e., combos of booking-office clerks and quantity-surveyors' assistants who've handed in their cards, and dedicated themselves to blowing what they believe to be the same notes as the wonderful Creoles who invented the whole thing, when it all long ago began."[14]

MacInnes appreciated the essentially—but barely—white-collar audience for trad in Britain ("booking-office clerks and quantity-surveyors' assistants"). In an age of drab austerity, leisure time identification with the musical stylings of a flamboyant and marginalized section of the turn-of-the-century South represented a low-risk, neatly compartmentalized gesture of nonconformity from the work-a-day world of trad's largely middle- and lower-middle-class adherents. Moreover, in the early to mid-1950s, when trad first really became a mass commercial phenomenon, British admiration for southern musical traditions still tended to revolve around nostalgic invocations of the region frozen in time and conveniently stripped of its more unsavory and retrogressive aspects. It was still possible to revel in images of an exotic hybrid South ("the wonderful Creoles") without seriously contemplating the real nature of southern race relations. As the decade wore on, however, fans of Dixieland and other southern-based music were forced to reconsider the connections between their love for the music and their frequently romanticized and anachronistic conceptions of the region.

Sometime during the early 1950s, Chris Barber became rather bored with the Dixieland-by-numbers style he had done much to popularize. While retaining his love of early jazz, Barber, with the support of his singing spouse, Ottilie Patterson, steadily moved his band (and elements of his audience) more in the direction of blues, gospel, and folk influences. This broadening of repertoire to embrace other overwhelmingly southern roots music laid the foundations for the skiffle boom of the mid-1950s. Surfacing just months before the civil rights conflagrations threw disturbing light onto the darker side of southern life, skiffle was generally spared the anti-southern slurs later leveled against rock and roll by some of its British opponents. Indeed, skiffle represented something of a last yee-ha for romantic notions of southern pastoral bliss.

The most important figure in the success of skiffle was Glaswegian Lonnie Donegan. A fan of Dixieland, the southern country blues of Josh White, Blind Lemon Jefferson, and Leadbelly, as well as of Oklahoma-born folk singer Woodie Guthrie and old-time country artists like the Carter Family, Donegan had formerly fronted his own band and worked as a banjoist and guitarist with Dixieland pioneers Ken Colyer and Chris Barber. During the intermission between sets by these trad bands, Donegan would perform a few southern folk and blues staples like "Frankie and Johnny" and "House of the Rising Sun," backed by a rudimentary rhythm section of stand-up bass and drums. These interludes became increasingly popular, and in 1955 Donegan was allowed to include a few such songs on the Chris Barber Jazz Band's *New Orleans Joys* album. This Decca release sold a remarkable sixty thousand copies at a time when the Barber band had probably not played before sixty thousand people in their entire career. One of the Donegan songs, a full-throttle reworking of Leadbelly's "Rock Island Line," proved especially popular and was released as a single in February 1956. It eventually sold some 3 million copies, making the British top ten and, more astonishingly, the American top twenty—a very rare achievement by any British artist at that time.

Powered by the classic skiffle line-up of propulsive rhythm guitar, a manically scraped wash-board, and a fiercely slapped upright bass—replaced in more impecunious bands by a tea-chest bass where the bass line was picked out on a single piece of string attached to the top of a broomstick which in turn was mounted on an upturned tea-chest—"Rock Island Line" inspired a massive outbreak of primitive youthful music making in Britain. Initially, much of the skiffle repertoire comprised traditional southern blues and country songs, or new songs cast in a similar style. Donegan himself recorded much more southern folk material, like "John Henry," "Pick a Bale of Cotton," "Cumberland Gap," and A. P. Carter's "Wabash Cannonball." These recordings, together with his regular live shows and appearances on British television and radio, did much to popularize both skiffle and its American antecedents among a new generation of fans.

Like both their trad predecessors and their rock and roll heirs, skiffle fans registered their impatience with some of the dominant social conventions of the day by very consciously adopting alien musical and cultural styles rooted in the South. Skiffle's substitution of southern musical standards for those associated with classical music and the more mainstream popular music fare of the day was an obvious enough declaration of this independence. Yet these southern affectations went beyond simply mimicking the region's favorite musical devices. Barely months before the rise of Massive Resistance seriously tarnished the South's image, it was still possible to revel fairly uncritically in southern style and use it to show a rather cool detachment from middle Britain and its values. As Britain's foremost folk singer, Ewan MacColl, said of the skiffle groups that suddenly swarmed the country, emptying the kitchens of the land in their feverish search for washboards, thimbles, rope, and broomsticks, "With the guitar went the frayed and faded blue-jeans with the washed-out horizontal stripes which proclaimed you a fugitive from a chain-gang. The more extreme cultivators of the American image sent to the U.S. for those little sacks of Bull Durham tobacco and learned to roll their own with one hand. ... And everywhere, in every dialect of English, Scots and Welsh you heard the 'Rock Island Line,' 'The Midnight Special,' and 'The House of the Rising Sun.'" Few of these disciples of Dixie paused long to consider the real implications of southern chain gangs, or to dwell upon the mixture of poverty and racism that had spawned much of the region's most impressive music.[15]

Clearly there was a common understanding in Britain that skiffle, with its rudimentary instrumentation and direct lyrics, was derived from the rural South. Sometimes this carried connotations that were more hick than hip, but most still found charm and sincerity, rather than ignorance and barbarism, in the music's apparent simplicity and lack of guile. Fans embraced the idea that skiffle was rooted in earthy, unadulterated, and largely spontaneous forms of southern music that had somehow evaded the cynical and contaminating touch of the mass popular music industry. In the village of Brewood, near Wolverhampton, for example, bassist Mo Foster's first group proudly called themselves the Peasants, jettisoning the name only when their playing matured and they traded the raw energy of skiffle for a more sophisticated pop sound.[16] The tabloid *Daily Mirror* also recognized the craze's southern lineage. "It dates back to the days of slavery in the Southern States of America when every Friday—rent day—groups of musicians would go round with homemade instruments, singing the old prison and slavery jazz songs to raise enough money to pay the rent. They were called Skiffleboys."[17] Years later, George Harrison would reiterate this line, claiming simply that skiffle was rooted in "black slave culture."[18]

If such accounts left something to be desired in terms of historical accuracy—not too many slaves paid rent on Friday, or any other day for that matter, and none of them played anything that might reasonably be called jazz—it nonetheless helped to cement in place the notion that skiffle had a real southern heritage. Moreover, the *Mirror* clearly saw nothing problematic or unsavory in acknowledging the style's indebtedness to black culture. This attitude would later sharply distinguish British critics of rock and roll from many of their American counterparts.

The heyday of skiffle lasted barely eighteen months, although its influence was felt for much longer, registered in the birth of a thousand eager British bands. Ultimately, skiffle appealed to the same youngsters who were inspired by Elvis Presley, Fats Domino, Little Richard, Buddy Holly, and the other American rock and rollers who stormed the British charts after 1956. Indeed, once rock and roll had burst upon the scene, the main British musical response was to apply skiffle's Do-It-Yourself musical techniques to that idiom. What little there was that was distinctive or potent about British rock and roll music of the late 1950s and early 1960s was the result of blending these two southern-derived musical forms.

As in America, rock and roll music was initially greeted in Britain with a combination of rapture and revulsion. On both sides of the Atlantic much of the hostility congealed around objections to its raw sexuality, fears that the frenzied responses it produced among its delirious young fans might herald a wider outbreak of teenage rebellion and anti-social behavior, and abhorrence of what was viewed as its crude musicianship and cheap commercialism. "Do we want this shockin rockin?" asked the *Daily Mirror*, speculating on whether a music that "has been blamed for starting riots, rape and alcoholism among the youngsters" could have a similar impact in Britain.[19] Meanwhile, Steve Race, the *Melody Maker*'s influential jazz critic, performer, and broadcaster, snootily dismissed rock and roll for its "cheap, nasty lyrics." Loathing the way that the style seemed to eschew traditional hallmarks of good musicianship, and the fact that it was dramatically eroding the audience and radio airtime for jazz, Race declared that "Viewed as a social phenomenon, the current craze for rock 'n' roll material is one of the most terrifying things ever to happen to popular music."[20]

None of this early criticism had a specifically southern focus. Indeed, whereas Dixieland and skiffle had immediately been identified with southern musical influences and cultural affectations, there were initially few signs of any British awareness of the southern roots of rock and roll among either supporters or opponents of the style. Given that the kiss-curled Yankee imposter Bill Haley and his "Rock Around the Clock" was the music's first great emissary in Britain, this was perhaps not surprising. It would take the emergence of Elvis Presley to cement the connection between rock and roll and the American South in British minds. After Presley's debut on the U.K.

record charts in May 1956 with "Heartbreak Hotel," rock and roll's southern credentials gradually became more conspicuous, although the reputation of neither the music nor the region necessarily benefited from the association.

The rise of rock and roll and Presley coincided with a series of racially charged events in the American South that significantly altered British attitudes toward the region. In late 1955 and especially in early 1956, highly publicized civil rights confrontations in Montgomery, Tuscaloosa, and elsewhere highlighted southern prejudice and racial repression, the depths of which most trad and skiffle fans had been unaware, or at least able to ignore. One incident that had a particularly profound effect on British perceptions of the modern South occurred in Birmingham, Alabama, and involved one of the Britain's foremost dance bands, the Ted Heath Orchestra.

Ted Heath visited America in the spring of 1956 as part of an integrated "Show of Stars" package headlined by the elegant jazz pianist-cum-balladeer Nat King Cole. From the outset the tour had attracted an unusual level of interest in Britain. Heath's orchestra was the first British act to play live in the United States in some twenty years, during which time the dispute between the two countries' musicians' unions had effectively barred transatlantic exchanges of talent. *Melody Maker* featured weekly reports from Heath on the road, while many other newspapers kept close tabs on his progress. In the wake of press coverage of the *Brown* decisions, the ongoing bus boycott in Montgomery, and the efforts of Autherine Lucy to integrate the University of Alabama, there was a good deal of interest in how Heath and the tour would fare in the South, where most of the concerts were scheduled. There was even optimism that this integrated tour might actually help to ease racial divisions and tensions in the region. When the show reached San Antonio, for example, it was hailed by the *Melody Maker* as "a smash hit" which "smashed the colour bar." At the first desegregated concert ever to be held at the city's Municipal Auditorium, "Negroes and whites together gave the British musician an enthusiastic welcome."[21]

If the San Antonio concert conjured up comforting images of racial progress and interracial bonhomie founded upon shared musical tastes, events in Birmingham offered much less edifying images. At a segregated, whites-only concert at the Municipal Auditorium on April 10, Nat King Cole was roughed up on-stage by members of Asa Carter's Alabama White Citizens Council before being rescued by local policemen. Most American press reports interpreted the assault as part of a Council campaign that was really directed against rock and roll music, with Cole serving as an unfortunate surrogate in the wrong place at the wrong time. To Carter and his followers, rock and roll with its black and white stylistic influences, black and white artists, and black and white fans, represented a lewd metaphor for the sort of mongrelized and debased South they feared would emerge if integration was allowed to proceed.[22]

While few contemporary American reports dwelt long on the connection between the Council's physical attack on Cole, its extended publicity campaign against rock and roll, and its dedicated resistance to the desegregation of the South, the British press focused heavily on those links. The Cole incident seemed to confirm just how retrograde southern racial practices were at a time when the civil rights movement was just beginning to garner increased British attention and sympathy. Indeed, whereas Nat King Cole himself repeatedly tried to downplay the political aspects of the assault to American journalists, failing to associate it with the intensification of Massive Resistance and expressing incredulity that he should be attacked when he was "not a crusader" for civil rights, he was much more forthcoming about the real motivations of the attackers when speaking to Christopher Dobson of the *Daily Express*. "The attack was not a personal affront," Cole agreed, but it did symbolize desperate white efforts to preserve Jim Crow. "It was part of the fuss over Autherine Lucy at the University of Alabama and the bus boycott in Montgomery," he explained. Similarly, Cole and the American press were keen to portray the incident as an act of aberrant hooliganism; they uniformly stressed the sympathetic ovation the singer had received from the mortified white audience in Birmingham when he returned to the stage to announce that he could no longer continue. The *Daily Express* complicated this image of southern contrition by noting that "through the cheering could be heard some booing and shouts of 'Nigger go home!'"[23]

Most British accounts emphasized that the attack on Cole had happened in a South that was clinging to an anachronistic system of racial oppression with no parallel at home. The most elaborate discussion of the incident and its transatlantic implications came from jazz expert Steve Race in his *Melody Maker* column. Race noted the irony of the fact that the Cole attack took place barely three weeks after American bandleader Stan Kenton had assured him that integrating his orchestra had aroused no opposition. "Fortunately, we do not have any more problems like that in the States," Kenton explained, "It seems like the battle has been won—at least in music." Race picked up on Kenton's rider that prejudice was dead "at least in music," as if to stress that the attack on Cole had come from beyond the allegedly more equalitarian world of music fans. More significantly, Race argued that such an incident was virtually inconceivable in Britain. And even if something similar had occurred in Britain, he insisted that there would have been a very different audience response. "We, who live in a country where society not only considers all men equal but tries to treat them as such, have reason to be proud that no coloured musician here need fear for his safety. Anyone who tried to attack a Negro on a British stage would have to contend with the entire audience as well as 15 policemen." While Race accepted that most Americans were appalled by the Cole attack, the implication was that far too many of those southerners attending the Birmingham concert accepted—or at least failed to oppose—the racism of which the assault was but an extreme and dramatic manifestation.[24]

Much of this served to reinforce a rather smug British confidence that they were somehow immune to American-style racial prejudices. This view persisted more or less unchallenged until 1958, when race riots in Nottingham and Notting Hill and the exposure of blatant color-bars operating in many British nightclubs punctured some of that complacency. Nonetheless, Race at least sounded several less self-congratulatory notes, foreshadowing some of the British debates on race relations and immigration policies that characterized the 1960s—debates which would frequently take place with one eye firmly on the unfolding racial situation in America. First he reminded British jazz fans that they carried a special responsibility to take a firm stand against racial discrimination wherever they found it. There was, he wrote "no excuse for the person who deliberately hides his head in the sand when such evils are around; least of all the Jazz enthusiast, who owes much more than he can repay to the Negro and his music. That is why racial intolerance, whenever and wherever it occurs, is the business of this paper and of this columnist. And of you."[25]

Second, Race reiterated comments made earlier in the *Observer* newspaper concerning Autherine Lucy's attempt to desegregate the University of Alabama in February 1956. The paper had pointed out that at least Lucy's right to attend the previously segregated university was now protected in law, even if the enforcement of that law in the face of white mob violence in Tuscaloosa had left much to be desired. Race and the *Observer* both reminded their readers that there was no counterpart to this legal protection against segregation in those British African territories where apartheid still reigned: "It will be a long time before we see a Miss Lucy able to claim similar rights in South Africa, or indeed, in Rhodesia and Kenya." Anxious to puncture misplaced British condescension toward the United States regarding its racial record, the *Observer* noted that "If an African girl who defied segregation were sure of the backing, not only of the law but of the British press and public opinion—as Miss Lucy has the support of the federal law and most of the press and public opinion in the Northern States—the British Commonwealth would be as advanced in matters of racial liberalism as the United States of America." What was needed to hasten the legal protection of civil rights for peoples of color in Commonwealth Africa was for British people of goodwill to "play the role the American northerners have played from the Civil War onwards" and support African rights. Moreover, Race assigned to music fans and artists a special role in challenging racism wherever they encountered it, at home or abroad. Referring to British Commonwealth policy, he urged music fans to "keep a keen eye on developments, and bring to bear on our representatives the pressure which is the birthright of free citizens in a still free country. We owe it to our fellow men—the ones with darker skins than ours happen to be. And at the very least, we owe it to Jazz."[26]

Race's heartfelt plea may have been hopelessly over-optimistic about the level of concern among jazz fans, let alone other Britains, for the plight of Africans in the Commonwealth, certainly in the days before the Sharpeville massacre in South Africa. And it painted a rather simplistic and rosy picture of racial toleration in the northern states of America. More significantly, it also had the rhetorical effect of placing all right-thinking Britains, especially music fans, in potential opposition to an intransigent, wrong-headed South—a region whose whites were increasingly equated with the embarrassing and unpalatable guardians of apartheid in Commonwealth Africa. Coinciding with the reports of racial unrest from elsewhere in the region, the Cole incident helped to push the more odious discriminatory aspects of southern history to the forefront of British consciousness, where it began to eclipse the comfortable nostalgia and Old South romanticism that had long dominated attitudes toward the region. In turn, images of southern racism revitalized all sorts of stereotypes of southern uncouthness, violence, moral laxity, and general backwardness.

This trend was even evident in Ted Heath's own reports, which, perhaps not surprisingly, became increasingly jaundiced toward the region following the Cole attack. Heath even managed to criticize the poor quality of southern highways. "The roads in the South are no better than those in England," he commented archly. Given the generally woeful state of British roads and the fact that the new Eisenhower interstates, conveyor belts for all those enviably sleek chromed and finned cars, were a potent symbol of American technological prowess and high living standards, this was about as stinging an indictment as one could imagine.[27] In his postmortem on the tour, Heath continued to suggest that the South lagged behind the rest of the nation not just in amenities but also in basic refinement and taste. The South, Heath complained, did not really have the sophistication necessary to appreciate quality entertainment. "Remember, we've just played in the hillbilly areas of Kentucky, the Dixieland area of New Orleans, the Cow-Boy song area of Texas, and missed the keen awareness of good jazz that you get in such cities as St. Louis and New York."[28]

There was nothing new in the British recognition that the South was not like the rest of the United States. The difference was that after the spring of 1956 there was much greater sensitivity to the fact that some aspects of southern distinctiveness were more a curse than a blessing. While this added some healthy realism to excessively romantic images of the South, the new focus on southern flaws could sometimes spill over into an excessive demonization of the region. Once associated primarily with magnolia and moonlight, the region was in danger of becoming almost exclusively associated with mayhem and malevolence. While never absolute, this shift of emphasis within a discourse of the South where violence and honor, crudeness and grace had always coexisted, had particular significance when rock and roll first burst upon the British scene. Seeking ammunition with which to attack the new style for its alleged sexual impropriety, encouragement of antisocial behavior, and musical primitivism, many British critics saw its southern origins as a potent part of their armory. In this changing climate of opinion about the region, simply drawing attention to rock and roll's southern roots was sometimes enough to raise serious doubts about the music's basic morality. Conversely, many of the more lurid tales emerging from the rock and roll scene seemed merely to confirm the accuracy of stereotypes about the depraved nature of the South.

In September 1956, the *Times* noted that Elvis Presley had ousted Bill Haley as leader of the rock and roll craze. Indeed, the newspaper admitted that all previous teen sensations "paled before the delirious triumphs of a raw young southerner, Elvis Presley, now only 21, whose combination of a hill-billy style of wailing with bodily contortions which are supposed to suggest the 'fundamental human drive', took him even beyond the peaks of popularity enjoyed most recently by the tearful Mr. Johnny Ray and Mr. Frank Sinatra." The article continued by describing Presley in his "real element"—the "personal performances which have filled halls all over the country, mostly in the south and south-west, with excited teenagers—the great majority seem to be girls—many of whom he reduces to shrieks and outbursts of weeping by his moaning and sinuous swayings."[29]

The language used here, especially the adjectives, revealed much about attitudes toward rock and roll in polite British society, but also toward the South from whence it and Elvis came. "Raw," "delirious," "bodily contortions," and "sinuous swayings" all evoked the sensual and visceral side of the South, hinting at the source of much of its appeal to British teenagers. In the wake of Montgomery, Tuscaloosa, and the Cole incident, however, such language could also conjure up images of lost self-control; and lost control was now accepted as a typically southern vice that manifested itself in both rock and roll's unrestrained sexuality—and the frenetic dancing which acted as both expression and surrogate for that "fundamental human drive"—and in the unrestrained mob violence associated with Massive Resistance.

The *Times*'s language also implied that Presley's music was from a region so full of blood and passion that everyone before him—Ray, Sinatra, Haley—paled by comparison. Maybe this pallor-sanguine contrast was a subtle acknowledgment of rock and roll's huge debts to African American musical style, but those links were not explored, or even hinted at elsewhere in the *Times*'s article. Unlike in so many American critiques, there was no effort to trace Presley's potent and deeply disturbing sexual charge to the lascivious influence of black music. Indeed, what was missing—or much muted—in British opposition to rock and roll was the deep sense of racial transgression that dominated attacks on rock and roll in America, especially in the South. The Reverend Albert Carter of Nottingham may have sounded much like Asa Carter of the Alabama White Citizens Council when he ranted that "the effect of this music on young people is to turn them into devil worshippers; to stimulate self-expression through sex, to provoke lawlessness, to impair nervous stability and to destroy the sanctity of marriage." Reverend Carter, however, did not try to explain the grave threat rock and roll clearly posed to western civilization in terms of its racial provenance.[30]

As with skiffle, most British commentators, irrespective of whether or not they were favorably inclined toward rock and roll, tended to acknowledge the style's black influences rather matter-of-factly, with no overt or implied criticism. The *Daily Mirror*, for example, simply noted, "this new boogie-style rhythm has been described as a mixture of western music and Negro jazz."[31] The *Times* similarly observed that rock and roll "derives from Negro church music."[32] It is also important to remember that in many British minds during the mid- to late 1950s, simply acknowledging the black roots of rock and roll had the effect of intensifying any association with the South. This was a time when, as one young fan recalled, many—if by no means all, Britains—"understood that 'negroes' were entirely from the South." Outside a coterie of British aficionados it was often assumed that even popular northern-based black rock and rollers like Chuck Berry and Bo Diddley lived and recorded in the South.[33]

Generally unalarmed by rock and roll's black influences, critics seemed much more concerned that British kids should be besotted by music from a place where the despicable treatment of African Americans was seen as symptomatic of a much deeper moral malaise and ignorance. If anything, the relative absence of anxiety about rock and roll's mixed racial heritage had the effect of making its regional and class credentials much more significant as lightning rods for British criticism. Certainly the *Times*'s dismissive description of Presley's uninhibited singing as a "hill-billy style of wailing" explicitly invoked his white lower-class credentials. It also had the effect of linking rock and roll, like skiffle before it, to a specifically rural southern heritage. Yet it was apparent that in the year or so separating the emergence of the two styles the implications of that rural link had changed in tandem with changing attitudes toward the region. Whereas skiffle's folk roots had inspired a pastoral nostalgia with positive images of rural simplicity and homespun honesty, rock and roll's country dimension was usually invoked to characterize the style as crude and unsophisticated, an emblem of pervasive southern backwardness.

What made this stress on rock and roll's rural primitivism particularly ironic was that, unlike much of the black and white southern folk music that inspired skiffle, it was primarily an urban phenomenon; the product of black and white migrations off the land into the cities of the South, most famously the Memphis of Sun Records. This misapprehension was even reflected in the early marketing of rock and roll in Britain. When Sun recording star Roy Orbison had his first British release on London Records in 1957, the four-song disk was titled *Hillbilly Rock*. The cover art featured a sketch of a bearded country yokel in suspenders reclining on a flour sack while he picked an acoustic guitar and sucked on a corncob pipe. This was light years away from the ultra cool self-image of Orbison and the other habitués of Sun Records, with their penchant for blue suede shoes and the most feline of cat clothes. Moreover, British rock and roll fans were generally uninterested in revisiting the bucolic southern yokeldom of yore; they were thrilled by the buzz of the music's urban electricity and captivated by the sharp urbanity and bold sexual swagger of its artists.[34]

At least the *Times* appreciated that Presley had come a long way from the farm—or more accurately, from small-town Tupelo, Mississippi. Yet, it still depicted him as an unsophisticated rube who exhibited the tasteless, if highly conspicuous, consumption of the newly monied. Presley, the paper noted, is "now the proud owner of three Cadillacs and hundreds of the violent sports shirts he affects." The condescending coverage continued with a verbatim reproduction of Presley's comments on his future career plans. Given that few British fans would have actually heard Presley speak prior to the release later in the year of his first film, *Love Me Tender*—itself a hackneyed Civil War drama set on the southern domestic front—this was an important step in casting him and rock and roll as quintessentially southern. "I wouldn't want no regular spots on no T.V. programme," Elvis explained. "Movies are the things. I love to act. I don't care nothing whatsoever about singing in no movie...." In case its readers—well-used to reading immaculately parsed Queen's English in every paragraph—did not immediately appreciate that the *Times* was poking fun at the King's English, the piece ended with the snide observation that "Mr. Presley adds ... that English was what he liked best at school."[35]

Presley's humble beginnings and meager formal education provided countless opportunities for the British press to belittle the singer, his musical idiom, and his region of birth. In 1958, the *Times*, for example, gratuitously reprinted the comments of Millyon Bowers, head of the Memphis draft board, which inducted Elvis into the army: "after all, when you take him out of the entertainment business what have you got left? A truck driver."[36] The *Times*'s disdain for Presley's lower-class southern roots and the diction and grammar that in British minds appeared to betray it was neither an isolated incident, nor a habit restricted to the "quality" press. British stereotypes of southern backwardness, ignorance, and even moral lassitude were always closely associated with the sound of the southern drawl, in which it seemed that southern minds and tongues were forever at odds, stumbling uncertainly toward something that might be identified as an intelligent thought. This linkage became even clearer in the coverage of Jerry Lee Lewis's aborted British tour in the spring of 1958.

Lewis arrived in England in late May, eager to capitalize on the success of his recordings "Whole Lot of Shaking Going On," "Great Balls of Fire," and "Breathless" by joining a nationwide package tour. Intrigued by advance publicity about the wild piano-pumping rock and roller raised in Ferriday, Louisiana, representatives from most of the British press were on hand as Lewis and his entourage flew into Heathrow on May 22. One member of that entourage was his young wife, Myra. When reporters asked how old she was, Jerry Lee replied, "Fifteen." The following day, the *Daily Herald* sported the headline "Rock Star's Wife Is 15: And Its His Third Marriage." *Daily Mirror* journalist John Rolls elaborated on the story following an interview with Myra at London's Westbury Hotel. "I didn't tell my parents for a fortnight," admitted Myra. "When they knew, they had a fit," she confessed. Still, those parental misgivings seemed a thing of the past, since it transpired that Myra's mother Lois and her father J. W. Brown, were also on the tour, with J. W. playing bass in Lewis's back-up band. When Myra was asked if she thought she was too young to marry, she was quite affronted. "Gosh, no, back home you can marry at ten. One girl got wed at nine."[37]

As if this was not enough to scandalize vast sections of the British public, worse was to follow. Further investigations revealed that young Myra was not fifteen years old at all. She was just thirteen. Then it turned out she was actually Jerry Lee's cousin. To cap it all, the marriage was bigamous: the wedding had taken place five months before Lewis's previous marriage was legally annulled. As Jerry Lee tried to explain himself to the press, he became ever more deeply mired in cliché and stereotype. At one point he admitted that he had been remiss in not asking Myra's father for prior permission to wed his daughter, and in failing to wait until his own divorce had come through. Yet he excused himself with reference to his fierce religious beliefs. Declaring that he and Myra were both members of the Pentecostal church and therefore against "make-up, drink, tobacco and divorce," the twice divorced, hard-drinking Lewis explained, "I consider that Myra is my wife morally. ... My divorce is a matter for God."[38]

A day later, Jerry Lee had changed his story again. He explained to journalist Anne Lloyd, "It was only mah second marriage which wasn't legal." Rather like the *Times* with Presley, the *Mirror* saw fit to print a phonetic version of Lewis's explanation of his matrimonial career to an incredulous British public. "Ah was a bigamist when ah was 16. Ah was 14 when ah was first married," he announced. "That lasted a year. Dorothy was a good girl, but she was too good for me. She was 17. Then ah met Jane. One day she said she was gonna have mah child. Ah was real worried. Her father threatened me. Her brothers were hunting me with whips."[39] This last point provided an important twist. These events took place long before 1976, when Jerry Lee immortalized himself as a true gun-toting son of the South by accidentally shooting his bass player Norman "Butch" Owens, and then turning up drunk at Elvis Presley's Graceland home brandishing a loaded pistol.[40] It was all very well marrying a barely pubescent cousin, but until this point the Lewis story was rather lacking in the violent overtones long associated with the South. Coverage of contemporary civil rights events—especially of the mob violence at Little Rock in 1957—made sure that such associations were very much to the forefront of British minds.

Anyway, the threat of violence to satisfy besmirched family honor was apparently enough to encourage Jerry Lee Lewis to marry the pregnant Jane Mitchum. Although Mitchum would later deny his version of events, Lewis claimed that his second marriage had taken place a week before his divorce from Dorothy, his first wife, had come through. Employing inscrutable logic, Lewis argued that since his second marriage had been illegal, he could not possibly have committed bigamy when he took Myra as his third bride. Somewhat dolefully he concluded by suggesting, "Mah father should have put his foot on mah neck and whipped the hide off me."[41] That was certainly what Iain Murray recommended in a letter to the *Melody Maker*: "Any adult who leads a girl of 13 into what can only be described as sin should be horsewhipped."[42]

The Lewis saga played neatly into a whole range of stereotypes about unsuppressed southern sexual appetites and unhealthy regional predilections for incest and child brides that had titillated British audiences for some time. A front-page story in the *Daily Mirror* for March 9, 1956, had featured a picture of the recently married Susie Goode from Spartanburg, South Carolina. Just twelve years old, Susie was shown clutching a baby doll in a clear allusion to the recent film *Baby Doll*, in which Carol Baker had epitomized the steamy allure of sexually precocious southern nymphets. Not that it was only young southern women who suffered from such stereotyping. When a reporter from the *Daily Herald* managed to smooth talk his way into Myra's mother's hotel room, he delighted in the cheap salaciousness of the scene, portraying Lois Brown like some kind of down-market Blanche DuBois: "*She lay in bed, nylon-nightie clad, smoothing her dark hair with one hand and holding a sheet close to her throat with the other.*" When the same reporter knocked on the door of Myra and Jerry Lee Lewis's room, the Killer shouted, "*I can't come out, I haven't got any clothes on.*"[43]

This was all a very long way from visions of chivalrous cavaliers and chaste belles, or even of honest yeoman farmers and their pious, hardworking spouses. To British audiences, it seemed as if the Lewises and Browns, like many white southerners in the midst of the civil rights maelstrom, simply did not know how to control their baser instincts and behave in a civilized manner. And rock and roll was their music. The *Daily Sketch*'s review of one Lewis concert offered a striking image of primal, almost feral, redneck activity as it described how, "Drooling at the piano, Lewis moans, grunts, wails and sneezes so close to the microphone he might be eating it."[44]

Battered by the rising tide of adverse publicity, the Lewis tour disintegrated. The *People* newspaper called for a boycott of the shows and for the home secretary to institute deportation proceedings.[45] While the police checked the legality of the Lewises' paperwork, Minister of Labour Sir Frank Medlicott rose in the House of Lords to denounce the rock and roller's visit and formally raise the subject of deportation. Protests began to mount at the theatres where Lewis was appearing. Cries of "baby snatcher" could be heard from the audience at a May 26 concert in Tooting. While headlines in the *Daily Sketch* screamed, "Get Out Lewis!" the paper explained, "We have a lot of time for Americans. We also have time—but not nearly so much—for rock'n'roll." The paper made it clear that it was the South, increasingly cast as a debauched and sordid netherworld, somehow adrift from the rest of America and civilization, which was the source and site of this affront to common decency. "Where did this story begin?" it asked rhetorically. "In the Southern United States, where early marriage is common," the paper reminded its readers. That was "where Jerry Lee Lewis began his rocket-like career to stardom."[46]

After a couple of days of this incessant criticism, the Rank Organization cancelled Lewis's appearances for the remainder of the tour. Young Myra was relieved. "Ah don't wanna see no more of Britain," she said. "Ah just wanna get back to mah lovely home in Memphis, Tennessee."[47] The following day, the couple was back in New York and Jerry Lee was answering questions on the tour and his marriage. No, he had not been deported. Yes, his wife was thirteen. "She'll be fourteen in July, but she's ALL woman," he assured anyone who wanted to know, including those in Britain who had followed this little southern soap opera so closely.[48]

As the press treatment of Elvis Presley and Jerry Lee Lewis revealed, British critics of rock and roll often referred to its "typically" southern traits as a means to question the style's moral rectitude. For British fans of the music, however, those same "southern" traits often accounted for much of rock and roll's appeal. This at least suggested the continued existence of a broadly shared set of British ideas about the region: opponents and enthusiasts simply had different responses to many of what both factions saw as typically southern characteristics. For example, while critics ridiculed southern performers for their speech and for the undesirable regional and class characteristics that this speech supposedly revealed, their fans adored them for having exotic diction and a vocabulary whose very strangeness announced that they, their music, and their social values came from somewhere far beyond the mainstream of British—and, indeed, American—society. Thus rock and roll's initial appeal depended largely on its outsider credentials. British fans found in rock and roll a variant on what their trad and skiffle predecessors had also found in southern musical culture: a marker of social difference and a vehicle for some measure of cultural and generational rebellion. The way in which this worked was clearly evident among the Teddy Boys, who represented Britain's most conspicuous early rock and roll fans. Indeed, as Christopher Booker wrote from the perspective of the late 1960s, "Only three things did the revivalist jazz fans have in common with the Teddy Boys of South London—their youth … their sense of apartness from conventional society and their reverence for a particular romantic image of America."[49]

The working-class Teddy Boys scene, with its stylistic and very occasionally violent rebellion against conventional values and established authority, predated the rock and roll explosion by several years. Highly visible because of their curious sartorial blend of Edwardian formal wear and the American city slicker duds associated with frontier villains and riverboat gamblers, the Teds had struggled to find a suitable musical accompaniment to their counter-cultural posturing. Modern jazz was too rarified and too associated with a despised intellectual elite. Trad was too closely linked with an equally reviled radical politics—the Teds were generally a-political and hostile to most formal ideologies and social crusades, preferring to register their boredom and vague resentment of the status quo by means of their loud style politics and occasional acts of hooliganism. Skiffle sounded closer to the mark, as did some of the uptown southern country sounds associated with the likes of Hank Williams, but both styles retained their rustic overtones and lacked the requisite slick urbanity. Consequently, there was an especially intense response, an outpouring of relief almost, when after years of searching, rock and roll appeared as the long overdue soundtrack to a working-class youth movement which had always had a special reverence for Hollywood-style southern chic. As sociologist Simon Frith observed, "chronologically, the teds' look predated ted music and rock 'n' roll, but these teenagers were already committed to a fantasy of hillbilly cool—the move from Tennessee Ernie Ford to Elvis Presley was no more peculiar in London's Elephant and Castle than it had been in Tennessee itself."[50]

The Teds were enraptured by a music and a set of performers who embodied their own sense of rebelliousness, of being outsiders who were busy creating a parallel universe in which they were the insiders, the cognoscenti, the definers of a brash style and founts of cool wisdom. Most of their heroes—Elvis Presley, Jerry Lee Lewis, Carl Perkins, Little Richard—were hard-rocking southern artists who, much like their initial audiences, felt themselves to be excluded from the levers of power and prestige in American life as a consequence of their race, region, youth, or class—or of some combination of these factors.

Significantly, unlike trad and skiffle fans, the Teds and other British fans of early rock and roll appeared to have no qualms about the unabashed commercialism of their favorite music. They welcomed its novelty and saw the rapid turnover of new artists, dance crazes, and one-hit wonders less as a sign of superficiality than of vibrancy. Above all, they enjoyed the pleasures of conspicuous consumption—consumption of the records, distinctive clothing, and other paraphernalia that loudly announced both their devotion to the music and their distance from their parents and less hip peers. After all, rock and roll came from the South—America *in extremis*, a region that was simultaneously admired and despaired of for its brashness, its gaudiness, the size of its sensual appetites, and the enormity of its passions. In this world, it made perfect sense that Presley would sport "violent shirts" and flamboyant gold lame suits ("snazzy, jazzy outfits," as his first British advertisement put it), and own more Cadillacs than most of his British fans owned neckties.[51] And of course Little Richard, the extravagant "Georgia Peach," would pile his pompadour sky-high and ladle mascara, lipstick, and rouge onto his face. They were after all southerners, glamorous mavericks, steeped in the redemptive joys of excess, keen to party and eager to dazzle. Little wonder, then, that the hero of MacInnes's *Absolute Beginners* should adopt Elvis as the patron saint of his search for kicks, swearing, "By Elvis and all the saints that this last teenage year of mine was going to be a real rave."[52]

Although not all British fans of rock and roll in the late 1950s were comb-carrying Teddy Boys, to a greater or lesser extent most shared the Teds' sense that the music initially represented a musical sign of individuality and nonconformity, and that the South was the prime source of that rebellious élan, that attractive sense of outsiderhood. John Gustafson, bassist with Merseybeat pioneers The Big Three, explained the mix of bewilderment and exhilaration that accompanied his first exposure to this alien, exotic southern sound on the radio. "On came a record by Little

Richard called 'Rip It Up', and that changed my whole life. ... I thought: 'What is this? Music from outer space or what? What is it?' I was so excited that I couldn't sleep at all that night."[53]

Gustafson's fellow Liverpudlian John Lennon similarly recalled "having my hair stand on end" the first time he heard Presley's "Heartbreak Hotel" in 1956. "We'd never heard American voices singing like that. They'd always be like Sinatra or enunciated very well. Suddenly there's this hillbilly hiccupping on tape echo and all this bluesy background going on. And we didn't know what the hell Presley was singing about." For Lennon as for many of his contemporaries, the sheer emotional power of the recording, its visceral power, obviated any need for a literal understanding of the lyrics. The strange, barely decipherable cadences of the voice simply added to the mystique. "It took a long time to work out what was going on. To us, it just sounded like a noise that was great."[54]

Such responses were hardly unique. Indeed, one could do worse than consider each of the Beatles' most important early musical inspirations to demonstrate the sheer pervasiveness of southern influences on their generation of British musicians.[55] However, that generation's deep admiration for southern music and its rebel rockers was often tempered by a much greater appreciation of the region's racial shortcomings. While youngsters like John, Paul, George, and Ringo could easily accept the music's lower-class southern credentials, embracing them along with its perceived sexual abandon and disregard for other middle-class niceties as part of their own gestures of nonconformity, they often found it less easy to ignore the continuing disregard for black rights in the region. In effect, what had happened was that press coverage of the early civil rights movement and the rise of Massive Resistance, coupled with a growing awareness of racial problems at home and in the Commonwealth, had changed the context and raised the stakes for British fans of southern-derived music forms. It became much more difficult to cling uncritically to romantic visions of southern charm, honor, grace, rural idyllicism, or even urban outlaw cool as stories from Montgomery, Tuscaloosa, Birmingham, Little Rock, and Clinton rolled off the presses and flickered across the television screens. Certainly, while black southern artists like Little Richard, Fats Domino, and Larry Williams were celebrated in Britain alongside their white counterparts, Elvis, Jerry Lee, Carl Perkins, and Buddy Holly, it became virtually impossible to hear the marvelously hybrid sounds of the South as the unproblematic products of joyous interracial cultural exchanges.

The author gratefully acknowledges the assistance of Steve Klinge, Helen McQuinn, Andreu Walker, Colin Ward, and Jenny Ward while researching aspects of this essay.

Notes

Epigraph: Helen Taylor, *Circling Dixie: Contemporary Southern Culture Through a Transatlantic Lens* (New Brunswick: Rutgers Univ. Press, 2001), 21.

1 *London Times,* August 20, 1977, 13.

2 Mo Foster, *Play Like Elvis: How British Musicians Bought the American Dream* (Bodmin: MPG Books, 2000), 55.

3 *London Times,* December 30, 1958, 3.

4 Ibid., November 22, 1957, 7; Grady McWhiney, *Cracker Culture: Celtic Ways in the Old South* (Tuscaloosa: Univ. of Alabama Press, 1988).

5 *The Beatles Anthology* (London: Cassell and Co, 2000), 28.

6 Jim Godbolt, *A History of Jazz in Britain, 1919–50* (London: Quartet, 1984), 17; Foster, *Play Like Elvis,* 199.

7 Foster, *Play Like Elvis,* 268.

8 *The Stage,* September 6, 1956, 7.

9 *Newcastle Evening Chronicle,* March 7, 1957, 19.

10 *The Stage,* September 13, 1956, 7.

11 George Melly, *Revolt into Style: The Pop Arts in Britain* (1970; reprint, London: Penguin, 1972), 60.

12 *Jazz Journal,* January 1950, 17.

13 *Melody Maker,* November 13, 1943, 6–7.

14 Colin MacInnes, *Absolute Beginners* (1959; reprint, London: Allison and Busby, 2001), 62.

15 Ewan MacColl, *Journeyman: An Autobiography* (London: Sidgwick and Jackson, 1990), 273.

16 Foster, *Play Like Elvis,* 191–93.

17 *Daily Mirror,* September 8, 1956, 7.

18 George Harrison, quoted in *Beatles Anthology,* 28.

19 *Daily Mirror,* August 16, 1956, 5.

20 *Melody Maker,* May 5, 1956, 8.

21 Ibid., April 7, 1956, 24.

22 For a detailed account of the Cole incident, and the links between Massive Resistance and the southern campaign against rock and roll, see Brian Ward, *Just My Soul Responding: Rhythm and Blues, Black Consciousness and Race Relations* (Berkeley: Univ. of California Press, 1998), 95–105.

23 *Daily Express,* April 12, 1956, 9.

24 *Melody Maker,* April 21, 1956, 8.

25 Ibid.

26 Ibid.

27 Ibid., April 14, 1956, 7.

28 Ibid, May 26, 1956, 3.

29 *London Times,* September 15, 1956, 4.

30 Reverend Albert Carter, quoted in Ian Whitcomb, *Whole Lotta Shakin'* (London: Arrow Books, 1985), 13. Clearly, a crucial factor here was that rock and roll's black heritage was associated specifically with African Americans, not with the Afro-Caribbeans or Asians who occupied a more conspicuous place in Britain's racial landscape and who were the subject of increasingly tense debates about race relations, immigration policies, and anti-discrimination laws.

31 *Daily Mirror,* September 5, 1956, 3.

32 *London Times,* September 15, 1956, 7.

33 Colin Ward, interview with author, June 20, 2001.

34 *Mojo,* July 2001, 138.

35 *London Times,* September 15, 1956, 4.

36 Ibid., January 6, 1958, 7.

37 *Daily Mirror,* May 23, 1958, 2; *Daily Herald,* May 23, 1958, 1. For the best coverage of Lewis's tour, see Nick Tosches, *Hellfire: The Jerry Lee Lewis Story* (New York: Dell, 1982), 151–61.

38 *Daily Mirror,* May 26, 1958, 1.

39 Jerry Lee Lewis, quoted in ibid., May 27, 1956, 10.

40 See, Tosches, *Hellfire,* 245–46.

41 Jerry Lee Lewis, quoted in *Daily Mirror,* May 27, 1956, 10.

42 *Melody Maker,* June 7, 1958, 12.

43 *Daily Herald,* May 26, 1958, 1, 3.

44 *Daily Sketch,* May 25, 1958, 5.

45 *People,* May 25, 1958, 1.

46 *Daily Sketch,* May 26, 1958, 1.

47 *Daily Mirror,* May 28 1958, 2.

48 Ibid., May 29, 1958, 2.

49 Christopher Booker, *The Neophiliacs: The Revolution in English Life in the Fifties and Sixties* (1969; 2d ed., London: Pimlico, 1992), 34–35.

50 Simon Frith, *Sound Effects: Youth, Leisure and the Politics of Rock 'n' Roll* (New York: Pantheon, 1982), 184–85.

51 *New Musical Express,* March 3, 1956, 5.

52 MacInnes, *Absolute Beginners,* 12.

53 John Gustafson, quoted in Foster, *Play Like Elvis,* 44.

54 John Lennon, quoted in *Beatles Anthology,* 192.

55 Paul McCartney, whose father led his own Dixieland combo, frequently cited Elvis and Little Richard as his greatest rock and roll idols, with Buddy Holly and the Everly Brothers not too far behind. George Harrison had similar heroes, but recalled Cajun legend Fats Domino's "I'm in Love Again" as the first rock and roll record he ever heard. Harrison credited hearing his father's copy of Jimmy Rodgers's "Waiting for a Train" with making him want to take up the guitar in the first instance; he had a similarly paternal exposure to the blues, folk, and country sounds of Josh White, Bill Broonzy, and Slim Whitman. Ringo Starr's infatuation with southern music, indeed the whole notion of the South, was if anything even more intense. "I thought about emigrating to the USA ... I wanted to go to Texas to live with Lightin' Hopkins—the blues man, my hero. I actually went to the embassy and got the forms. This was in 1958 ... we'd got a list of jobs to go to in Houston." *Beatles Anthology,* 27–28, 37 (Starr quote on page 37).

Whose "Rock Island Line"?

Originality in The Composition of Blues and British Skiffle

Bob Groom

Airplay has always been the major key to creating a hit record, particularly in the era before television exposure, celebrity reputations, and wider media coverage became significant. Over the years DJs have made hits out of the most unlikely records—David Seville's "Witch Doctor" and Chipmunks' records in America, "Happy Wanderer" by the Obernkirchen Children's choir and three hits by the Royal Scots Dragoon Guards Military Band in Britain are just a few examples that spring to mind. Surely at the time it first became popular, before it spearheaded a whole popular music phenomenon, "Rock Island Line" must have been seen in this novelty category. Despite the seemingly exotic nature of the lyrics, something about it appealed to British disc jockey Eamonn Andrews,[1] who was credited with "discovering" Lonnie Donegan's recording for BBC radio's *Pied Piper* series. With repetition, listeners also became intrigued with this railroad saga from the Deep South. (Jack Train's version of "The Runaway Train," originally a hit by Vernon Dalhart, was another BBC favorite at this time.) Not that they would be entirely unfamiliar with genuine American folk music, thanks to the efforts of Alistair Cooke, whose pioneering BBC radio series *I Hear America Singing* in 1938 contained an appreciable element of jazz and black music, drawn from commercial recordings and the Library of Congress Archive of folk song, folklorist Alan Lomax (resident in the United Kingdom in the 1950s), and BBC producer/presenter Charles Chilton, perhaps better known for the sci-fi thriller series *Journey into Space*. When Lonnie Donegan's "Rock Island Line" was first broadcast, it was simply one track of a popular eight-track ten-inch LP by Chris Barber's Jazz Band[2] on Decca (*New Orleans Joys*), but such was its popularity on air that Decca eventually issued it as a single (Decca F-J 10647) with "John Henry" on the B-side. It was also later made available on a Decca EP (DFE 6345) and so was available in all vinyl formats then in commercial use.

Record charts based on sales rankings had been introduced in Britain in 1952 by the *New Musical Express*, the "Hit Parade" having previously been constructed from sheet music sales (which still continued to be important for some years). By the autumn of 1955 all the major music papers featured record charts and "Rock Island Line" quickly made an appearance in them, climbing rapidly through January 1956 to reach its highest position at No. 8 during the first week of February. However, quite different from the "shooting star" path of most pop singles today—zooming to the top, and then quickly dropping off the chart—records often spent months on the charts, selling steadily. "Rock Island Line" spent twenty-two weeks on the chart, and when the Top 20 was extended to become a Top 30 in April 1956, it was back in at No. 16 and was listed at No. 19 the week before its last placing in June. (By which time Lonnie was at No. 2 with his first Pye-Nixa single, "Lost John.") Even more improbably, "Rock Island Line" became a major hit in America. Its raw excitement, a quiet opening, followed by acceleration to a fast and furious climax, hit the spot with U.S. record buyers. Lonnie himself was astonished by the record's huge popularity.[3] Ironically he derived no direct income from its sales (just a session fee as a member of the band when the recordings were made back in July 1954), although it gave him a seven-year career as a major pop star. While Decca shilly-shallied (instead of offering royalties and putting Lonnie on contract), Pye-Nixa signed up the new young sensation. Suddenly Donegan the jazzman was a pop star.

Those in the know felt that Lonnie had ripped off a composition of Leadbelly (Huddie Ledbetter) by claiming authorship of the song. "New words and music by Lonnie Donegan" was the credit, but neither element of this claim was correct. Essex Music first credited the song to Donegan on the sheet music, later changing it to "words and new music" by Donegan. On recent CD issues Ledbetter, J. and A. Lomax, and Donegan are co-credited with a song that none of them composed! Only later (long after the skiffle craze had died) did it come to light that Leadbelly himself had acquired the song from prisoners (Kelly Pace leading a group of seven axemen cutting pine logs) at the Cummins State Farm, Arkansas, when he was chauffeuring and acting as intermediary for John Lomax during a 1934 field recording trip for the Library of Congress. The prisoners sang about a train running from Memphis, Tennessee, to Little Rock, Arkansas, on a railroad line,[4] also celebrated in unrelated blues by Furry Lewis ("Rock Island Blues," Vocalion, 1927), Lonnie Coleman ("Old Rock Island Blues," Columbia, 1929), and Leroy Ervin ("Rock Island Blues," Gold Star 628, 1947), among others.[5] The chorus ran:

> Well the Rock Island Line is a mighty good road,
> Said the Rock Island Line is a road to ride
> If you want to ride you got to ride it like you find it,
> Buy your ticket at the station on the Rock Island Line

After the commercial comes a two-line religious verse, also repeated as verse four. Only verse three describes an actual train schedule on the railroad. Several times through the recording a hoot is heard, simulating the warning note of the engine approaching a crossing or halt.

Although the October 5, 1934, version by Kelly Pace and his fellow convicts (248-A-1) is the only one that has been issued, other group versions were recorded. According to the standard discography one was made only a few days earlier (236-A-1) by a different convict group at Little Rock, Arkansas. A text different from the lyrics heard on 248-A-1 was reproduced on page 474 of *Long Steel Rail* by Norm Cohen,[6] and it may be that this is from the earlier recording; if so its seeming lack of coherence may have prompted John Lomax to seek another version at Cummins Prison Farm.[7] On May 21, 1939, John Lomax, with son Alan, was back at Cummins Prison Farm, Gould, Arkansas, for the Library of Congress and while there recorded another version of "Rock Island Line" (2671-A-1) from a group of convicts led by Joe Battle. This has not yet been made available on vinyl or CD.

By this time Leadbelly had made his first recording of the song, for the Library of Congress in June 1937. Over the next twelve years he recorded it at least a dozen times. At first he referred to the song's work song origins[8] in a spoken introduction. Later he replaced this with an introduction to the action in the song as he developed this for dramatic effect. Realizing that it was parochial, he deleted the verse mentioning Memphis and Little Rock and substituted a story about an engine driver and a tollbooth official. The changes he made certainly were enough to entitle him to part-composer credit. Whether the credits accorded John and Alan Lomax represented any contribution to the lyrics by them is open to question.

A variety of artists covered the Donegan hit, including a then unknown Bobby Darin, who sang it on his first national television appearance in 1956, having just recorded it for American Decca. Established hit-maker Don Cornell's "cover" version for Coral at first threatened to outsell Lonnie's (issued on London Records in the United States), but it was Donegan who took it into the American Top Ten (No. 8 or No. 10, depending which chart you consult) in May 1956. A spoof version by master satirist Stan Freberg (on Capitol) made the lower reaches of the British Top 30 in July/August 1956. British actor/comedian Peter Sellers recorded a clever parody of Donegan's hits (including "Rock Island Line") called "Puttin' on the Smile"; Donegan hated it (although he had apparently been amused by the Freberg skit).

Blues artist Snooks Eaglin recorded "Rock Island Line" for Swedish Radio in 1964 and the great Little Richard performed it in a late 1980s film *A Vision Shared*, a tribute to Leadbelly and Woody Guthrie. Johnny Cash recorded "Rock Island Line" at Sun in 1956 and claimed ownership of the song. Cash may well have heard a Leadbelly version, or one by the Weavers (from 1951), but most likely his recording was a Sam Phillips-promoted "cover" of Donegan's. Cash inserts two "Casey Jones"-type verses to differentiate his from the Donegan version. Country hit maker Johnny Horton cut a version for Columbia, folksinger Ramblin' Jack Elliott recorded it for Prestige, and even smooth pop balladeer Brian Hyland included it in his *Rockin' Folk* album. The folk revival sparked numerous versions by groups like the Tarriers, the Brothers Four, and the Rooftop Singers. Inevitably Donegan eventually recorded "Rock Island Line" for Pye-Nixa, to complete his catalogue of hits, but by this time (August 1956) he must have performed it "live" at least a hundred times, and the re-cut lacks the raw excitement of the earlier Decca version.

With "Rock Island Line" red hot on the U.S. charts, Donegan was invited to do a ten-week American tour, commencing in June 1956 and including appearances on major television shows with Perry Como (who had him do a sketch with future American president, Ronald Reagan), Bill Randle, Howard Miller, and Paul Winchell, and package show performances with the likes of Chuck Berry, Clyde McPhatter, LaVern Baker, and Frankie Lymon and the Teenagers. The tour was a great success (at one point he was backed by the Rock and Roll Trio—Johnny and Dorsey Burnette and lead guitarist Paul Burlison!), but in August he made a swift return to the United Kingdom when his record company cabled that "Lost John" was No. 2 in the charts and he was needed for TV and concert dates. (Oddly "Lost John" was only a minor chart record in the United States, and Donegan had to wait until 1961 for his only other major American hit with a revival of the 1924 vaudeville song "Does Your Chewing Gum Lose Its Flavour on the Bedpost Overnight?")

Donegan's interest in black blues and gospel song dates back to his teenage years. Born Anthony (Tony) Donegan in Glasgow, Scotland, on April 29, 1931, he moved to London with his parents two years later and by the time he was fifteen he had developed an interest in American folk music. Donegan discovered jazz in 1947 and during National Service in the Army (1949–51) became an amateur jazz musician. In London he saw Josh White perform and gained access to blues, gospel, and old-time country records at the American Embassy (he later confessed to permanently "borrowing" their copy of the Muddy Waters Library of Congress 78!), Collet's Bookshop and elsewhere. Lonnie Johnson and Leadbelly were his favorites. The story, possibly apocryphal, of how Tony became Lonnie Donegan is that he, with his little jazz band of the day, appeared on the same bill as Tony's musical hero, Lonnie Johnson, at the Royal Festival Hall in 1952. The compere got the two mixed up and introduced Tony as Lonnie Donegan.

Donegan's success triggered a nationwide British enthusiasm for skiffle groups and spasm bands, usually consisting of washboard, guitar, washtub or tea-chest bass, and sometimes harmonica and banjo. In skiffle's peak year of 1957 there were thousands of amateur skiffle groups in Britain, many of them in big cities like London and Liverpool, where the Quarrymen skiffle group would later emerge as the Beatles. Many famous beat groups and solo artists of the 1960s evolved from skiffle groups. Hank Marvin of the Shadows started as a skiffler, as did Adam Faith and Cliff Richard. Donegan had a string of hits in Britain with songs like "Cumberland Gap" (1957), "Battle of New Orleans" (1959), and vaudeville/music hall numbers like "Does Your Chewing Gum Lose Its Flavour" and "My Old Man's a Dustman" (1960). His success was fairly short—he had little sympathy with the music of the rock 'n' rollers. His preference was for jazz, blues, and folk music, and when skiffle faded, he moved to country music and vaudeville songs. He had a brief revival of fame in the late 1990s when he recorded with Van Morrison and he was still performing when he died in November 2002.

The actual origins of skiffle are not entirely clear. The term seems to be a derivative of "scuffle," commonly used by African Americans in the sense of "scuffling for a living" or to describe a rough-and-ready party, or rent party, and by extension, impromptu music utilizing basic, often homemade or improvised instruments, performed at such gatherings. However, before 1900 the Razzy Dazzy Spasm Band with harmonica, cowbells, bullfiddle, pebble gourd, etc., played on the streets of Storyville in New Orleans. In the Windy City Jimmy O'Bryant and group recorded their "Chicago Skiffle" in 1925. In 1929 Paramount Records recorded (it was issued in 1930) a two-sided sampler of their blues hits under the generic title *Hometown Skiffle*. Folkways issued an LP titled *American Skiffle Bands* in 1957. This featured field recordings made by Sam Charters, including the Mobile (Alabama) Strugglers in 1957. Hokum blues, rent party music, and goodtime jazz have all been described as "skiffle." In 1940s Harlem, newspaper editor Dan Burley formed a skiffle group which made a number of recordings. Musically these little resemble what Lonnie Donegan et al. were to popularize as skiffle a decade later. So how did the British version get its name? Bill Colyer, brother of Ken and sometime musician, tells how he named the British music phenomenon, prior to a BBC broadcast. When pressed to find a less awkward name than "breakdown group music," he remembered a 1947 record by Dan Burley and his Skiffle Boys, coupling "Chicken Shack Shuffle" and "Skiffle Blues" (Arkay 1001/Exclusive 77) and dubbed the "new" music "skiffle." (Burley's group was also recorded live in 1951 performing a "Skiffle Jam.") Previously it had simply been the music of the "breakdown group" within a jazz band, a sparer, string band unit without brass instruments. British skiffle was born in 1953, named by October 1954, and became a musical phenomenon in 1956/7. At first, enthusiasm for it was mostly in jazz venues, but as its popularity mushroomed, it could be found in both coffeehouses and concert halls. Criticism in the press tended to dwell on the fact that most skiffle group guitarists didn't venture much beyond the three chord progression (C, F, G7) provided by a basic tutor. There was even a deliberate "dumbing-down" by some professional musicians. Washboards tended to be standard and can be heard on most records by McDevitt, the Vipers, et al. Oddly only Donegan's first hit featured washboard (by Beryl Bryden, a well-respected member of the jazz community), and when he went on the road in the United Kingdom he was quick to include drums in his line-up, giving a stronger, meatier sound than his rivals had.

What is the measure of originality? Was Leadbelly's "Rock Island Line" original? Not in the sense that the song already existed when he learnt it, but over a period of twelve years, beginning in 1937, Leadbelly re-shaped the song, effectively making it "his own," that is, personalized within his large repertoire. He gave it a preamble, describing the work gang that performed it for John Lomax at the Arkansas prison farm. As he worked on the song he extended the introduction to include a little story about the engineer (train driver) outwitting the tollgate keeper by pretending that the train is carrying "all livestock" when in fact he is hauling chargeable freight—"I fooled you, I fooled you, I got all pig iron ..." he calls back. The chorus is retained from the "original" performance and Leadbelly also uses the "Jesus died to save our sins" and "I may be right, I may be wrong" verses from it, adding the always mysterious "Cat's in the cupboard" verse.

Later the preamble about the work gang was omitted, and a dozen recorded performances of "Rock Island Line" by Leadbelly were made between 1942 and 1949, the year of Leadbelly's death. Probably the most widely heard of these was one made with Paul Mason Howard on zither at an October 1944 session for Capitol when the (self-styled) "King of the Twelve-String

Guitar" was trying his luck in Hollywood. The version that inspired Donegan may, however, have been a February 1945 version made in San Francisco and later issued by Folkways. Donegan had therefore inherited a fully-formed piece, developed by Leadbelly, transforming a work song (as Leadbelly first recorded it unaccompanied, for the Library of Congress in June 1937, and again at a June 1940 commercial session with the Golden Gate Quartet for Victor, which the company chose not to issue at the time) into a concert performance piece.

Although the songbooks of Leadbelly and Woody Guthrie were central to the repertoires of most skiffle groups, songs were acquired from a wide variety of sources, some homegrown such as the Vipers' splendid version of the Liverpool streetwalker song "Maggie May" ("and she'll never walk down Lime Street anymore"). Skiffle wasn't really a song genre, it was a particular approach to the instrumentation that gave it its distinctiveness, and when the novelty of that eventually wore off it spelled the end of skiffle as a commercial music phenomenon. The music industry has never really been comfortable with the do-it-yourself approach, and it is revealing to hear how many rock groups and performers had session musicians pressed on them at recording sessions by companies anxious to achieve the required standard. Out on the road there would be so much audience noise that a few fluffs wouldn't matter!

In the formative period of British skiffle, a traditional song from Texas became a favorite, and it was performed (and recorded) at a Copenhagen concert in 1953 with Lonnie Donegan and Ken Colyer duetting, and Lonnie, Dickie Bishop, and Chris Barber later did a studio recording of it (issued on Polygon) in May 1955. The overnight train to San Antonio, Texas, used to roll out of the Houston depot a few minutes past 11:00 every night. The Southern Pacific Railroad called it "The Alamo Special," but as it crossed the Brazos River Bottoms, twenty-five miles from the city and near the small town of Sugarland, an hour later, it passed close to Central Unit 2, part of the Texas prison farm system. The black prisoners there called it "The Midnight Special," a howl of noise, a stabbing core of light, and a glimpse of freedom, vanishing quickly into the night.[9] Inmates James Baker (known as "Iron Head"), Moses Platt ("Clear Rock") and Huddie Ledbetter ("Leadbelly," also sometimes "Lead Belly"), who was incarcerated at Sugarland between 1920 and 1925, all recorded a song about it for the Library of Congress.

> If you ever go to Houston, you better walk right,
> You better not stagger, and you better not fight.
> Oh let the Midnight Special shine its light on me,
> Oh let the Midnight Special shine its everlovin' light on me.

Mack McCormick has explained the origins of the title verse and some other elements of the song as probably deriving from an earlier song about Cowboy Jack Smith's unsuccessful jailbreak in Houston. The melody and the shape of the chorus may derive from an old spiritual.

At least two African American recordings of "The Midnight Special" were made up to 1930 (although a recording of that title, by Sodarisa Miller on Paramount dating to 1925 is unrelated). Southern blues singer and guitarist Sam Collins recorded "The Midnight Special" for Gennett in 1927. By the time Chicago pianist Romeo Nelson made his final recording in February 1930, "11.29 Blues," subtitled "The Midnight Special" (Vocalion 1494), the theme had become one of universal applicability:

> When you come to Chicago,
> said you better walk straight
> and you better not stumble,
> and you better not wait
> or the police will arrest you...

Big Bill Broonzy and the State Street Boys recorded "Midnight Special" (Okeh 8964/Vocalion 03004) in January 1935. In a somewhat tongue-in-cheek version, Broonzy places the action in Tennessee's Bluff City:

> Now if you ever go to Memphis, said you better walk right,
> The police will arrest you and carry you down,
> And take you to the station with the gun in his hand,
> Then the judge will tell you, you have been a naughty man.

Rosie, who comes to get her man out of jail, becomes Mary in this variant.

There have been numerous recorded versions of "The Midnight Special" by white country and folk artists starting with a 1926 version by Dave Cutrell with McGinty's Oklahoma Cowboy Band ("Pistol Pete's Midnight Special," Okeh 45057), and the song was also included in a 1927 song collection by Carl Sandburg published as *The American Songbag*. Woody Guthrie recorded the song on several occasions, but it was almost certainly Huddie Ledbetter who inspired its popularity with skifflers. Leadbelly recorded it for the Library of Congress in 1934 and again in 1935. In June 1940 he recorded it with the Golden Gate Quartet for Victor (27266). Amongst later versions of "Midnight Special," possibly the best is the 1948 recording for Fred Ramsey included in *Leadbelly's Last Sessions* (now available on Smithsonian/Folkways CD 40068/71). Notable among the other hundred plus commercially recorded versions are those by organist Jimmy Smith, Harry Belafonte (on his RCA-Victor album actually titled *Midnight Special*), blues shouter Big Joe Turner (Atlantic 1122), and Josh White (Elektra LP 114).

In his autobiography W. C. Handy recalls his youth in Florence, Alabama, when he heard old-time fiddle players like Uncle Whit Walker (born 1800) play a tune called "Sally Got a Meatskin Laid Away."[10] (As "Johnny Got a Meatskin Laid Away" it was recorded by black singer/guitarist Arthur "Brother-in-Law" Armstrong for the Library of Congress in Jasper, Texas, in October 1940.) "Sail Away Ladies," which was also performed by Walker, utilized the same tune. Popular white country artist Uncle Dave Macon recorded his excellent "Sail Away Ladies" for Vocalion (5155) in 1927. (Born in 1870, Macon was an exceptional musician with a huge repertoire, in some ways perhaps a white equivalent of Leadbelly.) The chorus includes the phrase "don't you rock me, daddy-o," repeated four times. Thirty years after this commercial recording was made, it was revived and partially rewritten by Wally Whyton to provide his skiffle group the Vipers with a UK Top Ten hit, "Don't You Rock Me Daddy-O," in February 1957. (Lonnie Donegan "covered" their version and took his version to No. 4 in the same month. It sold strongly for the following two months.)

Following "Daddy-O" the Vipers had several other hits, including "Cumberland Gap," which also reached the UK Top Ten but was overtaken by a bigger-selling Donegan "cover," which went on to No. 1, and a "skifflization" of the Red Nelson/Cripple Clarence Lofton classic "Streamline Train," that had been issued in Britain on a Brunswick 78. As skiffle faded the Vipers dropped the skiffle group title, but their transition to rock 'n' roll produced no hits.

Hot on the heels of the Vipers came the Chas McDevitt Skiffle Group. McDevitt had already been performing traditional music pre-skiffle and had discovered a potential hit song. Already fifty years old, the song about a freight train was about to leap up the charts. Elizabeth Cotten was a maid in the household of the folk-singing Seeger family in Washington, D.C., when her talents as a singer and guitarist were discovered. A compelling skiffle version by McDevitt of her song "Freight Train" was a top ten hit in the United Kingdom (peeking at No. 5 at the beginning of June 1957) and also made the American charts, although a cover version by Rusty Draper stole the biggest sales there. This led to a U.S. tour for the Chas McDevitt Skiffle Group, featuring singer Nancy Whiskey. (They had another, smaller hit with "Greenback Dollar," before Nancy left the group to go solo.) McDevitt has continued to be active in music and participated in several skiffle revivals. Elizabeth Cotten made a series of recordings issued on Moses Asch's Folkways label which became very influential in folk circles. Born near Chapel Hill, North Carolina, in 1893, she claimed the words and music of "Freight Train" as her own, composed in her youth, around 1910. The McDevitt hit record, enhanced by whistling, changes the perspective of the song from the first person to observer, perhaps justifying a co-composer credit. The standard discography gives the Cotten recording as ca. 1958, but that was when it was released in the United States on her first album *Negro Folk Songs\And\Tunes* (FG 3526). It was probably recorded in 1952 and brought to Britain by Peggy Seeger in 1956. (Seeger herself recorded "Freight Train" for Pye-Nixa around November, 1957, and this was issued on an EP entitled *Origins of Skiffle*.) Later versions included one by blues duo Brownie McGhee and Sonny Terry (Bluesville BV 1002), quite a number of country versions (e.g., Chet Atkins, Dave Dudley, Jimmy Dean), several folk recordings (Pete Seeger; Peter, Paul, and Mary), and even a jazz version (Bud Shank on *Folk 'n' Flute*), as well as popular versions by acts like Dick and Deedee, Margie Rayburn, and the Johnny Mann Singers.

Johnny Duncan, an American by birth, replaced Lonnie Donegan in the skiffle unit within Chris Barber's Jazz Band. In 1957 Duncan went solo and, with his Blue Grass Boys, scored a massive UK hit, "Last Train to San Fernando," which reached No. 2 on the charts. Although classified as skiffle it sounded more like country music, but surprisingly enough it started life as a 1950 Trinidadian road march, composed by calypsonian Dictator (Kenneth St. Bernard)! It was about the last train to run from Port of Spain, the island's capital, to its second city, San Fernando, before the railway line was closed. A later recording, made in New York by another calypso singer, the Duke of Iron

(Cecil Anderson), changed the lyrics somewhat, recounting how a lady wanted a last fling on the night before her wedding and the singer was happy to oblige: "You better beat this iron while it's hot!" The Duke of Iron 78 was issued in the United Kingdom (Melodisc 1316) and was the inspiration for the pop hit by Johnny Duncan, which was first credited to Randolph Padmore/Sylvester DeVere, before the Mighty Dictator was added on the sheet music and reissue credits.

Why did skiffle falter and fail while rock 'n' roll triumphed in the charts? I can offer some possible reasons. Firstly, it didn't produce marketable teenage idols like Elvis, Ricky Nelson, and Cliff Richard. Without doubt Lonnie Donegan was a major star, but hardly a teenage idol! Like Bill Haley before him, when Lonnie passed age thirty his chart success quickly came to an end. Secondly, skiffle was branded as home-made, anyone-can-do-it music, whereas rock relied on guitar wizardry or skilful sax work. Thirdly, the music industry was more comfortable with the adolescent lyrics and tamer sounds that tended to dominate the charts as the fifties gave way to the sixties. Songs about racehorses, like "Stewball," or murder ballads like "Frankie and Johnny," didn't really fit the bill. The traditional jazz boom of the early sixties also tended to favor softer material, and it was British blues that emerged as the next underground movement.

Although it spawned several records that became hits in America, the British pop skiffle craze was not repeated across the Atlantic. It was a peculiarly British phenomenon, although it also caught on in several other European countries. The do-it-yourself nature of the music, while not totally confined to working-class youth, was certainly at odds with the glamour of American culture in the mid-1950s. The smoldering rebellion represented by Marlon Brando and James Dean on film and Elvis Presley on TV in the affluence of America was light years away from spotty kids twanging guitars and playing washboards with thimbles in British coffee bars. But somehow skiffle seemed to fill a social need, channeling the restless energy of the young into popular music as Britain emerged from wartime and postwar austerity and social conformity. More recently there have been brief skiffle revivals in Britain, Germany, and elsewhere, probably as part of the general nostalgia for the music of the fifties.

So what of originality? A song whose origins predate the recording of black music is variously known as "Easy Rider," "See See Rider," or "C.C. Rider." Blues singer Ma Rainey recorded it for Paramount as "See See Rider Blues" in 1924. Blind Lemon Jefferson and Leadbelly also recorded it commercially. Big Bill Broonzy even claimed to have known its composer, an itinerant blues singer who probably called himself "C.C. Rider" after the song. Postwar it provided pop and R&B hits for Chuck Willis (1957), LaVern Baker, and Elvis Presley. It was also recorded by skifflers and traditional jazz bands. More recently it has been transmogrified into "Kootchie Rider" by a group called Freaky Realistic. The process of remolding and retreading songs continues. … It's a case of putting the song elements together in a different way to produce a "new" performance.

The $64,000 question is at what point does added value (a new arrangement; a change to the lyric; performing/recasting a song in a different style) constitute new or co-authorship? Several legal battles have been fought on this point, with variable outcomes. Did George Harrison plagiarize the Chiffons' "He's So Fine" by unconsciously borrowing the melody for his song "My Sweet Lord"? He lost the case, but lots of artists have got away with putting new lyrics to familiar tunes, from Woody Guthrie (whose "Grand Coulee Dam," later a Lonnie Donegan hit, put a new set of lyrics to the tune of the vintage song "Wabash Cannonball") to Chuck Berry (who borrowed the same tune for his "Promised Land" hit) to Bob Dylan. Judging the "added value" that renders a reshaping of a song original enough to merit a part-credit is certainly a matter of personal assessment and subjectivity. Ultimately our ears will judge the achievement of the artist in producing a new sound. A dictionary definition of "original" as "novel in character and style" would certainly fit Leadbelly's "Rock Island Line," and on that basis I would answer the question "Whose 'Rock Island Line'?" as "very definitely Leadbelly's"!

Appendix One

The well-established Chicago, Rock Island and Pacific Railroad Company took over the Choctaw, Oklahoma and Gulf Railroad in 1902, giving them control of a railroad line that crossed Arkansas, via Little Rock into the city of Memphis, Tennessee, a major Southern hub. This became known locally as the Rock Island Line.

The significance of Rock Island, a small town in Illinois across the river from Davenport, Iowa (where Bix Beiderbecke was born) is that it was here that the first bridge to span the Mississippi River was built in 1855, for the Chicago and Rock Island railroad, which had taken just two years (1852–54) to reach that point. Two weeks after the locomotive "Des Moines" crossed the long, wooden bridge (on April 21, 1855) a steamboat hit it, setting fire to itself and the bridge, which burned down but was later replaced as future president Abraham Lincoln, then the lawyer for the railroad, successfully defended an action by the steamboat company for damages and a nuisance to navigation. The case ended up in the Supreme Court, which held that building railroad bridges across navigable rivers was lawful.

Appendix Two

In 1933 Huddie Ledbetter, (later known as Leadbelly), then incarcerated in the Louisiana prison farm was recorded by John Lomax for the Library of Congress Archive of folk song. Lomax was excited at the discovery of a major black songster, with a huge repertoire, much of which would later be recorded. Following Leadbelly's release from Angola in 1934, Lomax agreed to Leadbelly becoming his chauffeur (and intermediary with black prisoners) on further field trips through the South. In October 1934 Leadbelly was present at the Cummins Prison Farm recordings, which included "Rock Island Line," and presumably learned the song there. (He may have also later heard the actual disc recording played.) Considerable publicity came from a nationally shown "March of Time" newsreel film, recreating Leadbelly's time on Angola and meeting with John Lomax.

In 1935 Leadbelly began performing for small white audiences. With encouragement from John Lomax and his son Alan, Leadbelly developed his natural flair for the dramatic to work up stories about and introductions to some of his songs. After falling out with John Lomax, Leadbelly tried for the big time, first in New York, later in California, but Hollywood humiliated and rejected him. He returned to the more modest career of entertaining white audiences and recording frequently, mostly for Moses Asch in New York. (Alan Lomax continued to document Leadbelly's repertoire for the Library of Congress.) A projected European tour was, due to illness, limited to one concert in Paris, France, before he was forced to return home. Leadbelly died in New York December 6, 1949, a victim of lateral sclerosis, and was buried in the Shiloh Baptist Churchyard.

Within months of his death, the Weavers folk group scored a massive international hit with "Goodnight Irene," a song that Leadbelly had made his own after learning it from his Uncle Terrell. (It originally derived from an 1886 published composition "Irene, Goodnight.") Nineteen fifty could have been Leadbelly's year, although it's doubtful if he could have achieved the huge sales of the smoother Weavers' version. Instead he didn't really become recognized until Lonnie Donegan made hits out of several of his best numbers—"Rock Island Line," "Bring a Little Water, Sylvie," "Take a Whiff on Me" (as "Have a Drink on Me"), and Donegan's last skiffle hit, "Pick a Bale of Cotton." (Film exists of Leadbelly performing this, impressive both musically and physically.) Donegan recorded at least fifteen other Leadbelly songs for albums or as "B" sides. His "The Cotton Song" became a major hit (as "Cotton Fields") for the Highwaymen in 1962, while Leadbelly's adapted "Hawaiian Song" became an American Top Ten hit (as "Hula Love") for Buddy Knox. The same year Jimmie Rodgers hit the Top Twenty with "Kisses Sweeter Than Wine," earlier a hit for the Weavers, using the melody of Leadbelly's "If It Wasn't for Dicky." A 1976 film of Leadbelly's life, starring blues singer/guitarist Hi-Tide Harris only had limited release, and the importance of this great American songster is still underestimated today.

Notes

1 Who had his own hit (in Britain) with "The Shifting, Whispering Sands," a 1955 American Top Ten entry for both Rusty Draper and the Billy Vaughn Orchestra.

2 Chris Barber, apart from leading a first-rate jazz band with a wide-ranging repertoire (for over fifty years), was largely responsible for bringing a number of major blues artists to the United Kingdom to tour successfully in the late 1950s and early 1960s, thereby helping lay the foundation for the sixties' Blues Boom that flourished in Britain and in turn sparked a Blues Revival in the music's homeland.

3 Donegan commenting about the success of "Rock Island Line" in interview with Michael Pointon (quoted in the notes to "More than Pye in the Sky").

4 See Appendix One on the significance of Rock Island. The Kelly Pace group recording is available on "Field Recordings Vol. 2," Document DOCD-5576.

5 In his 1936 "Mr. So and So Blues" (Bluebird B-6983) Arkansas Shorty sings "Well, I feel like ridin' on some Rock Island train."

6 I would suggest that this is from 236-A-1.

7 This version was supposedly issued on Document DOCD-5659, *Too Late, Too Late*, vol. 12, but the recording included turned out to be identical to 248-A-1, i.e., it is the Kelly Pace Group's version.

8 There is, of course, an outside chance that it was composed outside the prison system and then adapted as a work song at a later date. See Appendix Two for a brief outline of Leadbelly's career.

9 "A Who's Who of the Midnight Special" by Mack McCormick, "Caravan" no. 19, January 1960.

10 *Father of the Blues* (London: Sidgwick and Jackson, 1941), 6 and 139.

Bibliography

Booklet notes to *Leadbelly's Last Sessions*, originally issued on 4 LP records in 1994, re-issued in a 4-CD box set. Smithsonian/Folkways SF CD 40068/71.

Booklet notes to *More than Pye in the Sky*, Lonnie Donegan 8-CD box set. Bear Family Records BCD 15700, 1993.

Cohen, Norm. *Long Steel Rail: the Railroad in American Folksong*. Urbana: University of Illinois Press, 1981 ed.

Dewe, Michael. *The Skiffle Craze*. Aberystwyth: Planet, 1998.

Dixon, Robert M. W., and John Godrich, comps. *Blues and Gospel Records, 1902–1943*. Chigwell, Essex: Storyville Publications, 3rd edition, 1982.

Groom, Bob. *The Blues Revival*. London: Studio Vista, 1971.

Henry, Robert Selph. *Trains*. Indianapolis: The Bobbs-Merrill Company, 1934.

Leigh, Spencer. *Puttin' on the Style: The Lonnie Donegan Story*. Folkestone, Kent: Finbarr International, 2003.

McDevitt, Chas. *Skiffle: The Definitive Inside Story*. Robson Books, 1998.

Rees, D., B. Lazell, and R. Osborne. *40 years of NME CHARTS*. London: Box Tree, 1992.

Whitburn, Joel. *The Billboard Book of USA Top 40 Hits*. New York, 1989.

Wolfe, Charles, and Kip Lornell. *The Life and Legend of Leadbelly*. London: Secker and Warburg, 1993.

Rock'n'roll Comes to Britain

Andre Millard

S kiffle might have gotten each of the Beatles on stage, but rock'n'roll took over their lives and pushed them into becoming professional musicians. John Lennon was not alone when he said that rock'n'roll was like a religion to him. It encompassed a look, a lifestyle, and an attitude as well as music. While skiffle and trad jazz were played by amateurs having fun, rock'n'roll was a business, a dynamic and profitable business that brought significant changes to the British pop music industry. It also transformed the lives of the musicians who made up the Beatles.

Reading the histories of rock'n'roll today, you might be surprised that it got off the ground in England at all. Although the UK had a few small independent record companies, no Sun or Chess existed to discover the talent and start the movement with some historic records. Most of the new record labels formed in the UK after the war were subsidiaries of multinationals in electrical manufacturing (such as Pye and Philips) or of film studios that were eager to exploit the profitable record business (such as Top Rank).[1] These large diversified businesses saw opportunities in the postwar popular music market (just as their counterparts in the United States did), but preferred to be followers, rather than leaders, in the introduction of new music. The Oriole company was the only independent that might have made a difference in the UK. Formed by the Levy Company in the 1920s, Oriole was revived in 1950. It was a big operation with two pressing plants, but its business was mainly in cover records, which were sold in Woolworth's stores. Oriole became an important presence in the Liverpool music scene under the direction of A&R man John Shroeder. He signed local singer-songwriter Russ Hamilton from a skiffle group in 1957 and pushed Hamilton's "We Will Make Love" to Number 2 on the English pop charts.[2] But this was a romantic ballad that was not much different from all the other easy-listening records, and perhaps its success kept Shroeder from recording more innovative Liverpool music. He did not see the potential of the Afro-Caribbean groups who might have come up with a musical hybrid similar to rock'n'roll.

The spread of new music in England was hampered by the state-owned British Broadcasting Corporation (BBC), which acted as a conservative gatekeeper to the airwaves. Unlike the highly competitive American radio industry, broadcasting in the UK was a monopoly. The war years strengthened the BBC's hold on broadcasting and established the ruling oligarchy of EMI and Decca in the record business. All of them dismissed rock music as another American fad that would soon go away like the other short-lived musical novelties of mambo and calypso. The industry professionals on both sides of the Atlantic were often biased in their assessment of youth music, condemning it as the work of amateurs with low musical standards and poor recording facilities, which was often the case. They perceived the youth market as fickle and unsophisticated, and they continually underestimated its size. There was almost a professional pride in ignoring the youth audience in the offices of the BBC. Disc jockey and television presenter Jack Payne summed up this attitude in an article he wrote for the *Melody Maker*: "Should We Surrender to the Teenagers?" The powerful A&R man Mitch Miller was asking the same question in the United States. The answer was always no.

The BBC had often discriminated against popular music on aesthetic or moral grounds, and because it had the monopoly on broadcasting, its refusal to play a song was usually the end of it. Yet Bill Haley's "Shake, Rattle and Roll" was never played by the BBC and still managed to slip into the NME chart at Number 13 in December 1954, and by January the next year it was in the Top 5. How could anyone have heard this record before they bought it? The answer could be found in broadcasting media on the periphery of British entertainment, the jukeboxes found in select coffee bars (like the 2i's) and the record shops that catered to the growing number of rock'n'roll cognoscenti. These few outlets for new music managed to circumvent the oligarchy that controlled the marketing of records in the UK and brought the sound of rock'n'roll to adventurous teenagers.

American armed forces radio still broadcast in Europe in the 1950s and 1960s, and it was popular with listeners. The English newspapers published its schedules along with the BBC's Light, Home and Third programmes. It was joined by Radio Luxembourg, a commercial station established in the grand duchy by a French company in 1933. During the war it became part of the American propaganda effort, and the U.S. Armed Service planned to make it the "Voice of America" in Europe in the postwar years, but commerce prevailed over propaganda, and the British-language service of Radio Luxembourg gained strength in the 1950s as an important new vehicle for diffusing American music.

Established at 208 meters on the medium wave, the station broadcast prerecorded commercial programs produced by European and American record companies, who sent their latest releases to Luxembourg, where the biggest radio transmitter in the world spread them far and wide. You could only pick up Radio Luxembourg's signal well after dark in England, and it was a struggle to keep the dial fixed on 208 and the signal coming in. Yet thousands of English teenagers did it (including all the Beatles and me), and it became a ritual to listen to the popular music segments broadcast on Saturday and Sunday nights. The highlight was the two-hour *Jamboree* that started at 8 p.m. on Sundays, an "exciting, non stop, action packed" program that starred thirty minutes of deejay Alan Freed babbling from New York City and playing records that we never dreamed existed. It was Radio Luxembourg that brought Elvis's "Heartbreak Hotel" to the attention of four young men living in Liverpool in the 1950s.

Radio Luxembourg dramatically increased the profile of rock'n'roll in Europe, and there cannot have been many English schoolboys who had not heard some of it by the end of the 1950s. Soon the British record companies were digesting the sales numbers for rock records in the United States and their distribution over several different audiences—Elvis scored hits in the American pop, country, and R&B charts simultaneously—and thinking that this might not be a short-lived fad. By this time Elvis Presley was no longer the Nashville Cat representing a tiny record label in Memphis but the King of Rock'n'roll in the pay of RCA-Victor, a major presence in the American music industry. Smaller independents like Sun and Atlantic had led the way into rock'n'roll, but as soon as the big companies realized the potential of the new music, they overtook the independents and their African American stars with more palatable white singers.[3] RCA had taken a big gamble on Elvis, paying a record fee to get his contract from Sun and hoping to turn a regional attraction into a national figure. This it accomplished with help from NBC radio, CBS television, and movie studios Paramount and MGM. The music and image might have seemed rebellious, but Elvis Presley the film star and celebrity was the perfect employee of the Empires of Sound.

These multinational business organizations imported rock'n'roll into the UK. It crossed the Atlantic in the same way as all the other American entertainments that had delighted English audiences, and once established, it was copied by European musicians and record companies in a practice that went all the way back to the minstrel show. As soon as the English entertainment industry realized that rock'n'roll appealed to a mass market, they began to make copies of American originals. This practice of "covering" was especially strong in Great Britain and reflected the special conditions of broadcast entertainment. The BBC had a complete monopoly of Britain's radio waves and resisted the move into programming based on disc jockeys playing records—the "needle time" that was the mainstay of American radio broadcasting after the war. In fact, the influential rock deejays who did so much to spread the music in the United States were entirely absent in Great Britain. British radio preferred to reproduce popular records with its own in-house artists, cutting down royalty payments and keeping British musicians fully employed, a strategy supported (and sometimes enforced) by the British Musicians' Union. Their American counterparts had also recognized the threat of pre-recorded musical programming after the war and tried to ban it using strikes in the 1940s, but to no avail. The rise of the disc jockey in the United States, a professional broadcaster of recorded music, played an important part in the introduction of rock'n'roll.

The first English rock records were covers made by pop singers or large dance orchestras. Bill Haley's 1953 "Crazy Man, Crazy" was covered by a popular singer from Liverpool called Lita

Roza, who also produced copies of R&B songs originally performed by Ruth Brown and Ella Mae Morse. Roza was the vocalist for the Ted Heath Band, which had mined the American R&B charts for songs that might appeal to the stodgy, elderly listeners of the BBC's Light Programme. They even found a Sun record written, sung, and recorded by Alabama country singer Hardrock Gunter about his hometown. "Birmingham Bounce" was a local hit in Alabama and Tennessee that had caught the attention of Sun Records, who purchased Gunter's master and re-released the song on its label. In England you could purchase the Ted Heath version on a 78 rpm disc!

The BBC liked to talk about "harmonizing" American songs to fit the particular musical tastes of the British public, which in the minds of rock fans meant watering the excitement down and slowing the tempo to a leisurely pace. It rearranged two classics of early rock'n'roll from Bill Haley for the sedate tempos of the dance orchestras that dominated English radio: "Shake, Rattle and Roll" was reinterpreted by Jack Parnell and his orchestra, and "Rock Around the Clock" was mutilated by the Big Ben Accordion Band.

The English record companies scanned the advance copies of American records in search of hits. The innovations of small "unbreakable" 45 rpm vinyl discs and the transatlantic jet service facilitated the rapid diffusion of American records. Such was the speed of the transportation and distribution that the cover might appear in the same chart as the original. In 1956 American pop crooner Guy Mitchell covered a Marty Robbins country song, called "Singing the Blues," for Columbia Records under the guidance of Mitch Miller. It topped the U.S. charts in November and entered the British Top 20 on the European Philips label on December 8 that same year. One week later Tommy Steele's version challenged Mitchell's song in the English charts, and throughout that month his Decca record followed Mitchell's to the top. During January they swapped the Number 1 and 2 positions and stayed in the charts until February. Two years later Michael Holiday quickly took another Marty Robbins song to the top of the British charts, beating out other covers by English entertainers Alma Cogan, Dave King, and Gary Miller.

An alternative to covering American songs with in-house talent was the more expensive licensing agreement that allowed a British record company to release an American recording on its own label. EMI and Decca were international operations, and thus identifying and obtaining foreign master recordings was part and parcel of their daily business. They kept an especially close watch on American teen music because it constituted the major part of their own popular music catalogs. EMI had licensing agreements with the two major players in the United States— RCA-Victor and Columbia—and records produced by them accounted for more than half of EMI's sales in the early 1950s. As a multinational company EMI had recognized the importance of American music in the global entertainment business since the 1930s, yet its conservative attitude to new technology would hinder its acquisition of American product. The Empires of Sound were linked together, but each part could exercise the option not to adopt the new machines or music coming from the other side of the Atlantic. The management of EMI was not ready to accept the new vinyl records developed by Columbia and RCA, and this was the reason these American companies broke the licensing link. After losing these licensing deals, EMI purchased a controlling interest in America's third largest company—Capitol—in 1955 to get access to the American recordings that filled up its pop music catalog.[4]

The English majors were licensing so much music from America that they set up special labels to market it in Europe. British Decca had formed London Records to sell its recordings stateside because the split with U.S. Decca in the 1940s did not allow it to trade under its name in the United States. Decca then used the London label in the UK to distribute selected recordings licensed from American independents like Chess, Dot, Atlantic, Sun, and Specialty, including some R&B masterpieces like "Tutti Frutti" that would have such an impression on the Beatles. Decca pressed the discs in England but added the imprint "American Recordings" beneath the London title on the label. British Decca also managed the Coral label, which brought Britons the music of Buddy Holly and the Crickets. EMI created its Stateside label to compete with Decca's London discs in the UK, issuing such important records as the Isley Brothers' "Twist and Shout."

As rock'n'roll grew more popular in England, the majors moved from licensing records from the giants like RCA to approaching the smaller American independents that had discovered the R&B talent. Ironically, EMI's Stateside made licensing agreements with the American independents Vee Jay and Swan—the first American companies to release Beatles recordings. The licensing process worked both ways. The Searchers followed the success of the Beatles in the English charts, and their hits on the Pye label were licensed for American release on Mercury and Liberty discs.

If discriminating English record buyers were repulsed by half-hearted covers of American hits from local bands, they could soon buy the American original from a British company who had licensed it. For example, Bill Haley's recordings appeared on Brunswick in the UK—the label American Decca used to market its recordings overseas. Even the rare and exotic R&B records that could claim to be the forerunners of rock'n'roll were gradually made available in their original form to English record collectors. The Chords' "Sh-Boom" of 1954 was one of the first R&B records to get the attention of white America. It appeared on the B side of a single on the Atlantic label and was quickly covered by several American, Canadian, and English groups, but it was also licensed from Atlantic by EMI and appeared on its Columbia label in England.

The British record industry quickly mastered the techniques of processing American songs into English records or acquiring the licensing rights and releasing the original. The hit songs of R&B performers like Little Richard took some time to work their way through American companies' A&R organizations, licensing agreements, and British distribution deals. It could take as long as eighteen months to bring a Little Richard or Chuck Berry song to English listeners in the mid-1950s, but by 1957 the process had been streamlined. Buddy Holly's "That'll Be the Day" equaled Elvis Presley's "Heartbreak Hotel" in the effect it had on budding British musicians. Each of the Beatles took notice of this record when it appeared in English record shops only about a month after its American release in August 1957.

Not only was "That'll Be the Day" a great song, it had some spectacular guitar playing that was not too difficult to copy. Holly's basic country licks did not have the cool articulation of Chet Atkins', but he played with so much confidence and volume that his guitar breaks simply jumped out of the disc. He covered both lead and rhythm guitar, and he used nice, easy chords effectively. Consequently, "That'll Be the Day" was quickly inserted into the repertoire of every skiffle band, and the Quarry Men were so pleased with their version that they chose it for their first recording, as did many other Liverpool skiffle groups. Holly's records became an instruction manual for a generation of English rock guitarists, including George Harrison, who borrowed them from a friend so he could copy them, and Brian Rankin (Hank Marvin of the Shadows), who impressed record producer Mickie Most: "He had all the Buddy Holly licks off before anyone else could play them."[5] Buddy Holly was an ordinary-looking young man with a big smile and thick, black-framed glasses, but his guitar playing and songwriting talents impressed the amateurs who listened to him. John Lennon said that hearing what Buddy Holly could do with three chords made a songwriter out of him. True to form, a British company quickly produced a cover version of "That'll Be the Day." EMI picked a young singer who worked in their factory, and Larry Page actually got to pack his own single, described by Pete Frame as "among the most excruciating records ever made."[6]

The British record companies had mastered licensing by 1960, when a homegrown cover could be quickly eclipsed by the speedy release of a licensed original. "Will You Love Me Tomorrow" was written by composers Carole King and Gerry Goffin, who made the Brill Building in New York City rock'n'roll's Tin Pan Alley. It was recorded by a vocal group called the Shirelles, who formed in Passaic, New Jersey, and were discovered by local entrepreneur Florence Greenberg and signed to her small in-house Scepter label. Greenberg often sold promising Shirelles masters to American Decca, who marketed them nationally and started a trend of all-female singing groups that would have tremendous implications for African American pop music (think Tamla-Motown) and an influence on the music of the Beatles. "Will You Love Me Tomorrow" sold very well in the United States, and at the same time that a copy was being circulated around the corridors of British Decca as suitable material for a cover, the newly formed Top Rank label acquired the license to issue the record in the UK and quickly put it out in January 1960. Decca gave the song to Mike Berry, one of its rock'n'roll starlets, but Top Rank's Shirelles original crushed it in the charts. The Beatles must have got hold of the Top Rank single because they gave the B side, "Boys," to their drummers to sing, and Ringo Starr's version appeared on their first album. Passaic, New Jersey, to Liverpool, England, is a long way, but the international record industry was making the connection easier and easier as it mined the mother lode of rock'n'roll.

Both big and small companies became involved in the international movement of records as rock'n'roll grew more popular, and small English independent labels made licensing deals with their American counterparts. Joe Meek's record company was based in his home studio at his London apartment, but he still managed to distribute his songs in the United States through licensing arrangements with independents like Dot Records.[7] Oriole obtained the rights to release the first Motown records in the UK, including songs by the Contours ("Do You Love Me") and the Miracles ("You Really Got a Hold on Me"), which were Mersey Beat standards. (Later the rights were acquired by EMI and issued on Stateside.) Oriole's hit record by Russ Hamilton was picked up by the American independent Kapp in 1957, but the A and B sides were mistakenly switched, and instead of "We Will Make Love," the B side "Rainbow" broke the American Top 5. Hamilton later recorded with MGM in Nashville.[8]

The coming of rock'n'roll to Liverpool wasn't accidental, or lucky, or due to a special geographic and commercial situation. It was part of the operations of the Empires of Sound. Their experience in exploiting new music and seamlessly incorporating it into their networks of promotion and distribution brought the sound of rock'n'roll and rhythm and blues to England just as it had delivered swing, trad jazz, and country. Yet the Cunard Yank mythology was so attractive that it refused to go away. John Lennon embraced the myth when he was interviewed in the 1970s. He said that Liverpool was a cosmopolitan city: "It's where the sailors would come home with the blues records from America on the ships." Pete Frame could not resist the story of an Elvis fan that went to a London record store whose owner had made a profitable arrangement with a merchant seaman to bring in American records. The customer wanted a copy of Elvis's "Hound Dog," and once it was located, the store manager asked if he was interested in hearing the original, as performed by Big Mama Thornton on the independent Peacock label based in Houston, Texas.[9]

Yet by the end of the 1950s, there were enough formal links between the English and American record producers to make such exertions, and so many good stories, unnecessary. In 1962 a correspondent of *Mersey Beat* complained about the difficulty of obtaining R&B and blues records in Liverpool and wrote about a flourishing black market based on "cherished" personal collections of American discs. A spokesman from a record wholesaler immediately corrected him by pointing out that the records he discussed were available for purchase at NEMs in Liverpool and at record shops in Birmingham, Coventry, Manchester, Sheffield, Cambridge, and Bournemouth! The spokesman added that his company distributed a wide range of blues and R&B in the UK, including records from Little Walter, Howlin' Wolf, and Bo Diddley.[10] There was never any need for Cunard Yanks to bring precious American R&B and rock'n'roll records to eager teenagers in Liverpool, for the Empires of Sound were already doing it for them.

An English Elvis

With rock'n'roll so popular with English youth, the search for a homegrown Elvis, an English rock'n'roller who could make the music his own (and keep the profits in the UK), took on some importance. The men who took the lead in creating truly English rock'n'roll came from backgrounds in artist and theatrical management, record retailing, and independent studios. They combined their knowledge of distributing records with their promotional sense to manufacture the first wave of English rock'n'roll stars, starting with Joe Meek, whose "Telstar" by the Tornadoes went to Number 1 on the *Billboard* charts. He produced a string of rock and pop records with vocalists who had faultless good looks (like John Leyton), lukewarm covers of American hits, and lots of special effects in the background. In his memoirs Meek stressed the importance of making records for a teenage market, and he was well ahead of all the British record companies in this respect. The most important rock Svengali was Larry Parnes, who came from a Jewish family background in the clothing business and pursued a career in the theater. Parnes had the connections with the venues (including the all-powerful Delfont booking organization) and record companies but was not that interested in the music. Some of his signings were completed before even listening to the performer. For Parnes it was the look—the gold lamé suits, the mass of Brylcreemed hair, and the photographs he could place in the tabloids—that was more important than the songs he bought from Tin Pan Alley writers. Parnes was a showman with theatrical flair rather than a manager committed to the music.

Parnes groomed Tommy Steele to be the first British Elvis, organizing a record contract from Decca, a tour of provincial music halls, and some well-choreographed press stories. Although billed as the country's answer to Elvis Presley, Steele's career took much the same course as the other successful variety entertainers he was destined to follow: extensive touring around the country, radio and television appearances, a turn on the *Royal Variety Performance* at the London Palladium before the royal family, and finally films. Steele's Elvis-like ascent attracted the media, and he also bore the brunt of growing fan hysteria. The screaming at his shows was quickly noted in the press, and he narrowly escaped injury when a concert in Scotland got out of hand.

Although Parnes was based in London, he "discovered" the first generation of Liverpool rock'n'rollers. Ronald Wycherley used the same Liverpool recording service to make his own demo that the Quarry Men employed for their first record. He sent this to Parnes along with his photograph (very important) and was signed to a contract with Decca. As Billy Fury, Wycherley enjoyed a successful career in the early 1960s with a string of hits. Another Liverpudlian singer, John Askew, also wrote to Parnes and was signed to Philips Records. He was given the name Johnny Gentle. Parnes dominated the early years of rock'n'roll in England with a stable of handsome young men who wore the suits he chose for them, sang the American songs he found for them, and adopted the names he coined for them.

Larry Parnes' stable of attractive young singers followed the well-established tradition of copying Americans. They joined a long line of English entertainers who built their careers on copying African American material and sounding American. It started with those music hall performers, like Jack Lennon, who took songs and dances from the minstrel shows that toured Europe in the late nineteenth century. After nearly seventy years of imitating black Americans, this tradition was so strong in England that skiffle players like Lonnie Donegan could offer up weak imitations of American southern accents with no hint of embarrassment or self-consciousness. (Donegan had copied Lead Belly's version of the song exactly.) Similarly, Liverpool's country bands did impressions of American accents. Hank Walters reported that when the American servicemen heard the Drifting Cowboys, they "couldn't believe it cos we sang American style."[11]

When it came time for the Beatles to audition for Larry Parnes, they did their best to look and sound American too. They had tried to engage the nascent British rock industry at ground level, a year before Epstein turned up at the Cavern Club to take a look at them. Larry Parnes visited Liverpool to engage backing bands for a package show starring American rockers Eddie Cochran and Gene Vincent. The Quarry Men were still struggling along without a regular drummer and with very few gigs, but Parnes allowed them to audition. On the big day he turned up with his protégé Fury and announced that one lucky band would get to back up Fury on tour. Alas, the Quarry Men did not get the Billy Fury gig, but the group was overwhelmed at winning a consolation prize—backing Johnny Gentle and Duffy Power for ten exhausting, freezing nights in Scotland. They changed their name and took the first step toward becoming professional musicians. The Quarry Men had covered several bases of imported American music, country and western along with skiffle, but the Silver Beetles was now a rock'n'roll band.

The search for a suitable English Elvis continued while the Silver Beetles served their apprenticeship. An ex-variety player called George Ganjou saw a skiffle band called the Drifters, and although he had no previous experience in artist management, he was so impressed with the way the girls reacted that he took the band on. They were led by Harry Webb, a good-looking young man who could do perfect imitations of Elvis. Webb's rock'n'roll epiphany came when he saw Bill Haley play the Edmonton Regal cinema in London in 1957; he was inspired to form a band and make a demo at the HMV record store in London. Norrie Paramor, the recording manager of EMI's Columbia label, signed the group and gave it a bland American record to cover, "Schoolboy Crush," by Bobby Helms. On the B side of their single was a song written by Ian Samwell, a guitarist for the Drifters. Paramor used his influence to get them on Jack Good's *Oh Boy!* television program, which was an important showcase for pop music. Good did not think much of "Schoolboy Crush" and insisted the Drifters play the B side, "Move It." They did, and this song caused a sensation in British rock'n'roll circles when it was released in 1958. Considered by many music critics and musicians (including John Lennon) to be the first British rock song, "Move It" sounded so authentically American that it came as a surprise to many listeners that it was performed by an English band. Ian Samwell admitted that the Drifters copied the American masters of rock and R&B but argued that they did it better than the rest of the English groups: "We were closer to the real thing than anyone else around."[12] That is to say, their copy was considered the most accurate.

The Drifters had to change their name because the American group of the same name objected to it and threatened legal action if the band released records in the United States—an indication of the importance of the American market to British rock and pop acts. So the band became the Shadows, Harry Webb became Cliff Richard, and his guitarist, Bruce Rankin, now went by the name Hank Marvin—an American name for an English guitarist playing American music with an American guitar. Hank Marvin wore those thick glasses that everyone associated with Buddy Holly and took great lengths to acquire the same Fender Stratocaster that his hero played. Although everyone thought of the Shadows as the pioneer English rock band, the sound was all American. Marvin's Stratocaster produced bright upper registers that were recognized as the "Fender sound," shorthand for a clean, trebly sound with stinging highs. Rock'n'roll guitar was usually manipulated by reverb—the echoing, ominous sound that had made the early Elvis records so distinctive. Hank Marvin used an Italian echo device, the Meazzi, and cranked out heavy vibrato with the tremolo arm of his Stratocaster.

Cliff Richard and the Shadows started the trend of having the singer fronting the instrumentalists, in the three-electric-guitars-and-drums lineup that became the standard for rock groups.

Liverpool was full of them, with names like Gerry and the Pacemakers and Billy J. Kramer and the Dakotas. Cliff Richard became the most successful and long-lived English Elvis, but it was the Shadows that had the most influence on the Beatles. They were the first important guitar band in England that did not need a handsome singer up front to have a hit record. Their guitar instrumental "Apache" was a Number 1 hit in 1960 and set the stage for the British adoption of the rock instrumental genre that made American guitarists like Duane Eddy and Link Wray stars. The Shadows followed "Apache" with a string of instrumentals all constructed the same way, a solid repetitive beat produced by an electric bass, with a reverb-laden lead guitar picking out the notes of the simple melody. In the first four years of the sixties, they produced three or four instrumental records each year, and most of them made the Top 5. Even the names of their hits reflected the English admiration for American popular culture: "Apache" was inspired by the 1954 Western of the same name, and it was followed by "FBI," "The Frightened City," "Shindig," and "Mustang."

The Shadows were extremely important in the development of the Beatles' music. The first original song the Beatles ever recorded (for Polydor in Germany in 1962) was a Shadows-like instrumental appropriately entitled "Cry for a Shadow." Much of the Silver Beetles' repertoire was instrumentals, and the people who listened or auditioned them noticed the Shadows' influence.[13] Although Cliff Richard and the Shadows are virtually unknown in the United States today, they dominated British pop music at a critical time. In 1963 George Harrison said that if the Beatles did as well as Cliff and the Shadows, "we won't be moaning." Brian Epstein is famous for his belief that the Beatles would be "bigger than Elvis," but when he wrote to the record companies in 1961, he claimed that his band had written a song as good as a Cliff Richard and the Shadows hit.[14] In his liner notes for the album *Please Please Me*, Tony Barrow quotes the BBC's Brian Matthew's tribute, that the Beatles were "visually and musically the most exciting and accomplished group to emerge since the Shadows."

Record companies in North America had scant knowledge of the British rock scene except for Cliff Richard and Shadows. They were the standard against which the Beatles were to be measured. But the Shadows were definitely not cool; their bass player, Jet Harris, was cool—he had dramatic good looks, a blond quiff, and an impressive Fender Precision bass (the first in England)—but after he left, the band as a unit was not cool at all. There was no hint of rock'n'roll rebelliousness in their music or in their stage show, where they made the same choreographed steps—the "Shadows walk"—which was copied by an infinite number of amateur bands. For all his pouting and Elvis moves, Cliff Richard was safe and predictable, and the members of the Shadows were bland and silent.[15] This was the norm in the British popular music scene when the Beatles burst into the spotlight.

Breakthrough

Historians of the Beatles and many of their fans point to a concert at Litherland Town Hall on December 27, 1960, as a turning point in their career. It happened about eight months after the Larry Parnes audition in Liverpool, and in this time the band had played shows all across the United Kingdom and in Hamburg, Germany. When they left for Germany, they were still pretty much amateurs, but the band that returned to England in the winter of 1960 was tight, ambitious, and professional. They came back with a much larger repertoire and greatly improved musicianship. A fellow musician described the transformation: "They wore black leather, had brand new instruments and played brilliantly."[16] They also played loudly and with a confidence that had been sorely lacking in the Quarry Men and Silver Beetles, a confidence that impressed fans, journalists, and fellow musicians alike.[17]

Both John Lennon and George Harrison felt that this was the high point in the development of the Beatles as a rock band. When the group left for Hamburg, the Shadows were top of the pile of English pop music, and most of the Liverpool beat bands copied their sound as well as their stage outfits and guitars. The Shadows had helped inspire the crowded beat scene, and it was hard to get away from their sound of three electric guitars and drums. The Litherland Town Hall billed the Beatles as straight "from Germany," and the fact that many in the audience thought them to be foreigners shows how much their music differed from the other Mersey Beat groups.

It was not a good night for a concert. Tony Bramwell remembered it as freezing and snowy, and contrary to the legend, not that many people were there.[18] As soon as the band started up with a blast of amplified guitars, the crowd rushed toward the stage, and the excitement never let up. Brian Kelly, the promoter, was impressed; this was the loudest group he had heard, and he recognized that their "pounding, pulsating beat ... would be big box office." One fan remembered them as young, rough, and sexy.[19] Even though their leather outfits were now considered low class, they added weight to the contrast with the Shadows, whose dinner jackets now looked distinctly unexciting. The Beatles came across as wild and unrestrained, especially when they incorporated the little vocal tricks and slurs they had picked up from their store of R&B records. This was the big difference, and as George Harrison concluded, "that's why we became popular."

The Beatles were able to stand out among the numerous guitar bands in the city because they kept true to their American inspiration: in 1960 the Beatles were rock purists. In John Lennon's opinion, when it came down to playing "straight rock," nobody in the country could touch them. In a column in *Mersey Beat,* Bob Wooler said that many people had approached him after the Litherland concert and asked him why the Beatles had become so popular. His answer was that the band had resurrected the excitement and rebellion of the early years of rock'n'roll and had "exploded on a jaded scene" dominated by pale imitations of Presley and play-by-the-numbers Shadows clones.[20] The Beatles were, in the words of Ian Samwell, closer to the real thing than anyone else around. Their copies were more attentive and respectful to the American originals. When the Rolling Stones challenged their popularity a few years later, they did it on the same grounds; they were closer to the American masters than the most successful band in the world, which had sold out and gone pop.

The crowd at Litherland Town Hall was not an easy audience. Like the venues in Bootle and Garston, it was notorious for fights, and even the young ladies in the crowd put fear into the Beatles' entourage. Yet Litherland was a triumph and marked the beginning of a new phase for the band. John remembered, "That's when we first stood there being cheered for the first time."[21] Brian Kelly immediately booked them for scores of gigs over the next few months, and they hired Neil Aspinall to be their full-time road manager. The crowds were getting bigger and more excitable. At a return engagement at Litherland Town Hall on Valentine's Day, 1961, the bouncers had to protect the band as the audience rushed the stage. Many more girls were hanging around them, and soon they moved from steady girlfriends to playing the ever-growing field.

During 1961 they competed for birds and audiences in the frantic Liverpool beat scene, which consisted of at least three hundred amateur and semiprofessional groups. The enthusiasm for rock'n'roll was strong in Liverpool, and there was a great deal of scouser pride in the size and vitality of the local music scene, which encompassed not only beat groups but also folk, blues, jazz, and R&B. The new music coming from America had swept up the large Afro-Caribbean community as well, and there were probably more interracial bands—such as Derry and the Seniors—around Merseyside than in any other city in the country. Rock'n'roll might have made the most noise, but there was still enough support to maintain a thriving jazz scene on Merseyside, which encompassed everything from trad jazz, New Orleans style, to cool jazz, the latest musical import from America. By the end of 1961 the Beatles were acclaimed as the best band in Liverpool in a vote organized by *Mersey Beat*. They were on their way.

Being Different

Just like the crowd at Litherland Town Hall, the American fans found the Beatles' music loud, fresh, and different—a remarkable accomplishment if you consider that much of their repertoire at the time consisted of covers of American records. But what struck Americans when they first heard the Beatles was the newness of the sound. The consensus among fans everywhere was that the Beatles sounded different; "fresh" is the adjective that crops up again and again. They had the same effect on the engineers when they first played at Abbey Road: "It was the freshest music I'd ever heard," one said. The historian of rock'n'roll Charlie Gillett thought that the vocals made the Beatles sound different to English listeners. The vocals were a new combination of two American styles, the hard-rock style of singers like Little Richard and the call-and-response, gospel-tinged style of the girl groups.[22]

Since many Americans knew nothing of the rockabilly and R&B roots of rock'n'roll, the Beatles' early repertoire must have sounded refreshingly different to their ears. Its delivery, in scouse-inflected English, stood somewhere between the perfect enunciation of Julie Andrews and the American ersatz of Cliff Richard—the opposing poles of English pop music as discerned by American listeners. The Beatles might have incorporated Americanized pronunciation and rock or soul vocalizations for effect, but they kept to their own voices without succumbing to the temptation to impersonate Americans in the grand old English music hall tradition. This made an important difference, as a fan explained: "Everything was so new, between the British accents and a different beat, and different lyrics, especially."[23]

Nevertheless, parts of the American press corps, including *Newsweek,* found the band's sound "achingly familiar," and both American and English record companies came to the same conclusion: the guitar sound was out of style, and the Beatles did not bring anything new to pop music. Certainly John Lennon's harmonica work added a lot to their early hits, but was it markedly superior to Delbert McClinton's piece on Bruce Channel's "Hey Baby" or that of any of Bob Dylan's early records?[24] Their harmonies were beautiful, but were they markedly better than those of the Everly Brothers—whose records the Beatles copied and whose sound many people heard in the first Beatles records? The Beatles did play with energy and excitement, but they were far from the only band resurrecting the good old days of rock'n'roll. Was their "Twist and Shout" rawer or more aggressive than the Kingsmen's "Louie Louie," a record that exploded onto the rock scene in 1963, or louder than the Kinks' "You Really Got Me," which amazed English record buyers in 1964? The Beatles were not the only guitar band that played R&B covers in an African American style, but somehow they made it sound original. At the same time black musicians credited the Beatles with introducing their blues and R&B to the white audience in America, the kids in the crowd were being swept away with its novelty: "It was a totally new style of music, totally exciting," said one American fan. Another said: "They're different! They're so different!"[25]

The look played a large part in this perception of difference. In England the Beatles differed from the nondescript Shadows, and in the United States they contrasted with perfectly groomed pretty boys crooning romantic ballads on *American Bandstand.* Rock music was as much seen as heard, and this was especially true for the Beatles. The English journalist Maureen Cleave concluded that it was "the looks that got people going."[26] The 1963 *Newsweek* article that introduced the band to American readers pointed out that the music was "even more effective to watch than to hear. They prance, skip and turn in circles."[27] If a fan accessed new music by listening to it across the vast American airwaves, he or she might not have received the Beatles' sound as original and fresh, but on television the band came across as different. This sense of newness was linked to the perceived foreignness of the Beatles and the innovative ways in which their carefully crafted image was presented to the fans.

Notes

1 Some small labels were set up by artist management to distribute recordings made by their clientele. For example, Polygon Records was established in 1949 by the father of singer Petula Clark and was quickly gobbled up in 1955 by Pye, a leading manufacturer of radios, televisions, and electronics.

2 Oriole recorded many of the beat groups who failed to make a connection with a major company in London, but it did so after the event and had no role in creating the Mersey Sound. One of the first Liverpool groups to get a record contract was Derry and the Seniors, followed by the Blue Mountain Boys, who in 1962 released "Drop Me Gently" on the Oriole label; McManus, *Nashville of the North,* 31.

3 Charlie Gillett, *The Sound of the City* (New York: Pantheon, 1983), 70.

4 Gould, *Can't Buy Me Love*, 121. George Martin places the blame squarely on the chairman, Sir Earnest Fisk; *All You Need Is Ears*, 40–41. When Columbia ended its licensing agreements with EMI in 1953, Philips was waiting in the wings. One of the largest electrical manufacturers in Europe, Philips was attracted to Columbia's catalog because two of its biggest stars, Frank Sinatra and Doris Day, were also movie stars whose films were very popular in Europe; Marmorstein, *The Label*, 205.

5 Frame, *Restless Generation*, 317.

6 In 1974 Jim Dawson sent a questionnaire to John Lennon, which Lennon filled in and returned. At the bottom of the sheet he wrote, "I WAS Buddy Holly!" See everything2.com/index.pl?node_id=979603; Frame, *Restless Generation*, 285.

7 Joe Meek was a highly innovative recording engineer and an astute businessman who could "smell" a hit record. His Triumph and RGM labels were among the few independents in the UK that dealt in youth music and developed new sounds. Nevertheless, he rarely strayed from the American pop paradigm and dismissed the Beatles' records as derivative when they first came out.

8 Harry, *Liverpool*, 39–40.

9 Wenner, *Lennon Remembers*, 184; Frame, *Restless Generation*, 271.

10 *Mersey Beat*, 28 March 1963, 2.

11 McManus, *Nashville of the North*, 4.

12 Frame, *Restless Generation*, 334.

13 *Mersey Beat*, 20 June 1963, 2.

14 Frame, *Restless Generation*, 437; Geller and Wall, *Epstein Story*, 38.

15 Cliff and the Shadows made movie after movie with virtually the same plot, like *The Young Ones* (1961). Twenty-five years later, the Shadows' safe, squeaky clean, bland entertainment was satirized in an English comedy show with the same name as the film.

16 Harry, *Liverpool*, 80.

17 Maureen Cleave, "Why the Beatles Create All that Frenzy," *Evening Standard*, 2 Feb. 1963, in Egan, *Mammoth Beatles*, 25.

18 Bramwell, *Magical Mystery Tours*, 3.

19 *Mersey Beat*, 20 June 1963, 8; Lennon, *Twist of Lennon*, 36.

20 *Mersey Beat*, 11 April 1963, 7.

21 Miles, *Diary*, 31.

22 Emerick, *Here, There and Everywhere*, 59; Gillett, *Sound of the City*, 263.

23 Janet Lessard, quoted in Berman, *See the Beatles*, 50.

24 The Beatles played with Bruce Channel at the Tower Ballroom, Liverpool, on 21 June 1962. Considering "Hey Baby" came out in March, John Lennon probably learned it from Channel's harmonica player, Delbert McClinton, that night; Harry, *Liverpool*, 77.

25 Carol Moore, quoted in Berman, *See the Beatles*, 39; *New York Times*, 17 Feb. 1963, 1.

26 Maureen Cleave, "All that Frenzy," in Egan, *Mammoth Beatles*, 24.

27 *Newsweek,* 18 Nov. 1963, 104.

Post-Reading Questions for Part II

1   What distinguished the appeal of rock and roll for young British fans from their counterparts in the United States? How did the southern origins of rock and roll contribute to that appeal? What were some of the misconceptions that the British had regarding the American South in the 1950s?

2   How did the reception of rock and roll differ in Britain from that which it received in the United States? Did acceptance or rejection of rock and roll represent a political statement in addition to being a reflection of musical taste?

3   How derivative of American popular culture was skiffle and rock and roll in Britain? What were some of the creative elements that Lonnie Donegan and his British contemporaries contributed to these genres? What factors does Groom use to explain the relatively swift demise of the skiffle craze and the long-term success of rock and roll in Britain?

4   How does Millard account for the early popularity of the Beatles in Britain and the United States? Based on the readings in this section, do you think it owed more to their originality or their appropriation of America's own cultural traditions? According to Millard, what distinguished the Beatles and the Rolling Stones from their British predecessors such as the Shadows?

PART III

THE BEATLES' INFLUENCE ON AMERICA

Introduction

The third and final set of readings in this volume turns its attention from the impact American popular culture had on the Beatles to the impact the Beatles had on American popular culture. The Beatles had by 1964 fully absorbed a wide spectrum of American musical and cultural influences and filtered them through their experiences in Britain and Hamburg, Germany to form a style and musical sensibility unique to them. Thus, when they arrived in the United States for the first time in February 1964 they brought with them a sound both familiar and new to American audiences. Perhaps most importantly, they encountered an audience of teenagers now accustomed to seeking out their own musical icons heedless of the wishes, taste, or influence of their parents or teachers. Sales of Beatles' records sky-rocketed, far exceeding the original expectations of their US label, Capitol, forced by demand to quintuple the two hundred thousand copies they originally planned to press of the Beatles' smash single, "I Want to Hold Your Hand." The Beatles went on to crank out hit after hit through 1964 and 1965, but even in these early years, albums such as *Beatles for Sale* would indicate that they had broader musical interests and serious artistic inclinations, many of them rooted in the traditions of blues, early rock and roll, and country and western that originally inspired them. They would also continue to absorb American influences in the 1960s, particularly from the folk revival associated with Bob Dylan, but through the phenomenon of

Beatlemania and their own maturation of artists, they made their own distinct contribution to American popular culture.

In the first selection in this section, Andre Millard discusses the meteoric rise of the Beatles' popularity in the United States, which caught everyone off guard, including the Beatles themselves. The Beatles' relatively short—about thirty minutes—concerts left their screaming teenage fans breathless while their television appearances on *The Ed Sullivan Show* affected and inspired millions, who viewed it as a turning point in their lives. Millard describes in detail the hysteria and almost religious fervor that animated Beatlemania, providing an excellent vehicle for thinking about the audience's role in the making of popular culture. Tracing its origins in Britain, Millard's account shows the ways in which the appeal of the Beatles far transcended their music, although their hit records fueled the frenzy of a fan base that had begun to emerge based solely on the group's live performances. Yet, as Millard notes, the phenomenon of Beatlemania received more attention than the Beatles' music prior to their arrival in the United States in February 1964. Finally, Millard surveys the contemporary and historical explanations for Beatlemania, finding each one of them wanting. Although his larger explanation for Beatlemania lies outside the scope of this volume (interested readers can turn to the longer work in which this chapter originally appeared), he challenges us not to settle for easy answers to explain a complex historical and cultural phenomenon.

Barbara Ehrenreich, Elizabeth Hess, and Gloria Jacobs approach the topic of Beatlemania from a different angle than does Millard—the perspectives of individual fans who participated in the hysteria and obsession that accompanied Beatlemania. The authors cite contemporary psychological explanations for the manic behavior of young teenage girls responding to the Beatles, but move beyond them in their analysis of a phenomenon many still find inexplicable. They explore in some depth the sexual expectations of girls in early-sixties American society and root them in the larger conformist culture that rock and roll had already begun to challenge in the previous decade. They note the timing of the appearance of Betty Friedan's feminist manifesto, *The Feminine Mystique* in 1963, just a year before Beatlemania exploded in the United States. In doing so, the authors firmly situate the mass hysteria accompanying the Beatles' first US visit in the context of American popular culture in a way that goes beyond the simple appeal of rock and roll. However, the authors do not neglect the role that rock and roll played in causing the hysteria, especially since very few of the teenage fans screaming their lungs out over the Beatles would have likely had an awareness yet of Friedan's work, except by osmosis. Perhaps that is the point, however; something was in the air and this article captures an important moment in the history of American popular culture in a way that supplements Millard's treatment.

The sixties moved rapidly after the explosion of the Beatles onto the American pop culture scene in 1964. The Beatles were growing up and so were their fans; the group began cultivating more adult themes in their music in 1965 and 1966, while the civil rights movement and the Vietnam War began to make their impact on American popular culture and youth sensibilities. The evolution of the counterculture centered in San Francisco and the Summer of Love coincided with the release of the Beatles' most innovative album, *Sgt. Pepper's Lonely Hearts Club Band* in June 1967. In my essay on the Beatles and the political culture of the 1960s, I place the Beatles and American Popular Culture within the larger context of the sixties and the national global developments that shook the world in 1968. In particular, this essay examines the evolving role of the Beatles in the youth culture of the time with regard to their response—or lack thereof—to the growing importance of political issues. The Beatles and rock and roll had come a long way by the end of the 1960s from its origins discussed in the first part of this book. My essay concludes with some thoughts on the significance and meaning of that journey.

Pre-Reading Questions for Part III

1   Do pop stars and celebrities have the same rights to privacy as ordinary citizens? Do fans have ethical obligations not to intrude too much on the space and privacy of the stars they idolize?

2   Does a double standard still exist today regarding the sexual expectations of teenage boys and girls? What cultural messages do teenagers receive today from music, films, and the media regarding sex? Does society still expect "good girls" to refrain from sex?

3   Do artists have an obligation to respond to the political concerns of their generation?

4   How did/do the artists of your generation reflect the issues and events of their time?

Beatlemania

Andre Millard

As Ringo Starr pointed out during the Beatles' first tour of the United States, the Americans had all gone out of their minds. This sentiment was repeated by his band mates and everyone else there, from the promoters to the security detail. The cop who told an English reporter "I think the world has gone mad" summed up the general reaction to Beatlemania.[1] The mass hysteria when the group first touched down at the newly named Kennedy Airport in New York City on February 7, 1964, was only the beginning of the highly visible public events that would dwarf the adulation previously directed at pop stars. Young women had screamed and hurled themselves at Elvis Presley and Johnny Ray in the 1950s; they had idolized the young Frank Sinatra in the 1940s; and they had even danced in the aisles to the swing music of Benny Goodman in the 1930s, but none came close to the scale and ferocity of the public outpourings of affection directed at the Beatles in 1964 and 1965.

The band was a national obsession in the United Kingdom, yet no one could have imagined the response from the United States; it even caught the Beatles and their management by surprise. In addition to being seen as "one of the most extraordinary and significant events in the history of American show business," Beatlemania marked a turning point in millions of young lives. It was a magical time, a historic moment in the minds of an influential generation, and people who were there tell us that you had to be there to experience it. For those who were there, the Beatles were changing the world, and as one fan said later, "There is no question in my mind that The Beatles had the MOST profound impact on history."[2] Since those halcyon days, nobody in popular entertainment has been able to repeat this moment in all its economic and cultural significance.

Beatlemania was bigger than the Beatles, drowning out the music and eventually over-shadowing the musicians themselves. It was much more than screaming fans. Entertainment industries capitalized on it to promote concerts, records, films, magazines, books, clothes, and toys. It inspired countless copy cat bands, ranging from the very successful Monkees to the quickly forgotten Liverpools and their *Beatlemania in the U.S.A.* record. Beatlemania was one of the largest and most successful merchandising campaigns in American history. As one magazine explained, "Today's modern Beatle fan can wear Beatlemania, speak Beatlemania, play Beatlemania and even eat Beatlemania."[3]

In the long run Beatlemania was a significant chapter in the history of celebrity, a major cultural event that highlighted important social trends, like the rise of the counterculture. The Beatles' music went far beyond mere entertainment, acquiring significance and providing meanings deeper than the lyrics of those well-remembered songs. In a decade remembered by its popular music, the Beatles have become an essential part of our collective memories of the 1960s. Understanding Beatlemania is part of making sense of that tumultuous decade.

Madness. That was Beatlemania. *Time* magazine called it "The New Madness." Eyewitnesses found it difficult to describe this "frenzied scene that beggared belief," and as many observers pointed out, it was impossible to imagine it if you had not seen it with your own eyes and heard it with your own ears.[4] Larry Kane was a deejay on a Miami radio station who got the opportunity of a lifetime to join the press corps accompanying the Beatles during their first two historic tours. In a book appropriately titled *Ticket to Ride*, he described the frenzied crowd behavior that was repeated all over the country wherever the band played. He remembered screaming so loud it hurt his ears. Girls screamed at top volume for the entirety of the Beatles performance (that clocked in at around thirty minutes), maintaining a high-pitched cacophony from the moment Ringo Starr's drums were brought onto the stage until the final desperate news that the band had left the auditorium. The noise levels were painful and often compared to thunder or an earthquake—the waves of sound an oppressive, physical force, beating down on people, forcing their hands over their ears. A reporter described it as a jet engine streaking through a summer thunderstorm: "It had no mercy."[5] The screaming drowned out all in its path, and everyone left the show with a ringing in their ears that lasted for a day or two.

Larry Kane was shaken by the almost animalistic behavior of the fans—nice young affluent Americans with good schooling and careful upbringing. He was alarmed by the tidal waves of young female bodies hurled against the stage: "Girls and some boys close together, standing screaming, moaning, groaning, ripping at their hair, pushing, shoving, falling on the floor and crying, real tears streaming down hundreds of faces, smearing their mascara and lipstick, and mothers and fathers hiding in the back, some of them dancing to the music."[6] The young women were usually described as hysterical or frenzied—squealing, wailing, screaming, weeping, and beating their heads with their fists in the agony of not being close enough to their idols: "I remember ripping part of my hair out of my head, screaming—we couldn't talk after the concert we were screaming so bad."[7] Some girls laughed with joy; others cried within the "deafening ecstasy" and "screaming pandemonium" of the Beatles' audience. A considerable number were overcome by this massive assault on the senses: "I had fainted. I think the emotions, the hot August night, it was the first time I saw them, it was exciting."[8]

Figure 8.1 The Beatles arrive at Kennedy Airport to begin an American tour in 1964. Behind them stands their manager, Brian Epstein; in front of them are thousands of screaming girls. Paul and Ringo are looking upward at the packed galleries of fans that had spent hours waiting for the arrival. (New York Daily News Archive, Getty image 97269347, courtesy Getty Images)

These were not seasoned rock fans; many of them were attending their first concert. Although the 1960s are remembered as a decade of permissiveness, the fans' personal accounts of Beatlemania reveal that much of the strict 1950s was still in place in 1964. For many of the lucky ones who went, not only was it the first show they attended, but it was the first time out without a chaperone, and even the first time they got to stay up after 11 p.m. Seeing the Beatles in person was an important step in growing up, the significant event that began the sixties for them. The girls came in their best clothes: "We wore canary yellow dresses so that the Beatles would see us, and [we] would stand out. And apparently everyone else had the same idea," and brought with them Beatles' merchandise, photographs of their favorite band member, cameras with a supply of flashbulbs, homemade signs, and gifts and tributes to hurl at the band on stage.[9] During the tour all four musicians were hit by flying objects, John, Paul, and George sustaining cuts and bruising while Ringo cowered behind his drums. When a teen magazine revealed that George Harrison liked jelly beans, the band was bombarded with them—about two tons a night as George remembered—while they tried to play. This practice spread by word of mouth and the press (although the Beatles went out of their way to discourage it), and it became "the obligatory throwing of jelly beans," a ritual invented by the fans that was repeated at every performance. Other objects thrown at the band included food, dolls, clothing, and used flash bulbs.[10]

Such was the emotional energy generated by the Beatles that more than one concert turned into a riot. Squads of police, some on horseback, had to hold back the crowds—no easy task when you consider the size of the attacks they had to repulse, which ranged from five hundred to several thousand (the police estimated that about six thousand fans stormed the stage one night), and the feral determination of young girls to get close to their idols. The police used dogs, horses, nets, barricades, lassoes, and their batons in attempts to control the fans. In two concerts in Cleveland, the Beatles faced full-scale riots of thousands of people and had to flee for safety. Mindful that these dedicated fourteen-year-olds "could break through the defensive line of the Cleveland Browns if they wanted to," the police had to threaten to cancel the show to restore order.[11]

At Vancouver about 135 young people were injured in a melee during the show, suffering broken limbs, concussions, contusions, and what Larry Kane described as the consequences of Beatles-induced combat—"bloody lips and noses, bruises, welts and abrasions." In the aftermath of a rock concert, one expects to find litter, food wrappers, and empty alcohol containers, but Kane noticed that the food concession stands at a Beatles concert did very little business—the audience did not want to miss a minute of the show. Instead he saw gauze, medicine bottles, and bandages

Figure 8.2 Caught in mid-shriek, these two girls were among the 55,000 fans who packed into Shea Stadium in August 1965 to watch a historic Beatles concert. According to the promoters, this was the biggest crowd, and the biggest gross, in the history of show business. It was also the loudest. Security guards had to cover their ears because of the intensity of the crowd noise. The Beatles were deafened by the screams and could not hear themselves play. Many of the fans are holding cameras; the girl on the right holds an 8 mm movie camera. (New York Daily News Archive, Getty image 97340351, courtesy Getty Images)

left by the temporary triage stations set up at the back of the concert halls as well as spent flashbulbs and lost shoes scattered around everywhere.[12] After the Beatles' Cleveland concert at a baseball stadium, hundreds of shoes (singles not pairs) were piled on top of the pitcher's mound. Their official biographer, Philip Norman, described performances as "cops and sweat and jelly beans hailing in a dream like noise ... faces ugly by shrieking and biting fists; it was huge amphitheatres left littered with flashbulbs and hair rollers and buttons and badges and hundreds of pairs of knickers, wringing wet."[13]

The fans' enthusiasm for the music was so intense that it produced moments of sheer terror when all that adolescent energy and excitement threatened to turn into violence. When John Lennon was asked how he felt after a near riot at the Cow Palace in San Francisco—the first date of their second American visit of 1964—he confessed: "Not safe. Can't sing when you're scared for your life." (But this was also the person who encouraged a noisy response: "I like a riot.")[14] Larry Kane thought that the Beatles seemed to be running for their lives when they left the stage. When they got to the end of their last song, they unclipped their guitars from the straps on their shoulders, and the moment the music ended, they dropped their instruments and ran.

The madness was not restricted to the concerts, and this gave Beatlemania the extra dimension that lifted it above all other incidents of fan worship: the home invasions, the besieging of hotels, and the assaults on recording studios. Fans mobbed the Beatles as they traveled to and from concerts. They permanently picketed their hotels on tour and their residences in the UK. Often they physically attacked the musicians, ripping off their clothes and forcibly removing pieces of their hair. They took anything that could be torn off, including Ringo's St Christopher's medal. As one of their entourage admitted, "To see three thousand almost deranged girls heading your way was quite terrifying." And the consequences to the band if they were caught by this mob were frightening: "They could be stripped naked and knocked unconscious ... or worse, scalped."[15] In San Francisco their limousine did not leave the stage quickly enough, and the weight of fans on the vehicle caved in the roof. In Houston fans broke through the barricades and climbed on the wing of the Beatles' airplane before it had reached the terminal. After the mayhem of two concerts at Forest Hills Stadium, critic Robert Shelton warned that the Beatles had created "a monster" and that "they had better concern themselves with controlling their audiences before this contrived hysteria reaches uncontrollable proportions."[16]

By necessity the security arrangements for their concert tours were as meticulously planned as military operations, involving elaborate ruses like decoys and deliberately misleading the waiting press corps. Some American cities gave the Beatles the level of protection reserved for the president; others provided more. Ringo once said that being a Beatle was like being in "the bloody secret service."[17] One journalist compared the band's transportation plans to a shipment of gold from Fort Knox. The security involved hundreds of police officers, miles of cyclone fencing, and even an iron cage to protect them en route. They traveled in police cars, ambulances, armored cars, and even fish trucks to avoid the mob. They exchanged clothes with policemen to dupe the waiting throngs and often disguised themselves if they had the nerve to leave the hotel and walk outside.

The positions of road manager and personal assistant, filled by Mal Evans and Neil Aspinall respectively, were dangerous jobs that required a mixture of careful planning, guile, and courage. After a few months of field testing, they chose limousines for ease of entry: the Austin Princess had the widest doors, and it was easier to throw people into them. The work was more than a matter of conveying the musicians and their valuable equipment; it involved defending their charges against threats as diverse as fans hidden in hotel rooms (some armed with knives), mothers of fans getting stuck in air-conditioning ducts, photographers who stormed dressing rooms, and attractive young ladies who were not going to take no for an answer. (The job was not without the perks that came with hundreds of women willing to do anything to get close to John, Paul, George, or Ringo.)

The rest of America struggled to find the words to describe Beatlemania and the reasons for such "dangerous mass hysteria among young people." The record industry likened it to a disease spreading rapidly through the teenage population, "and doctors are powerless to stop it." They spoke of a "sales epidemic" that had swept through Europe and now was appearing in North America. *Newsweek* reported that the concerts were "slightly orgiastic" because of the power of amplified electric guitars.[18] Beatlemania was interpreted as a religion by commentators trying to find the root causes for so much teenage emotion. Ken Ferguson described it as a cult and "a form of hysterical worship" in an article written for *Photoplay* magazine. He experienced the "full blast and fury" of the fanatical fans who had been mesmerized by the Beatles' "savage, pulsating, hypnotic sounds." Brian Epstein told the press that he was going to the United States to "spread the gospel" of his band.[19] Some of the Beatles' most devoted followers experienced a powerful spirituality that went beyond the music. Throughout the tours parents brought sick, crippled, and blind children backstage to receive the healing touch of the four embarrassed musicians. John Lennon told his friend Pete Brown that dealing with these sick children and their parents was by far the worst part of the tours.

The fans were the objects of both fascination and disdain by those adults who observed them. The conservative papers *Daily Express* and *Daily Telegraph*, the bastion of British middle-class fears and values, deplored the animalistic behavior of the young and voiced concerns that these masses of easily impressed youth might be open to more sinister suggestions than "She Loves You." In an editorial, the *Telegraph* compared Beatlemania to the hysteria and barbarian fantasies of the Nazi rallies at Nuremberg. The fans were seen as mindless, "pitiable victims," hypnotized by their grotesque idols: "the huge faces, bloated with cheap confectionary and smeared with chain store makeup, the open sagging mouths and glazed eyes, the hands mindlessly drumming in time to the music." Paul Johnson described them as pathetic, dull, and vacuous—the least fortunate of their generation.

What Beatlemania represented to critics like Johnson was the triumph of the entertainment industry, a commercial machine that had turned a generation into "fodder for exploitation." These views followed the criticisms made by Theodor Adorno and Max Horkheimer of what they called "the culture industry" back in the early twentieth century. The purely capitalist operations manufactured standardized mass entertainment that not only brought profit but also provided ideological legitimization of the system. Adorno thought that mass entertainment integrated consumers into capitalism and manipulated them into a process of response mechanisms that undermined the ideal of individuality in a free society. Conformity had replaced consciousness, and this process depended on the star system propagating "great personalities" and "heart throbs."[20] Beatlemania is the outstanding example of the effectiveness of these culture industries.

Creating Beatlemania

Americans might have established Beatlemania as the significant cultural event of the decade and made the band global celebrities—but they did not invent it. Beatlemania emerged in 1963 as the Beatles rose to the very top of British entertainment in an amazingly short time, capturing the attention of nearly everybody on the island, from preteens to the royal family. During 1963 the voracious English press, especially the mass-circulation tabloids, weaved together this annus mirabilis of record sales, chaotic concerts, and screaming fans into a major news item. English newspapers did not report about popular music and only noticed rock'n'roll when it inspired incidents of delinquency. The up-market broadsheets like the *Times* kept to their reviews of classical performances, while the tabloids thought up nasty words to describe the sound of the new youth music. The press interpreted rock'n'roll as another teenage craze, "The Big Beat Craze" that the *Daily Mirror* expected to burn out quickly: "Beat Bubble Could Burst Overnight." Yet pop music celebrity grabbed the tabloids' attention with the excesses (financial, sexual, and alcoholic) of the rock'n'roll lifestyle, which seemed as out of control as the fans. Like their counterparts in the United States, the English newspapers were always interested in the rags to riches (and then back to rags) story, and popular music was becoming one of those mythical but carefully observed domains where fame and money could transform the lives of ordinary people with the magic wand of stardom.

The rise of Elvis Presley or Cliff Richard had provided some titillating copy for the press, but this was nothing compared to the Beatles, who exploded from an obscure regional pop scene into national prominence almost overnight. As John Lennon's half-sister Julia Baird remembered about the friends and family watching from Liverpool, "We knew they were going to be big, but we didn't know what big was." This sentiment was repeated in London by the professionals at EMI who saw the Beatles break all the records for sales, concerts, awards, and fan mania.[21] The band quickly moved into other arenas, such as film and television, and repeated their triumphs. Their star had ascended so quickly and shone so brightly that it overpowered every other one in the entertainment firmament. As the band continued to reinvent what it was to be rich and famous, Beatlemania grew larger.

The story had appropriately humble beginnings. Exactly a year before they touched down in New York, the Beatles played the Regal Theatre in Wakefield—a bleak and gloomy town in the industrial North that does not even justify a mention in the British Tourist Association's *Touring Book of England*. The night before, they had played Bedford in the Midlands, and after Wakefield, they had to travel all the way up to Carlisle, which is on the border with Scotland. They were one of the supporting artists on a package tour headlined by Helen Shapiro, a sixteen-year-old who already had several hit records, an American tour (including an appearance on *The Ed Sullivan Show*), and a film to her credit. The Beatles were way down at the bottom of the bill, but they were still happy to be on a bill anywhere—at this point in their career, the object of the exercise was to keep working, and it didn't really matter where. Outside Liverpool, they were pretty much unknown. They could walk about the streets of Wakefield unmolested and grab a cup of tea and a sandwich at a greasy café before going on stage.

From a strictly historical viewpoint, the first buds of Beatlemania had broken through in the early months of 1961, when the band members realized they had made an important transition. George Harrison said, "People were following us around, coming to see us personally, not just coming to dance."[22] They had returned from an extended stay in Hamburg as a greatly improved band, and the girls at the Liverpool clubs they played were indeed taking notice of them. In an amazingly prescient comment made in 1961, a writer for the Liverpool music newspaper *Mersey Beat* called them "the stuff that screams were made of," blissfully unaware of the noise that was to follow.[23] The Beatles were big in the Liverpool music scene, but Liverpool was a down-at-heel northern town that nobody in the music business took seriously. London was the center of popular entertainment, and Liverpool, as one record company executive put it, might as well have been Greenland.

The Beatles made their first record in 1962, an achievement that greatly pleased the four musicians, and for at least two of them, this might have generated enough pride and satisfaction to justify the whole journey had it ended then. They also made their first radio broadcasts. They acquired a new manager, got rid of their first drummer, Pete Best (something that happened all the time in pop groups), and finalized their lineup around three guitarists and their new drummer, Ringo. They were voted the best band in Liverpool in a *Mersey Beat* poll and drew impressive crowds whenever they played in their hometown. They also made a triumphant return to Hamburg—a return engagement that emphasized how far they had come from the loose band of amateurs who had arrived two years earlier with little idea how to play and no idea of what to expect. They ended the year with a successful recording session at the Abbey Road studios of EMI.

In January 1963 the police had to be called in to keep order at a concert. The Beatles' second record, "Please Please Me," entered the British charts in February at Number 16, sandwiched between the latest American singles from Brenda Lee and Duane Eddy. But by the end of the month, it had reached the top position. Along with thousands of other young musicians, the Beatles had dreamed the dream of reaching the top of the charts, but they had no idea how much it would change their lives. The English music press began to report that the fans were going wild. The band had started at the bottom of the bill on the Helen Shapiro tour, but now the kids were calling out "We want the Beatles!" throughout the shows. Articles about them and their fans began to appear in the press. In February Maureen Cleave of the London *Evening Standard* wrote a story that tried to answer the question on everyone's mind: "Why the Beatles Create All That Frenzy."

As "From Me to You" raced up the charts, the screams increased. The Beatles hardly noticed that their anonymity was slipping away. By the summer of 1963, thousands of fans were turning up at the stage doors of the small venues they played, blocking the entrances and threatening to riot.

In October they appeared on the country's most popular televised variety show, *Sunday Night at the London Palladium*—the British version of *The Ed Sullivan Show*. The whole country watched them play four songs, including their latest release, "She Loves You," but far more important to the newspapers was the crowd outside the theater. The hundreds of young girls who appeared at the stage door of the Palladium well before the concert had swelled to an unruly mob by the time the Beatles turned up. The next morning, October 14, the story dominated the English press. The *Daily Mail,* the *Daily Herald,* and the *Daily Mirror* made a great deal out of "the fantastic Palladium TV siege," and undoubtedly exaggerating the number of "frenzied" fans, but neverthe-less the pictures of them were dramatic.[24] Even the stuffy *Daily Express* carried the photographs.

On October 21, the *Daily Mail* put the Beatles on the front page and on page three used the term "Beatlemania" for the first time. By November it was in general use, and the band and its fans were major news items. The stories focused on the "squealing females," the "hordes of kids" that materialized as soon as the Beatles were spotted, followed by the rugby-like scrums of bodies, with the policemen's helmets rolling on the pavement, and the frantic escape of the musicians to cars that were almost submerged by mobs of young people.[25] As newspapers warmed to Beatlemania, they regularly reported the number of fans in attendance and usually inflated them, with estimates running as high as ten thousand. Even the staid *Sunday Times* got into the act, describing five thousand "hysterical youngsters" who had slept out on the pavement days before the Beatles arrived. With only an occasional cynical aside that these demonstrations might have been staged, the press eagerly joined in the enthusiasm for Beatlemania: "You have to be a real sour square not to love the nutty, noisy, happy, handsome Beatles!" said the *Daily Mirror,* doubtless trying to connect with a younger readership.[26]

The story in the English press gradually got some attention in the United States—a country that in 1963 was concerned with far graver issues than a pop group from Liverpool. So the first signs of Beatlemania were small. Martin Goldsmith provides an appropriate metaphor for its dawning: "Like an approaching thunderstorm, the Beatles' arrival in America was preceded by a few low rumbles and flashes of light, none of them giving more than the slightest hint of the potency to follow."[27] Articles in the press and on television often described the effect of the Beatles in terms of noise and light, as extraordinary occurrences in the natural world, and as signs that came as a premonition of something important to come.

Beatlemania began to seep into the American press by the end of 1963. On November 15, *Time* magazine ran a short story on the excesses of the fans. This was followed up by *Newsweek* on the 18th, which described their music as "one of the most persistent noises heard over England since the air raid sirens [from World War II] were dismantled." Then *Life* ran several articles in December and January, which leaned heavily on images taken of the fans in England. One eight-page article in *Life* carried seventeen photographs, and most were pictures of the fans and the police cordons they assaulted.

All three American television networks became interested, and *CBS Evening News* took the lead by broadcasting a three-minute story mainly about the "adolescent adulation" of Beatlemania that was the "modern manifestation of compulsive tribal singing and dancing." CBS repeated this story later in December, when the grief that followed the assassination of President Kennedy had abated slightly. By the time the press and record companies were preparing for the Beatles' arrival, Jack Paar (one of Ed Sullivan's competitors) ran some short performance clips on his show on January 4. He made light-hearted fun of the fans and said later that he had no idea that the Beatles "were going to change the culture of the country with music ... I brought them here as a joke."[28] Americans were learning about the Beatles not from listening to their music, but from the news reports about their fans.

What got Beatlemania noticed was its scale. When Pan Am Flight 101 left London airport, about one thousand fans screamed their farewells, but an estimated three to five thousand welcomed them to New York. The Beatles were somewhat apprehensive about their reception and thought that the throngs at the airport were there to meet someone else, a head of state or somebody like that. A harried airport official commented, "We've never seen anything like this before. Never. Not even for Kings and Queens."[29] This response, framed in shock and awe, was repeated throughout the tour. It came from security men, hotel staff, theater managers, and transportation officials: "It scares you ... It's just beyond me. I've never seen anything like this," "I've never seen anything like it, and I was here when Castro arrived, when Khrushchev came in, but this topped them all," and "This is kind of like Sinatra multiplied by 50 or 100."[30]

Despite the fervor of the American welcome, and the avid attention of the media, the people who were most excited on that first day in New York City were the Beatles themselves. They might have been surprised by their fantastic rise to fame in the UK, but these accomplishments paled against their amazement and delight at their American reception. On the journey between Kennedy Airport and the Plaza Hotel, Paul McCartney experienced feelings of elation: "It was like a dream. The greatest fantasy ever."[31]

A Televised Spectacular

When the Beatles finally established their tour headquarters in New York, one hundred thousand fan letters awaited them—all written by people who had never heard them perform a live concert. Ed Sullivan already had 50,000 applications for the 728 seats in the venue where his show was broadcast. He was not sure what he was getting when he signed the Beatles for three performances. Like other impresarios, he regularly crossed the Atlantic to look for talent for his variety show, and when he saw the Beatles fans going wild at Heathrow Airport, he told his entourage that this was exactly the same excitement that Elvis had aroused. By the time the broadcast was ready to go on air, Sullivan had overcome his second thoughts about top billing for an unknown band and was beginning to grasp the significance of the event he was about to present to the American people. Beatlemania had made its mark on America in just a few days.

Along with all those other grizzled professionals who had spent their careers in the capital of the entertainment industry, Sullivan was amazed at the frenzy of the fans. He told his viewers, "All these veterans agree with me that the city never has witnessed the excitement stirred by these youngsters from Liverpool."[32]

The screams began the moment he introduced them and continued through the show. After they finished their last song, "She Loves You," a bemused-looking Sullivan read out a congratulatory telegram from Elvis Presley (which had been composed by his manager, Colonel Tom Parker, without his knowledge). Presley's performances on Ed Sullivan had been a milestone in his career and in the acceptance of rock'n'roll by mainstream America, and this telegram was the symbolic passing of the baton to a new generation. In addition to Elvis's famous appearances (when he was shown only from the waist up), Buddy Holly and Bill Haley also enjoyed historic appearances on the Sullivan show—the latter's performance of "Rock Around the Clock" in August 1955 was the first time millions of adult Americans experienced the excitement of rock'n'roll. But nothing compared to the impact of the Beatles. The 73.9 million people who watched on that frigid February night were the largest television audience ever recorded up to that point, far exceeding the 60 million people who tuned in to Elvis. The Beatles had captured the attention of over a third of the population of the United States and a very high proportion of the country's 22 million teenagers. In New York City, three-quarters of the city's television sets were tuned into Ed Sullivan, and it was said that even the criminals took time off to watch the Beatles.

All over the country, there were millions of individual epiphanies as Beatlemania took hold: "When they struck that first chord it just sent something through me," "I was two inches from the screen, screaming," "I sat with my girlfriends to watch them. We were feeling the TV and touching it and screaming." The magic was not restricted to teenage girls, for four-year-old Jay Willoughby "went berserk!" with excitement. He more or less decided right then what he wanted to do with his life.[33] So did hundreds of thousands of other kids, sitting transfixed before tiny black-and-white screens. How many careers in pop music were activated that Sunday night we shall never know, but several important bands formed as a result of watching the program, including the Byrds and Creedence Clearwater Revival. A young man who watched the show from the wings went on (as Davy Jones) to become part of the Monkees. There must be a legion of rock stars and amateur strummers out there who wistfully look back to the Beatles on Ed Sullivan as their starting point. None of them had any idea that you could be a rock star until they watched the Beatles that night.

As important to Beatlemania as this broadcast was, the next day, a school day, millions of kids realized that something important had happened during this shared media moment: "The next day at school, that's all anybody talked about. And all of a sudden all of the boys that had their hair slicked back on Friday—on Monday it was all combed down."[34] Monday marked the formation of a nationwide Beatle-lovers community, as young people were drawn together by their shared experience. Seeing the Beatles for the first time was described by them as a religious conversion that brought feelings of elation and joy. In the months to come, Beatlemania evolved into a youth culture, where "Beatlepeople" interacted in "Beatleland."

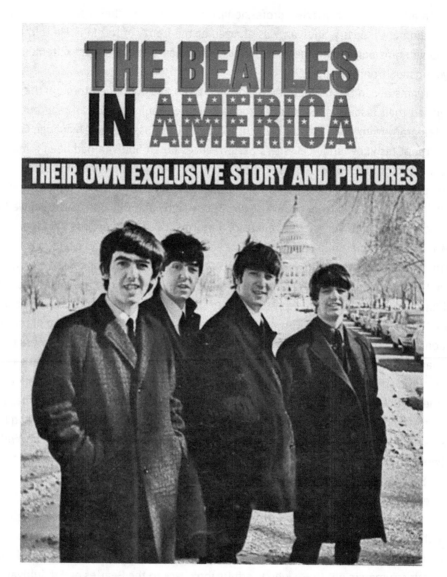

Figure 8.3 The Beatles in Washington, D.C., in February 1964, as captured on the cover of one of the many magazines and books that appeared during their various American tours. These mass publications hastily combined photographs and text and often included "personal" messages from the Beatles to give the purchaser a feeling of closeness with them. The signed message in the magazine Beatles in America said, "We made friends with a whole country of strangers by television." Quite true.

The superlatives that followed the Ed Sullivan broadcast increased with every new triumph in 1964, and everywhere the Beatles went, the crowds were bigger, the screams louder, and the pandemonium harder to comprehend. An American promoter, Sid Bernstein, had convinced Brian Epstein to put on two shows at the historic Carnegie Hall in New York—one of the most prestigious concert halls in the world. Part of the myth of Beatlemania was that no rock act had ever been allowed on its stage, not even Elvis Presley, but the careful research of Bruce Spizer shows that to be incorrect; several rock'n'rollers, including Bill Haley, played there in 1955. But no matter, the "first" at Carnegie Hall was added to the list of unprecedented achievements of the Beatles.[35]

Bernstein took an enormous risk in signing a virtually unknown band (at the time he made the deal over the phone with Epstein in October 1963) to a very large hall for two consecutive concerts. How he convinced the Carnegie Hall management to accommodate this group of long hairs from England is unclear, but he made no mention of rampaging fans. By the time the concerts were played in February 1964, *The Ed Sullivan Show* had made Bernstein's gamble a sure thing, and afterward he upped the ante by contracting with the 55,000-seat Shea Stadium for another concert in August 1965. Despite the unimaginable success of the Beatles up to this point, Brian Epstein was quite understandably concerned that no act in show business could fill a huge stadium, but Bernstein offered him $10 for every unfilled seat, and the deal was made. The show was a resounding success and a milestone in the entertainment business—the pop concert had now become an event. Bernstein "saw the top of the mountain" at Shea and so did scores of other promoters who realized that the sky was now the limit in youth music. Brian Epstein told the British press that the triumph of the Beatles was so total, so complete, that it would never be matched again. In his words, the Beatles had made history.[36]

The *Daily Mirror* called the Beatles' American tour "The Most Astounding Triumph in Pop History."[37] Superlatives like these were the defining feature of Beatlemania that elevated it above all other outbreaks of fan worship. At first the Beatles, like every other band, were compared to Elvis Presley—the gold standard in record sales and fan hysteria. They were introduced as the biggest sensation in pop music since Presley, but as they kept on breaking all the records that defined success in the entertainment industry, they were anointed as the biggest thing ever, "the most successful rock and roll band the world has ever seen." Since then the Beatles' yardstick has been used to evaluate all other pop acts.[38] The Shea Stadium concert had a special importance, and everyone there saw the significance of that night: "That's when it hit me. This is a big deal. This is no little rock 'n' roll band."[39]

No one had taken Brian Epstein seriously in 1962 when he patiently explained to all who would listen that he sincerely believed that the band "will be the biggest thing entertainment has ever known." Now journalists, promoters, and broadcasters were saying the same thing, only louder. Beatlemania took on a life of its own as it fed off the self-awareness and aspirations of its multitude of followers: "The Beatles ... had the lyrics to change the world. Beatlemania! It was and is very real."[40] The people around the Beatles sensed something different about the band. The musician and critic George Melly had the thankless task of introducing them on the Helen Shapiro tour. As a Liverpudlian and trad jazz player, he was in a better position than most to appreciate their appeal, and he was struck by something special in the Beatles.[41] Their American fans had no doubt: "At the airport, you could really feel that something was happening. We had been bored, and you felt like this was the beginning of the earthquake." Some of the girls were convinced that they were part of something important: "I know it's gonna go big and it's gonna go far."[42]

"Revolutionary" was soon being used to describe the Beatles. First they had revolutionized the production of music, then the world of entertainment as they brought more acceptance of youth music and more legitimacy for young musicians. Some even saw a social revolution in Beatlemania.[43] The Beatles and their management did make significant changes in the business of entertainment, pioneering the one-act performance, the music video, the stadium show, and the world tour. No musicians in the 1960s did a better job of merging music with image, and no entertainer could command as many star vehicles as the Beatles. By the end of the decade, they had enlarged the status of the pop star and helped make rock'n'roll mainstream entertainment. The bands that followed the Beatles enjoyed an entirely different environment and much greater ambition. The paradigm of success created by Beatlemania would dominate popular music for the next two decades.

Explaining Beatlemania

As much as the attainments of the band were seen as unprecedented, it was the behavior of the fans that really shocked observers and parents. As these outsiders recoiled from the outpouring of assertive sexuality from tens of thousands of young females, they reached for words like "revolutionary" to explain it.[44] An army of social scientists rushed in to make sense of Beatlemania. In an article in the *New York Times*, John Osmundsen broke down "every standard explanation in the book" from psychologists, sociologists, and anthropologists. The most common explanation he found was that teenagers needed to have a good time as a relief from the anxieties of living "in an uncertain world plagued with mortal dangers." Beatlemania took a generation's mind off the threats of the Cold War and acted as a relief valve for suppressed tensions and anxieties.

There also appeared to be links between Beatlemania and the growing affluence of teenagers and the rise of a consumer society. Yet socioeconomic theories were usually trumped by more emotional explanations. Anthropologists and journalists liked to depict Beatlemania as a tribal rite accompanied by jungle rhythms, a throwback to the "uninhibited, kinetic self expression" of primitive man. The musicians played the role of witch doctors, "who put their spell on hundreds of shuffling and stamping natives."[45] Adolescent psychology was a fertile and quite profitable ground for social scientists. Pop psychologists like Dr. Joyce Brothers, who plied their trade in newspapers and television, saw Beatlemania as another rebellion of youth against their elders. This was a popular theme of the 1950s, related to concerns about changing social roles and fears of delinquency.

Beatlemania did represent revolt to many Americans, mainly parents, but strong patterns of conformity in the fans' behavior fit the analysis of Theodor Adorno. In his theories, the fans' obedience to the beat expressed their desire to obey. There was a measure of conformity in not conforming! Sociologist Renee Claire Fox of Barnard College saw the contradictions of American society reflected in Beatlemania. The Beatles' androgynous looks contrasted female with male characteristics, and they managed to straddle both adult and juvenile worlds. They were good kids who posed as bad boys.[46] The last word has to go to John Lennon, who refused to explain the phenomenon, preferring "to leave it to the psychologists and let them get it wrong."[47]

Since the 1960s numerous accounts of Beatlemania have attempted to explain this phenomenon, ranging from scholarly books and articles written by professional historians and sociologists all the way to impressionist accounts produced by fans and posted on the Internet. Two main explanations of Beatlemania have emerged from these accounts. The first attributes the success of the Beatles as a relief for the depression that followed the assassination of President Kennedy. Thus the Beatles came to "a wounded country in its time of trouble" and "helped dispel the gloom of that death in November."[48] The second explanation places the success of the Beatles within the context of the stale and empty pop formulas that characterized American youth music at the time. In the words of Jonathan Gould, these were the "Dark Ages of Rock," the age of prepackaged teen idols, lush orchestral accompaniment, and juvenile novelty songs.[49]

All these explanations have firm foundations in the reminiscences of the people who were caught up in Beatlemania. The great national sadness that followed the death of John Kennedy was felt especially hard by teenagers. A youthful and optimistic president had spoken directly to young Americans, giving them hope and pride in this "new generation" that was making important changes in the world. Some of that hope and empowerment died with the president. After more televised bloodshed came the painful realization that the United States was a hopelessly violent and hateful place. And then came the Beatles, in the words of musician Jerry Garcia, "a happy flash. Post Kennedy assassination. Like the first good news."[50] Richard Manley remembered that the two months after the Kennedy assassination were "a sad scary time for thirteen-year-olds like me." Ron Monteleone thought that "the whole nation was in a deep depression over it. The Beatles came along and lifted the world's spirits."[51] For music critic Lester Bangs, they were the "perfect medicine" and "a welcome frenzy to obliterate the grief with a tidal wave of Fun [sic] for its own sake which ultimately was to translate into a whole new hedonistic dialectic."[52]

The gloom after the death of President Kennedy was largely felt in the United States, while Beatlemania was a global phenomenon, equally powerful and pervasive in places like Australia, which brought out the largest recorded gatherings of fans. Although the sadness after the tragic death of the president might have prepared the way for the joyous reception of the Beatles, it seems rather a stretch to assign the causes of Beatlemania to the aftermath of an assassination, especially when more than two months had elapsed before the Beatles arrived. This was the argument used by Ian Inglis in his careful debunking of this theory. He listed all the other significant events in the six months that followed the assassination and asked if they could be explained as a consequence of this event.[53] It cannot be disputed that many of the fans who took part in Beatlemania looked back at the joy as an antidote to the unhappy times, but plenty of others don't agree with the connection. There can be no better representative of the fans than author Bruce Spizer. He remembers his sadness after the events of November but adds, "by the holiday season of 1963, I was over it."[54]

As for the paucity of quality music available to American audiences in the early 1960s, many people scathingly affirmed that the Beatles had landed in a country with very bad pop music:

"I was waiting for something. Nothing was going on. It was crappy music like Paul Anka." Then the Beatles' performance on *The Ed Sullivan Show* opened eyes and ears to something much better: "I was 13 and in love with Fabian and no band from Britain was going to change that until Mom put on CBS."[55] Performers like Paul Anka, Frankie Avalon, Fabian, and Bobby Rydell produced the bland, safe popular songs that had replaced the energy and raw excitement of rock'n'roll. A few years later Don McLean sang about "the day the music died" in his song "American Pie." The passing of Buddy Holly was indeed a great blow to rock'n'roll, and after him came a deluge of mediocrity. If the Singing Nun could get to Number 1 in the charts with "Dominique" in November 1963, surely the time was right for a return to the excitement of rock'n'roll?

The Beatles came to the United States with some fresh sounds and finely crafted records, but was the competition that bad? American popular music of the early 1960s contained some outstanding creativity. These were the golden years for Motown and for artists like Ray Charles and James Brown. Even though Don McLean and his audience could lament that the music had died, more than enough rock'n'rollers were keeping the beat of Elvis and Buddy, such as Tommy Roe ("Sheila") and Del Shannon ("Runaway"). There were plenty of slicked-back crooners and fabricated pop records like "The Twist," but among them were some well-written songs that have stood the test of time: "Blue Velvet" (Bobby Vinton) and "Breaking Up Is Hard to Do" (Neil Sedaka).

The fans waiting for the Beatles at Kennedy Airport were ready for something different. It was in the air, a shared expectation that bound together thousands: "It was very electric, it really was, like something was going to happen."[56] Perhaps the key to explaining Beatlemania is timing, being in the right place at exactly the right time to exploit numerous strands of development that were coming together to form a critical mass. To unlock this particular puzzle, we have to go back before the 1960s and examine the business and technological networks that brought the Beatles to America and primed their audience for the experience of a lifetime.

Notes

1 Peter Brown, *The Love You Make: An Insider's Story of the Beatles* (New York: McGraw-Hill, 1983), 119; *Daily Mirror* 8 Feb. 1964, 1.

2 This was the view of the *Melody Maker*, a leading English music paper, on 26 Sept. 1964, reproduced in W. Fraser Sandercombe, *The Beatles Press Reports* (Burlington, Canada: Collector's Guide, 2007), 91; Virginia Maita quoted in www.thirteen.org/beatles/the-beatles.

3 Barry Miles, *The British Invasion: The Music, The Times, The Era* (New York: Sterling, 2009), 102.

4 *Time*, 15 Nov. 1963, 64; Kevin Howlett, *The Beatles at the Beeb: The Story of Their Radio Career* (London: BBC, 1982), 33–34; Sam Leach, *The Rocking City: The Explosive Birth of the Beatles* (Merseyside: Pharaoh Press, 1994), 130.

5 Bob Spitz, *The Beatles* (New York: Little Brown, 2005), 521; *San Francisco Examiner*, 19 Aug. 1964, quoted in Barry Miles, *British Invasion*, 105.

6 Larry Kane, *Ticket to Ride* (Philadelphia: Running Press, 2003), 86.

7 Martin Goldsmith, *The Beatles Come to America* (New York: John Wiley and Sons, 2004), 133; Penny Wagner quoted in Berman, *"We're Going to See the Beatles!" An Oral History of Beatlemania* (Santa Monica, CA.: Santa Monica Press, 2008), 129.

8 *Daily Mirror*, 10 Sept. 1963, 12–13; JoAnne McCormack quoted in Berman, *See the Beatles*, 121.

9 Claire Krusch, quoted in Berman, *See the Beatles*, 124.

10 Maggie Welch quoted in Berman, *See the Beatles*, 117; George Harrison said in *The Beatles Explosion* (Legend Films, 2008), DVD, that "two tons a night" were thrown at them.

11 Ron Sweed quoted in Dave Schwensen, *The Beatles in Cleveland* (Vermilion, OH: North Shore Publishing, 2007), 48.

12 Kane, *Ticket to Ride*, 49.

13 Philip Norman, *Shout: The Beatles and Their Generation* (New York: Simon and Schuster, 1981), 240.

14 Kane, *Ticket to Ride*, 35; Spitz, *The Beatles*, 522.

15 Tony Bramwell, *Magical Mystery Tours: My Life with the Beatles* (London: Portico, 2005), 90–91.

16 *New York Times*, 29 Aug. 1964, 6.

17 Bramwell, *Magical Mystery Tours*, 76.

18 Spizer, *The Beatles Are Coming: The Birth of Beatlemania in America* (New Orleans: 498 Productions, 2004), 70, 68, 56; *Newsweek*, 18 Nov. 1963, 104.

19 *Newsweek*, 18 Nov. 1963, 64; *Daily Mirror*, 22 Oct. 1963, 16–17.

20 Paul Johnson, "The Menace of Beatlism," *New Statesman*, 28 Feb., 1964, in June Skinner Sawyers, ed., *Read the Beatles* (New York: Penguin, 2006), 53; Theodor Adorno, *The Culture Industry* (London: Routledge, 1981), 98–101.

21 Julia Baird in *Long and Winding Road* (Koch International, 2003), DVD; Geoff Emerick, *Here, There and Everywhere: My Life Recording the Music of the Beatles* (New York: Gotham, 2007), 63.

22 Goldsmith, *Come to America*, 63.

23 *Mersey Beat*, 11 April 1963, 7. This article is part of Bob Wooler's retrospective history of the Beatles.

24 *Daily Mirror* 14 Oct. 1963, 2.

25 *Daily Mail*, 21 Oct. 1963, 1, 3.

26 Jonathan Gould, *Can't Buy Me Love: The Beatles, Britain, and America* (New York: Harmony, 2007), 164; Goldsmith, *Come to America*, 96; *Daily Mirror*, 6 Nov. 1963, 6.

27 Goldsmith, *Come to America*, 115.

28 *Time*, 15 Nov. 1963, 64; *Newsweek*, 18 Nov. 1963, 104; Spizer, *Beatlemania*, 88.

29 Barry Miles, *The Beatles: A Diary* (London: Omnibus, 2002), 106.

30 Spitz, *The Beatles*, 520; Goldsmith, *Come to America*, 154; Miles, *British Invasion*, 111.

31 Ibid., 462.

32 Michael R. Frontani, *The Beatles: Image and the Media* (Jackson: University Press of Mississippi, 2007), 31.

33 Charles Pfeiffer, Carol Cox, Betty Taucher, and Penny Wagner quoted in Berman, *See the Beatles*, 73–75; Jay Willoughby interview by Jay Dismukes, 1996, Beam Oral History Project, Birmingham, Alabama.

34 Betty Taucher, Shaun Weiss quoted in Berman, *See the Beatles*, 78.

35 Spizer, *Beatlemania*, 193.

36 Brian Epstein in the *Melody Maker*, quoted in Sandercombe, *Press Reports*, 84; Bernstein's account is in his foreword to Berman, *See the Beatles*, 8–10.

37 *Daily Mirror* 20 Jan. 1964, 7.

38 From *Record Mirror*, *Mersey Beat*, and *Disc*, quoted in Sandercombe, *Press Reports*, 44, 80, 143.

39 Jerry Bishop quoted in Schwensen, *Beatles in Cleveland*, 57.

40 Geller and Wall, *Epstein Story*, 50; Paul D. Mertz posted on www.thirteen.org/beatles/the-beatles.

41 Spitz, *The Beatles*, 397. George Melly went on to write an important book about the effects of pop music on British culture; *Revolt into Style* (London: Allen Lane, 1970).

42 Steven D. Stark, *Meet the Beatles* (New York: Harper, 2005), 15; June Harvey and Debbie Levitt quoted in Berman, *See the Beatles*, 59, 69.

43 From *Disc and Music Echo*, 11 Nov. 1967, quoted in Sandercombe, *Press Reports*, 214, 218.

44 Frontani, *Image and Media*, 38.

45 *New York Times*, 17 Feb. 1964, 1, 20.

46   Ibid., 23 Feb. 1964, 15, 69–70.

47   Lennon quote from *Long and Winding Road* (DVD).

48   Goldsmith, *Come to America*, 4, 3.

49   Gould, *Can't Buy Me Love*, 100.

50   Ibid., 217–18; Stark, *Meet the Beatles*, 32.

51   Posted on www.thirteen.org/beatles/the-beatles.

52   Lester Bangs, "The Withering Away of the Beatles," in Egan, *Mammoth Beatles*, 352.

53   Ian Inglis, "The Beatles Are Coming! Conjecture and Conviction in the Myth of Kennedy, America and the Beatles," *Popular Music and Society* 24, no. 2 (Summer 2000): 93–108.

54   Spizer, *Beatlemania*, 64.

55   Cathy McCoy-Morgan quoted in Berman, *See the Beatles*, 51; Susan Hanrahan quoted in www.thiteen. org/beatles/the-beatles.

56   June Harvey quoted in Berman, *See the Beatles*, 69.

Beatlemania

Girls Just Want to Have Fun

Barbara Ehrenreich, Elizabeth Hess, and Gloria Jacobs

... witness the birth of eve — she is rising she was sleeping she is fading in a naked field sweating the precious blood of nodding blooms ... in the eye of the arena she bends in half in service — the anarchy that exudes from the pores of her guitar are the cries of the people wailing in the rushes ... a riot of ray/dios ...

Patti Smith, 'Notice,' in *Babel*

The news footage shows police lines straining against crowds of hundreds of young women. The police look grim; the girls' faces are twisted with desperation or, in some cases, shining with what seems to be an inner light. The air is dusty from a thousand running and scuffling feet. There are shouted orders to disperse, answered by a rising volume of chants and wild shrieks. The young women surge forth; the police line breaks ...

Looking at the photos or watching the news clips today, anyone would guess that this was the sixties — a demonstration — or maybe the early seventies — the beginning of the women's liberation movement. Until you look closer and see that the girls are not wearing sixties-issue jeans and T-shirts but bermuda shorts, high-necked, preppie blouses, and disheveled but unmistakably bouffant hairdos. This is not 1968 but 1964, and the girls are chanting, as they surge against the police line, 'I love Ringo.'

Yet, if it was not the 'movement,' or a clear-cut protest of any kind, Beatlemania was the first mass outburst of the sixties to feature women — in this case girls, who would not reach full adulthood until the seventies and the emergence of a genuinely political movement for women's liberation. The screaming ten- to fourteen-year-old fans of 1964 did not riot *for* anything, except the chance to remain in the proximity of their idols and hence to remain screaming. But they did have plenty to riot against, or at least to overcome through the act of rioting. In a highly sexualized society (one sociologist found that the number of explicitly sexual references in the mass media had doubled between 1950 and 1960), teen and preteen girls were expected to be not only 'good' and 'pure' but to be the enforcers of purity within their teen society—drawing the line for overeager boys and ostracizing girls who failed in this responsibility. To abandon control—to scream, faint, dash about in mobs—was, in form if not in conscious intent, to protest the sexual repressiveness, the rigid double standard of female teen culture. It was the first and most dramatic uprising of *women's* sexual revolution.

Beatlemania, in most accounts, stands isolated in history as a mere craze—quirky and hard to explain. There had been hysteria over male stars before, but nothing on this scale. In its peak years—1964 and 1965—Beatlemania struck with the force, if not the conviction, of a social movement. It began in England with a report that fans had mobbed the popular but not yet immortal group after a concert at the London Palladium on 13 October, 1963. Whether there was in fact a mob or merely a scuffle involving no more than eight girls is not clear, but the report acted as a call to mayhem. Eleven days later a huge and excited crowd of girls greeted the Beatles (returning from a Swedish tour) at Heathrow Airport. In early November, 400 Carlisle girls fought the police for four hours while trying to get tickets for a Beatles concert; nine people were hospitalized after the crowd surged forward and broke through shop windows. In London and Birmingham the police could not guarantee the Beatles safe escort through the hordes of fans. In Dublin the police chief judged that the Beatles' first visit was 'all right until the mania degenerated into barbarism.'[1] And on the eve of the group's first US tour, *Life* reported, 'A Beatle who ventures out unguarded into the streets runs the very real peril of being dismembered or crushed to death by his fans.'[2]

When the Beatles arrived in the United States, which was still ostensibly sobered by the assassination of President Kennedy two months before, the fans knew what to do. Television had spread the word from England: The approach of the Beatles is a license to riot. At least 4,000 girls (some estimates run as high as 10,000) greeted them at Kennedy Airport, and hundreds more laid siege to the Plaza Hotel, keeping the stars virtual prisoners. A record 73 million Americans watched the Beatles on 'The Ed Sullivan Show' on 9 February, 1964, the night 'when there wasn't a hubcap stolen anywhere in America.' American Beatlemania soon reached the proportions of religious idolatry. During the Beatles' twenty-three-city tour that August, local promoters were required to provide a minimum of 100 security guards to hold back the crowds. Some cities tried to ban Beatle-bearing craft from their runways; otherwise it took heavy deployments of local police to protect the Beatles from their fans and the fans from the crush. In one city, someone got hold of the hotel pillowcases that had purportedly been used by the Beatles, cut them into 160,000 tiny squares, mounted them on certificates, and sold them for $1 apiece. The group packed Carnegie Hall, Washington's Coliseum and, a year later, New York's 55,600-seat Shea Stadium, and in no setting, at any time, was their music audible above the frenzied screams of the audience. In 1966, just under three years after the start of Beatlemania, the Beatles gave their last concert—the first musical celebrities to be driven from the stage by their own fans.

In its intensity, as well as its scale, Beatlemania surpassed all previous outbreaks of star-centered hysteria. Young women had swooned over Frank Sinatra in the forties and screamed for Elvis Presley in the immediate pre-Beatle years, but the Fab Four inspired an extremity of feeling usually reserved for football games or natural disasters. These baby boomers far outnumbered the generation that, thanks to the censors, had only been able to see Presley's upper torso on 'The Ed Sullivan Show.' Seeing (whole) Beatles on Sullivan was exciting, but not enough. Watching the band on television was a thrill—particularly the close-ups—but the real goal was to leave home and meet the Beatles. The appropriate reaction to contact with them—such as occupying the same auditorium or city block—was to sob uncontrollably while screaming, 'I'm gonna die, I'm gonna die,' or, more optimistically, the name of a favorite Beatle, until the onset of either unconsciousness or laryngitis. Girls peed in their pants, fainted, or simply collapsed from the emotional strain. When not in the vicinity of the Beatles—and only a small proportion of fans ever got within shrieking distance of their idols—girls exchanged Beatle magazines or cards, and gathered to speculate obsessively on the details and nuances of Beatle life. One woman, who now administers a Washington, DC-based public interest group, recalls long discussions with other thirteen-year-olds in Orlando, Maine:

> I especially liked talking about the Beatles with other girls. Someone would say, 'What do you think Paul had for breakfast?' 'Do you think he sleeps with a different girl every night?' Or, 'Is John really the leader?' 'Is George really more sensitive?' And like that for hours.

This fan reached the zenith of junior high school popularity after becoming the only girl in town to travel to a Beatles' concert in Boston: 'My mother had made a new dress for me to wear [to the concert] and when I got back, the other girls wanted to cut it up and auction off the pieces.'

To adults, Beatlemania was an affliction, an 'epidemic,' and the Beatles themselves were only the carriers, or even 'foreign germs.' At risk were all ten- to fourteen-year-old girls, or at least all white girls; blacks were disdainful of the Beatles' initially derivative and unpolished sound. There appeared to be no cure except for age, and the media pundits were fond of reassuring adults that the girls who had screamed for Frank Sinatra had grown up to be responsible, settled housewives. If there was a shortcut to recovery, it certainly wasn't easy. A group of Los Angeles girls organized a detox effort called 'Beatlesaniacs, Ltd.,' offering 'group therapy for those living near active chapters, and withdrawal literature for those going it alone at far-flung outposts.' Among the rules for recovery were: 'Do not mention the word Beatles (or beetles),' 'Do not mention the word England.' 'Do not speak with an English accent,' and 'Do not speak English.'[3] In other words, Beatlemania was as inevitable as acne and gum-chewing, and adults would just have to weather it out.

But why was it happening? And why in particular to an America that prided itself on its post-McCarthy maturity, its prosperity, and its clear position as the number one world power? True, there were social problems that not even *Reader's Digest* could afford to be smug about— racial segregation, for example, and the newly discovered poverty of 'the other America'. But these were things that an energetic President could easily handle—or so most people believed at the time—and if 'the Negro problem', as it was called, generated overt unrest, it was seen as having a corrective function and limited duration. Notwithstanding an attempted revival by presidential candidate Barry Goldwater, 'extremism' was out of style in any area of expression. In colleges, 'coolness' implied a detached and rational appreciation of the status quo, and it was de rigueur among all but the avant-garde who joined the Freedom Rides or signed up for the Peace Corps. No one, not even Marxist philosopher Herbert Marcuse, could imagine a reason for widespread discontent among the middle class or for strivings that could not be satisfied with a department store charge account—much less for 'mania'.

In the media, adult experts fairly stumbled over each other to offer the most reassuring explanations. The *New York Times Magazine* offered a 'psychological, anthropological', half tongue-in-cheek account, titled 'Why the Girls Scream, Weep, Flip'. Drawing on the work of the German sociologist Theodor Adorno, *Times* writer David Dempsey argued that the girls weren't really out of line at all; they were merely 'conforming'. Adorno had diagnosed the 1940s jitterbug fans as 'rhythmic obedients', who were 'expressing their desire to obey'. They needed to subsume themselves into the mass, 'to become transformed into an insect'. Hence, 'jitterbug', and as Dempsey triumphantly added: 'Beatles, too, are a type of bug ... and to "beatle," as to jitter, is to lose one's identity in an automatized, insectlike activity, in other words, to obey'. If Beatlemania was more frenzied than the outbursts of obedience inspired by Sinatra or Fabian, it was simply because the music was 'more frantic', and in some animal way, more compelling. It is generally admitted 'that jungle rhythms influence the "beat" of much contemporary dance activity', he wrote, blithely endorsing the stock racist response to rock 'n' roll. Atavistic, 'aboriginal' instincts impelled the girls to scream, weep, and flip, whether they liked it or not: 'It is probably no coincidence that the Beatles, who provoke the most violent response among teenagers, resemble in manner the witch doctors who put their spells on hundreds of shuffling and stamping natives'.[4]

Not everyone saw the resemblance between Beatlemanic girls and 'natives' in a reassuring light however. *Variety* speculated that Beatlemania might be 'a phenomenon closely linked to the current wave of racial rioting'.[5] It was hard to miss the element of defiance in Beatlemania. If Beatlemania was conformity, it was conformity to an imperative that overruled adult mores and even adult laws. In the mass experience of Beatlemania, as for example at a concert or an airport, a girl who might never have contemplated shoplifting could assault a policeman with her fists, squirm under police barricades, and otherwise invite a disorderly conduct charge. Shy, subdued girls could go berserk. 'Perky', ponytailed girls of the type favored by early sixties sitcoms could dissolve in histrionics. In quieter contemplation of their idols, girls could see defiance in the Beatles or project it onto them. *Newsweek* quoted Pat Hagan, 'a pretty, 14-year-old Girl Scout, nurse's aide, and daughter of a Chicago lawyer ... who previously dug "West Side Story,"

Emily Dickinson, Robert Frost, and Elizabeth Barrett Browning: "They're tough," she said of the Beatles. "Tough is like when you don't conform … You're tumultuous when you're young, and each generation has to have its idols.'"[6] America's favorite sociologist, David Riesman, concurred, describing Beatlemania as 'a form of protest against the adult world.'[7]

There was another element of Beatlemania that was hard to miss but not always easy for adults to acknowledge. As any casual student of Freud would have noted, at least part of the fans' energy was sexual. Freud's initial breakthrough had been the insight that the epidemic female 'hysteria' of the late nineteenth century—which took the form of fits, convulsions, tics, and what we would now call neuroses—was the product of sexual repression. In 1964, though, confronted with massed thousands of 'hysterics,' psychologists approached this diagnosis warily. After all, despite everything Freud had had to say about childhood sexuality, most Americans did not like to believe that twelve-year-old girls had any sexual feelings to repress. And no normal girl—or full-grown woman, for that matter-was supposed to have the libidinal voltage required for three hours of screaming, sobbing, incontinent, acute-phase Beatlemania. In an article in *Science News Letter* titled 'Beatles Reaction Puzzles Even Psychologists,' one unidentified psychologist offered a carefully phrased, hygienic explanation: Adolescents are 'going through a strenuous period of emotional and physical growth,' which leads to a 'need for expressiveness, especially in girls.' Boys have sports as an outlet; girls have only the screaming and swooning afforded by Beatlemania, which could be seen as 'a release of sexual energy.'[8]

For the girls who participated in Beatlemania, sex was an obvious part of the excitement. One of the most common responses to reporters' queries on the sources of Beatlemania was, 'Because they're sexy.' And this explanation was in itself a small act of defiance. It was rebellious (especially for the very young fans) to lay claim to sexual feelings. It was even more rebellious to lay claim to the *active,* desiring side of a sexual attraction: the Beatles were the objects; the girls were their pursuers. The Beatles were sexy; the girls were the ones who perceived them as sexy and acknowledged the force of an ungovernable, if somewhat disembodied, lust. To assert an active, powerful sexuality by the tens of thousands and to do so in a way calculated to attract maximum attention was more than rebellious. It was, in its own unformulated, dizzy way, revolutionary.

Sex and the Teenage Girl

In the years and months immediately preceding US Beatlemania, the girls who were to initiate a sexual revolution looked, from a critical adult vantage point, like sleepwalkers on a perpetual shopping trip. Betty Friedan noted in her 1963 classic, *The Feminine Mystique,* 'a new vacant sleepwalking, playing-a-part quality of youngsters who do what they are supposed to do, what the other kids do, but do not seem to feel alive or real in doing it.'[9] But for girls, conformity meant more than surrendering, comatose, to the banal drift of junior high or high school life. To be popular with boys and girls—to be universally attractive and still have an unblemished 'reputation'—a girl had to be crafty, cool, and careful. The payoff for all this effort was to end up exactly like Mom—as a housewife.

In October 1963, the month Beatlemania first broke out in England and three months before it arrived in America, *Life* presented a troubling picture of teenage girl culture. The focus was Jill Dinwiddie, seventeen, popular, 'healthy, athletic, getting A grades', to all appearances wealthy, and at the same time, strangely vacant. The pictures of this teenage paragon and her friends would have done justice to John Lennon's first take on American youth:

> When we got here you were all walkin' around in fuckin' Bermuda shorts
> with Boston crewcuts and stuff on your teeth ... The chicks looked like
> 1940's horses. There was no conception of dress or any of that jazz. We just
> thought what an ugly race, what an ugly race.[10]

Jill herself, the 'queen bee of the high school', is strikingly sexless: short hair in a tightly controlled style (the kind achieved with flat metal clips), button-down shirts done up to the neck, shapeless skirts with matching cardigans, and a stance that evokes the intense posture-consciousness of prefeminist girls' phys. ed. Her philosophy is no less engaging: 'We have to be like everybody else to be accepted. Aren't most adults that way? We learn in high school to stay in the middle.'[11]

'The middle,' for girls coming of age in the early sixties, was a narrow and carefully defined terrain. The omnipresent David Riesman, whom *Life* called in to comment on Jill and her crowd, observed, 'Given a standard definition of what is feminine and successful, they must conform to it. The range is narrow, the models they may follow few.' The goal, which Riesman didn't need to spell out, was marriage and motherhood, and the route to it led along a straight and narrow path between the twin dangers of being 'cheap' or being too puritanical, and hence unpopular. A girl had to learn to offer enough, sexually, to get dates, and at the same time to withhold enough to maintain a boy's interest through the long preliminaries from dating and going steady to engagement and finally marriage. None of this was easy, and for girls like Jill the pedagogical burden of high school was a four-year lesson in how to use sex instrumentally: doling out just enough to be popular with boys and never enough to lose the esteem of the 'right kind of kids'. Commenting on *Life's* story on Jill, a University of California sociologist observed:

> It seems that half the time of our adolescent girls is spent trying to meet
> their new responsibilities to be sexy, glamorous and attractive, while the
> other half is spent meeting their old responsibility to be virtuous by hold-
> ing off the advances which testify to their success.

Advice books to teenagers fussed anxiously over the question of 'where to draw the line', as did most teenage girls themselves. Officially everyone—girls and advice-givers—agreed that the line fell short of intercourse, though by the sixties even this venerable prohibition required some sort of justification, and the advice-givers strained to impress upon their young readers the calamitous results of premarital sex. First there was the obvious danger of pregnancy, an apparently inescapable danger since no book addressed to teens dared offer birth control information. Even worse, some writers suggested, were the psychological effects of intercourse: It would destroy a budding relationship and possibly poison any future marriage. According to a contemporary textbook titled, *Adolescent Development and Adjustment,* intercourse often caused a man to lose interest ('He may come to believe she is totally promiscuous'), while it was likely to reduce a woman to slavish dependence ('Sometimes a woman focuses her life around the man with whom she first has intercourse').[12] The girl who survived premarital intercourse and went on to marry someone else would find marriage clouded with awkwardness and distrust. Dr Arthur Cain warned in *Young People and Sex* that the husband of a sexually experienced woman might be consumed with worry about whether his performance matched that of her previous partners. 'To make matters worse,' he wrote, 'it may be that one's sex partner is not as exciting and satisfying as one's previous illicit lover.'[13] In short, the price of premarital experience was likely to be postnuptial disappointment. And, since marriage was a girl's peak achievement, an anticlimatic wedding night would be a lasting source of grief.

Intercourse was obviously out of the question, so young girls faced the still familiar problem of where to draw the line on a scale of lesser sexual acts, including (in descending order of niceness): kissing, necking, and petting, this last being divided into 'light' (through clothes and/or above the waist) and 'heavy' (with clothes undone and/or below the waist). Here the experts were no longer unanimous. Pat Boone, already a spokesman for the Christian right, drew the line at kissing in his popular 1958 book, *'Twixt Twelve and Twenty.* No prude, he announced that 'kissing is here to stay and I'm glad of it!' But, he warned, 'Kissing is not a game. Believe me! ... Kissing for fun is like playing with a beautiful candle in a roomful of dynamite!'[14] (The explosive consequences might have been guessed from the centerpiece photos showing Pat dining out with his teen bride, Shirley; then, as if moments later, in a maternity ward with her; and, in the next picture, surrounded by 'the four little Boones.') Another pop-singer-turned-adviser, Connie Francis, saw nothing wrong with kissing (unless it begins to 'dominate your life'), nor with its extended form, necking, but drew the line at petting:

> Necking and petting—let's get this straight—are two different things. Petting, according to most definitions, is specifically intended to arouse sexual desires and as far as I'm concerned, petting is out for teenagers.[15]

In practice, most teenagers expected to escalate through the scale of sexual possibilities as a relationship progressed, with the big question being: How much, how soon? In their 1963 critique of American teen culture, *Teen-Age Tyranny,* Grace and Fred Hechinger bewailed the cold instrumentality that shaped the conventional answers. A girl's 'favors,' they wrote, had become 'currency to bargain for desirable dates which, in turn, are legal tender in the exchange of popularity.' For example, in answer to the frequently asked question, 'Should I let him kiss me good night on the first date?' they reported that:

> A standard caution in teen-age advice literature is that, if the boy 'gets' his kiss on the first date, he may assume that many other boys have been just as easily compensated. In other words, the rule book advises mainly that the (girl's] popularity assets should be protected against deflation.[16]

It went without saying that it was the girl's responsibility to apply the brakes as a relationship approached the slippery slope leading from kissing toward intercourse. This was not because girls were expected to be immune from temptation. Connie Francis acknowledged that 'It's not easy to be moral, especially where your feelings for a boy are involved. It never is, because you have to fight to keep your normal physical impulses in line.' But it was the girl who had the most to lose, not least of all the respect of the boy she might too generously have indulged. 'When she gives in completely to a boy's advances,' Francis warned, 'the element of respect goes right out the window.' Good girls never 'gave in,' never abandoned themselves to impulse or emotion, and never, of course, initiated a new escalation on the scale of physical intimacy. In the financial metaphor that dominated teen sex etiquette, good girls 'saved themselves' for marriage; bad girls were 'cheap.'

According to a 1962 Gallup Poll commissioned by *Ladies' Home Journal,* most young women (at least in the *Journal*'s relatively affluent sample) enthusiastically accepted the traditional feminine role and the sexual double standard that went with it:

> Almost all our young women between 16 and 21 expect to be married by 22. Most want 4 children, many want ... to work until children come; afterward, a resounding no! They feel a special responsibility for sex *because* they are women. An 18-year-old student in California said, 'The standard for men—sowing wild oats—results in sown oats. And where does this leave the woman?' ... Another student: 'A man will go as far as a woman will let him. The girl has to set the standard.'[17]

Implicit in this was a matrimonial strategy based on months of sexual teasing (setting the standard), until the frustrated young man broke down and proposed. Girls had to 'hold out' because, as one *Journal* respondent put it, 'Virginity is one of the greatest things a woman can give to her husband.' As for what *he* would give to her, in addition to four or five children, the young women were vividly descriptive:

> ... I want a split-level brick with four bedrooms with French Provincial cherrywood furniture.

... I'd like a built-in oven and range, counters only 34 inches high with Formica on them.

... I would like a lot of finished wood for warmth and beauty.

... My living room would be long with a high ceiling of exposed beams. I would have a large fireplace on one wall, with a lot of copper and brass around.... My kitchen would be very like old Virginian ones—fireplace and oven.

So single-mindedly did young women appear to be bent on domesticity that when Beatlemania did arrive, some experts thought the screaming girls must be auditioning for the maternity ward: 'The girls are subconsciously preparing for motherhood. Their frenzied screams are a rehearsal for that moment. Even the jelly babies [the candies favored by the early Beatles and hurled at them by fans] are symbolic.'[18] Women were asexual, or at least capable of mentally bypassing sex and heading straight from courtship to reveries of Formica counters and cherrywood furniture, from the soda shop to the hardware store.

But the vision of a suburban split-level, which had guided a generation of girls chastely through high school, was beginning to lose its luster. Betty Friedan had surveyed the 'successful' women of her age—educated, upper-middle-class housewives—and found them reduced to infantile neuroticism by the isolation and futility of their lives. If feminism was still a few years off, at least the 'feminine mystique' had entered the vocabulary, and even Jill Dinwiddie must have read the quotation from journalist Shana Alexander that appeared in the same issue of *Life* that featured Jill. 'It's a marvellous life, this life in a man's world,' Alexander said. 'I'd climb the walls if I had to live the feminine mystique.' The media that had once romanticized togetherness turned their attention to 'the crack in the picture window'—wife swapping, alcoholism, divorce, and teenage anomie. A certain cynicism was creeping into the American view of marriage. In the novels of John Updike and Philip Roth, the hero didn't get the girl, he got away. When a Long Island prostitution ring, in which housewives hustled with their husbands' consent, was exposed in the winter of 1963, a Fifth Avenue saleswoman commented: 'I see all this beautiful stuff I'll never have, and I wonder if it's worth it to be good. What's the difference, one man every night or a different man?'[19]

So when sociologist Bennet Berger commented in *Life* that 'there is nobody better equipped than Jill to live in a society of all-electric kitchens, wall-to-wall carpeting, dishwashers, garbage disposals [and] color TV,' this could no longer be taken as unalloyed praise. Jill herself seemed to sense that all the tension and teasing anticipation of the teen years was not worth the payoff. After she was elected, by an overwhelming majority, to the cheerleading team, 'an uneasy, far-away look clouded her face.' 'I guess there's nothing left to do in high school,' she said. 'I've made song leader both years, and that was all I really wanted.' For girls, high school was all there was to public life, the only place you could ever hope to run for office or experience the quasi fame of popularity. After that came marriage—most likely to one of the crew-cut boys you'd made out with—then isolation and invisibility.

Part of the appeal of the male star—whether it was James Dean or Elvis Presley or Paul McCartney—was that you would *never* marry him; the romance would never end in the tedium of marriage. Many girls expressed their adulation in conventional, monogamous terms, for example, picking their favorite Beatle and writing him a serious letter of proposal, or carrying placards saying, 'John, Divorce Cynthia.' But it was inconceivable that any fan would actually marry a Beatle or sleep with him (sexually active 'groupies' were still a few years off) or even hold his hand. Adulation of the male star was a way to express sexual yearnings that would normally be pressed into the service of popularity or simply repressed. The star could be loved noninstru-mentally, for his own sake, and with complete abandon. Publicly to advertise this hopeless love was to protest the calculated, pragmatic sexual repression of teenage life.

The Economics of Mass Hysteria

Sexual repression had been a feature of middle-class teen life for centuries. If there was a sig-nificant factor that made mass protest possible in the late fifties (Elvis) and the early sixties (the Beatles), it was the growth and maturation of a teen market: for distinctly teen clothes, magazines, entertainment, and accessories. Consciousness of the teen years as a life-cycle phase set off between late childhood on the one hand and young adulthood on the other only goes back to the early twentieth century, when the influential psychologist G. Stanley Hall published his mam-moth work *Adolescence*. (The word 'teenager' did not enter mass usage until the 1940s.) Postwar affluence sharpened the demarcations around the teen years: fewer teens than ever worked or left school to help support their families, making teenhood more distinct from adulthood as a time of unemployment and leisure. And more teens than ever had money to spend, so that from a marketing view point, teens were potentially much more interesting than children, who could only influence family spending but did little spending themselves. Grace and Fred Hechinger reported that in 1959 the average teen spent $555 on 'goods and services not including the necessities normally supplied by their parents', and noted, for perspective, that in the same year school-teach-ers in Mississippi were earning just over $3,000. 'No matter what other segments of American society—parents, teachers, sociologists, psychologists, or policemen—may deplore the power of teenagers', they observed, 'the American business community has no cause for complaint.'[20]

If advertisers and marketing men manipulated teens as consumers, they also, inadvertently, solidified teen culture against the adult world. Marketing strategies that recognized the impor-tance of teens as precocious consumers also recognized the importance of heightening their self-awareness of themselves *as teens*. Girls especially became aware of themselves as occu-pying a world of fashion of their own—not just bigger children's clothes or slimmer women's clothes. You were not a big girl or a junior woman, but a 'teen', and in that notion lay the germs of an oppositional identity. Defined by its own products and advertising slogans, teenhood became more than a prelude to adulthood; it was a status to be proud of—emotionally and sexually complete unto itself.

Rock 'n' roll was the most potent commodity to enter the teen consumer subculture. Rock was originally a black musical form with no particular age identification, and it took white performers like Buddy Holly and Elvis Presley to make rock 'n' roll accessible to young white kids with generous allowances to spend. On the white side of the deeply segregated music market, rock became a distinctly teenage product. Its 'jungle beat' was disconcerting or hateful to white adults; its lyrics celebrated the special teen world of fashion ('Blue Suede Shoes'), feeling ('Teenager in Love'), and passive opposition ('Don't know nothin' 'bout his-to-ry'). By the late fifties, rock 'n' roll was the organizing principle and premier theme of teen consumer culture: you watched the Dick Clark show not only to hear the hits but to see what the kids were wearing; you collected not only the top singles but the novelty items that advertised the stars; you cultivated the looks and personality that would make you a 'teen angel'. And if you were still too young for all this, in the late fifties you yearned to grow up to be—not a woman and a housewife, but a teenager.

Rock 'n' roll made mass hysteria almost inevitable: It announced and ratified teen sexuality and then amplified teen sexual frustration almost beyond endurance. Conversely, mass hysteria helped make rock 'n' roll. In his biography of Elvis Presley, Albert Goldman describes how Elvis's manager, Colonel Tom Parker, whipped mid-fifties girl audiences into a frenzy before the appearance of the star: As many as a dozen acts would precede Elvis—acrobats, comics, gospel singers, a little girl playing a xylophone—until the audience, 'driven half mad by sheer frustration, began chanting rhythmically, "*We want Elvis, we want Elvis!*" When the star was at last announced:

> Five thousand shrill female voices come in on cue. The screeching reaches
> the intensity of a jet engine. When Elvis comes striding out on stage with
> his butchy walk, the screams suddenly escalate. They switch to hyperspace.
> Now, you may as well be stone deaf for all the music you'll hear. [21]

The newspapers would duly report that 'the fans went wild.'

Hysteria was critical to the marketing of the Beatles. First there were the reports of near riots in England. Then came a calculated publicity tease that made Colonel Parker's manipulations look oafish by contrast: five million posters and stickers announcing 'The Beatles Are Coming' were distributed nationwide. Disc jockeys were blitzed with promo material and Beatle interview tapes (with blank spaces for the DJ to fill in the questions, as if it were a real interview) and enlisted in a mass 'countdown' to the day of the Beatles' arrival in the United States. As Beatle chronicler Nicholas Schaffner reports:

> Come break of 'Beatle Day', the quartet had taken over even the disc-jockey
> patter that punctuated their hit songs. From WMCA and WINS through W-A-
> Beatle-C, it was 'thirty Beatle degrees', 'eight-thirty Beatle time' ... [and] 'four
> hours and fifty minutes to go.'[22]

By the time the Beatles materialized, on 'The Ed Sullvan Show' in February 1964, the anticipation was unbearable. A woman who was a fourteen-year-old in Duluth at the time told us,

'Looking back, it seems so commercial to me, and so degrading that millions of us would just scream on cue for these four guys the media dangled out in front of us. But at the time it was something intensely personal for me and, I guess, a million other girls. The Beatles seemed to be speaking directly to us and, in a funny way, *for us*.'

By the time the Beatles hit America, teens and preteens had already learned to look to their unique consumer subculture for meaning and validation. If this was manipulation—and no culture so strenuously and shamelessly exploits its children as consumers—it was also subversion. *Bad* kids became juvenile delinquents, smoked reefers, or got pregnant. Good kids embraced the paraphernalia, the lore, and the disciplined fandom of rock 'n' roll. (Of course, bad kids did their thing to a rock beat too: the first movie to use a rock 'n' roll soundtrack was 'Blackboard Jungle', in 1955, cementing the suspected link between 'jungle rhythms' and teen rebellion.) For girls, fandom offered a way not only to sublimate romantic and sexual yearnings but to carve out subversive versions of heterosexuality. Not just anyone could be hyped as a suitable object for hysteria: It *mattered* that Elvis was a grown-up greaser, and that the Beatles let their hair grow over their ears.

The Erotics of the Star–Fan Relationship

In real life, i.e., in junior high or high school, the ideal boyfriend was someone like Tab Hunter or Ricky Nelson. He was 'all boy', meaning you wouldn't get home from a date without a friendly scuffle, but he was also clean-cut, meaning middle class, patriotic, and respectful of the fact that good girls waited until marriage. He wasn't moody and sensitive (like James Dean in *Giant* or *Rebel Without a Cause*), he was realistic (meaning that he understood that his destiny was to earn a living for someone like yourself). The stars who inspired the greatest mass adulation were none of these things, and their very remoteness from the pragmatic ideal was what made them accessible to fantasy.

Elvis was visibly lower class and symbolically black (as the bearer of black music to white youth). He represented an unassimilated white underclass that had been forgotten by mainstream suburban America-more accurately, he represented a middle-class caricature of poor whites. He was *sleazy*. And, as his biographer Goldman argues, therein lay his charm:

> What did the girls see that drove them out of their minds? It sure as hell wasn't the All-American Boy …. Elvis was the flip side of [the] conventional male image. His fish-belly white complexion, so different from the 'healthy tan' of the beach boys; his brooding Latin eyes, heavily shaded with mascara … the thick, twisted lips; the long, greasy hair…. God! what a freak the boy must have looked to those little girls … and what a turn-on! Typical comments were: 'I like him because he looks so mean' … 'He's been in and out of jail.'[23]

Elvis stood for a dangerous principle of masculinity that had been expunged from the white-collar, split-level world of fandom: a hood who had no place in the calculus of dating, going steady, and getting married. At the same time, the fact that he was lower class evened out the gender difference in power. He acted arrogant, but he was really vulnerable, and would be back behind the stick shift of a Mack truck if you, the fans, hadn't redeemed him with your love. His very sleaziness, then, was a tribute to the collective power of the teen and preteen girls who worshipped him. He was obnoxious to adults—a Cincinnati used-car dealer once offered to smash fifty Presley records in the presence of every purchaser—not only because of who he was but because he was a reminder of the emerging power and sexuality of young girls.

Compared to Elvis, the Beatles were almost respectable. They wore suits; they did not thrust their bodies about suggestive; and to most Americans, who couldn't tell a blue-collar, Liverpudlian accent from Oxbridge English, they might have been upper class. What was both shocking and deeply appealing about the Beatles was that they were, while not exactly effeminate, at least not easily classifiable in the rigid gender distinctions of middle-class American life. Twenty years later we are so accustomed to shoulder-length male tresses and rock stars of ambiguous sexuality that the Beatles of 1964 look clean-cut. But when the Beatles arrived at crew-cut, precounterculture America, their long hair attracted more commentary than their music. Boy fans rushed to buy Beatle wigs and cartoons showing well-known male figures decked with Beatle hair were a source of great merriment. *Playboy,* in an interview, grilled the Beatles on the subject of homosexuality, which it was only natural for gender-locked adults to suspect. As Paul McCartney later observed:

> There they were in America, all getting house-trained for adulthood with their indisputable principle of life: short hair equals men; long hair equals women. Well, we got rid of that small convention for them. And a few others, too.[24]

What did it mean that American girls would go for these sexually suspect young men, and in numbers far greater than an unambiguous stud like Elvis could command? Dr Joyce Brothers thought the Beatles' appeal rested on the girls' innocence:

> The Beatles display a few mannerisms which almost seem a shade on the feminine side, such as the tossing of their long manes of hair. ... These are exactly the mannerisms which very young female fans (in the 10-to-14 age group) appear to go wildest over.[25]

The reason? 'Very young "women" are still a little frightened of the idea of sex. Therefore they feel safer worshipping idols who don't seem too masculine, or too much the "he man."'

What Brothers and most adult commentators couldn't imagine was that the Beatles' androgyny was itself sexy. 'The idea of sex' as intercourse, with the possibility of pregnancy or a ruined reputation, was indeed frightening. But the Beatles construed sex more generously and playfully, lifting it out of the rigid scenario of mid-century American gender roles, and it was this that made them wildly sexy. Or to put it the other way around, the appeal lay in the vision of sexuality that the Beatles held out to a generation of American girls: They seemed to offer sexuality that was guileless, ebullient, and fun—like the Beatles themselves and everything they did (or were shown doing in their films *Help* and *A Hard Day's Night*). Theirs was a vision of sexuality freed from the shadow of gender inequality because the group mocked the gender distinctions that bifurcated the American landscape into 'his' and 'hers'. To Americans who believed fervently that sexuality hinged on *la difference,* the Beatlemaniacs said, No, blur the lines and expand the possibilities.

At the same time, the attraction of the Beatles bypassed sex and went straight to the issue of power. Our informant from Orlando, Maine, said of her Beatlemanic phase:

> It didn't feel sexual, as I would now define that. It felt more about wanting freedom. I didn't want to grow up and be a wife and it seemed to me that the Beatles had the kind of freedom I wanted: No rules, they could spend two days lying in bed; they ran around on motorbikes, ate from room service. ... I didn't want to sleep with Paul McCartney, I was too young. But I wanted to be like them, something larger than life.

Another woman, who was thirteen when the Beatles arrived in her home city of Los Angeles and was working for the telephone company in Denver when we interviewed her, said:

> Now that I've thought about it, I think I identified with them, rather than as an object of them. I mean I liked their independence and sexuality and wanted those things for myself. ... Girls didn't get to be that way when I was a teenager—we got to be the limp, passive object of some guy's fleeting sexual interest. We were so stifled, and they made us meek, giggly creatures think, oh, if only *I* could act that way, and be strong, sexy, and doing what you want.

If girls could not be, or ever hope to be, superstars and madcap adventurers themselves, they could at least idolize the men who were.

There was the more immediate satisfaction of knowing, subconsciously, that the Beatles were who they were because girls like oneself had made them that. As with Elvis, fans knew of the Beatles' lowly origins and knew they had risen from working-class obscurity to world fame on the acoustical power of thousands of shrieking fans. Adulation created stars, and stardom, in turn, justified adulation. Questioned about their hysteria, some girls answered simply, 'Because they're the Beatles.' That is, because they're who I happen to like. And the louder you screamed, the less likely anyone would forget the power of the fans. When the screams drowned out the music, as they invariably did, then it was the fans, and not the band, who were the show.

In the decade that followed Beatlemania, the girls who had inhabited the magical, obsessive world of fandom would edge closer and closer to center stage. Sublimation would give way to more literal, and sometimes sordid, forms of fixation: By the late sixties, the most zealous fans, no longer content to shriek and sob in virginal frustration, would become groupies and 'go all the way' with any accessible rock musician. One briefly notorious group of girl fans, the Chicago Plaster Casters, distinguished itself by making plaster molds of rock stars' penises, thus memorializing, among others, Jimi Hendrix. At the end of the decade Janis Joplin, who had been a lonely, unpopular teenager in the fifties, shot to stardom before dying of a drug and alcohol overdose. Joplin, before her decline and her split from Big Brother, was in a class by herself. There were no other female singers during the sixties who reached her pinnacle of success. Her extraordinary power in the male world of rock 'n' roll lay not only in her talent but in her femaleness. While she did not meet conventional standards of beauty, she was nevertheless sexy and powerful; both genders could worship her on the stage for their own reasons. Janis offered women the possibility of identifying with, rather than objectifying, the star. 'It was seeing Janis Joplin,' wrote Ellen Willis, 'that made me resolve, once and for all, not to get my hair straightened.' Her 'metamorphosis from the ugly duckling of Port Arthur to the peacock of Haight Ashbury'[26] gave teenage girls a new optimistic fantasy.

While Janis was all woman, she was also one of the boys. Among male rock stars, the faintly androgynous affect of the Beatles was quickly eclipsed by the frank bisexuality of performers like Alice Cooper and David Bowie, and then the more outrageous antimasculinity of eighties stars Boy George and Michael Jackson. The latter provoked screams again and mobs, this time of interracial crowds of girls, going down in age to eight and nine, but never on the convulsive scale of Beatlemania. By the eighties, female singers like Grace Jones and Annie Lenox were denying gender too, and the loyalty and masochism once requisite for female lyrics gave way to new songs of cynicism, aggression, exultation. But between the vicarious pleasure of Beatlemania and Cyndi Lauper's forthright assertion in 1984 that 'girls just want to have fun,' there would be an enormous change in the sexual possibilities open to women and girls—a change large enough to qualify as a 'revolution.'

Notes

1 Lewis (1963, p. 124).

2 Green (1964, p. 30).

3 'How to Kick ...' (1964, p. 66).

4 Dempsey (1964, p. 15).

5 Quoted in Schaffner (1977, p. 16).

6 'George, Paul ...' (1964, p. 54).

7 'What the Beatles Prove ...' (1964, p. 88).

8 'Beatles Reaction ...' (1964, p. 141).

9 Friedan (1963, p. 282).

10 Quoted in Schaffner (1977, p. 15).

11 'Queen Bee ...' (1963, p. 68).

12 Crow and Crow (1965, pp. 248–9).

13 Cain (1967, p. 71).

14 Boone (1967, p. 60).

15 Francis (1962, p. 138).

16 Hechinger (1963, p. 54).

17 'Shaping the '60s ...' (1962, p. 30).

18 Quoted in Norman (1981, p. 200).

19 Grafton (1964, p. 36).

20 Hechinger (1963, p. 151).

21 Goldman (1981, p. 190).

22 Schaffner (1977, p. 9).

23 Goldman (1981, p. 191).

24 Quoted in Schaffner (1977, p. 17).

25 Quoted in Schaffner, ibid., p. 16.

26 Willis (1981, p. 63).

References

Beatles Reaction Puzzles Even Psychologists. 29 February 1964. *Science News Letter.*

Boone, Pat. 1967. *'Twixt Twelve and Twenty: Pat Talks to Teenagers*. Englewood Cliffs, N J: Prentice-Hall.

Cain, Arthur. 1967. *Young People and Sex*. New York: The John Day Co.

Crow, Lester D. and Alice Crow. 1965. *Adolescent Development and Adjustment*. New York: McGraw-Hill.

Dempsey, David. 23 February 1964. Why the Girls Scream, Weep, Flip. *New York Times Magazine*.

Francis, Connie. 1962. *For Every Young Heart*. Englewood Cliffs, N. J.: Prentice-Hall.

Friedan, Betty. 1963. *The Feminine Mystique*. New York: W. W. Norton.

George, Paul, Ringo and John. 24 February 1964. *Newsweek*.

Goldman, Albert. 1981, *Elvis*. New York: McGraw-Hill.

Grafton, Samuel. 15 December 1964. The Twisted Age. *Look*.

Green, Timothy. 31 January 1964. They Crown Their Country with a Bowl-Shaped Hairdo. *Life*.

Hechinger, Grace and Fred M. 1963. *Teen-Age Tyranny*. New York: William Morrow.

How to Kick the Beatle Habit. 28 August 1964. *Life*.

Lewis, Frederick. December 1 1963. Britons Succumb to 'Beatlemania'. *New York Times Magazine*.

Norman, Philip. 1981. *Shout! The Beatles in Their Generation*. New York: Simon & Schuster.

Queen Bee of the High School. 11 October 1963. *Life*.

Schaffner, Nicholas. 1977. *The Beatles Forever*. New York: McGraw-Hill.

Shaping the '60s ... Foreshadowing the '70s. January 1962. *Ladies' Home Journal*.

What the Beatles Prove About Teen-agers. 24 February 1964. *U.S. News & World Report*.

Willis, Ellen. 1981. *Beginning to See The Light*. New York: Alfred A. Knopf.

"You Say You Want a Revolution"

The Beatles and the Political Culture of the 1960s

Kenneth L. Campbell

T he Beatles released John Lennon's song "Revolution" in August 1968 in the midst of the most politically contentious year of the most politically charged decade of the twentieth century. Lennon acknowledged in the song that "we all want to change the world," but he raised explicit doubts about whether the kind of radical political change advocated by mostly young revolutionaries around the world would achieve positive results. Lennon's ambivalence (at best) about violent political change brought upon himself and the Beatles as a whole the animus of the leftist avant-garde who now thought the group completely out of touch with the needs of the times. 1968 was proving to be a cataclysmic year that saw student protests and anti-war demonstrations spread around the globe, a year in which the peace-loving counterculture of the hippies took a hard turn toward violence and increased radical activity among the fraying youth movement. The Beatles, meanwhile, had gone to India in February to learn more about the practice of Transcendental Meditation from their guru and spiritual mentor, Maharishi Mahesh Yogi. Far removed from the harsh realities of political conflict and radical rebellion, John Lennon gained a perspective he later expressed in "Revolution" through the lyric "it's all gonna be all right."

This was hardly the first time that the Beatles found themselves in the middle of a controversy related to the changes in political culture sweeping the world in the 1960s. While performing in Japan in 1966, the group became ensconced in a national narrative in which Japanese traditionalists viewed the Beatles as profaning the sacred Nippon Budokan Hall, previously reserved for revered martial arts demonstrations. In the Philippines, the Beatles created a firestorm by failing to attend a reception hosted by the country's atrocious dictator, Ferdinand Marcos and his spendthrift wife, Imelda.

The Beatles had been unaware of the invitation, but that did not prevent some rough treatment of the besieged group and its entourage and some tense moments prior to their leaving the country. After their traumatic experience in the Philippines, they took one of their first overtly political stances by denouncing the Marcos dictatorship, which had the support of the United States as an anti-Communist ally in the Cold War. Religious conservatives in the southern United States exhibited their hostility toward the Beatles during their 1966 US tour by advocating the burning and banning of Beatles' records because of John's statement in an earlier interview with British journalist Maureen Cleave that he thought the Beatles had become "more popular than Jesus." The Beatles, despite their relative lack of political engagement, had still come to symbolize for conservatives in Japan, the Philippines, and the United States the rebellious and potentially revolutionary nature of the 1960s youth movement.

One could make the case, however, that the Beatles had cultivated some level of political and cultural consciousness, even in their early years when they were mostly known as lovable mop-tops mainly performing pleasant and harmonious love songs. For example, by including a number of Motown songs in their repertoire and on their early LPs, they demonstrated an affinity with African-American music at a time of racial tension and the growing Civil Rights movement in the United States. Furthermore, their inclusion and performance of songs such as "Please Mr. Postman," "Chains," and even the female-centric "Boys," which were first popularized by girl groups, blurred gender lines and contributed to their appeal among young female fans, who in their own way were rebelling against societal norms for females (Douglas 112–20). Moreover, the Beatles opened their 1966 album *Revolver* with George Harrison wryly satirizing the British government for its draconian tax code in his song "Taxman." Bob Spitz called "Taxman" "as sly and critical as anything Dylan was writing" (Spitz 611).

The Beatles' use of marijuana and LSD had also found resonance in the emerging counter-culture, especially after thinly veiled references to the drugs began appearing on albums such as *Revolver* and 1967s *Sgt. Pepper's Lonely Hearts Club Band,* the last song of which, "A Day in the Life," was banned by the BBC for the inclusion of the phrase "I'd love to turn you on." When Paul McCartney not only admitted to using LSD but also extolled its virtues in the press, he confirmed the transformation of the entire band in the public eye from a naive group of wide-eyed inno-cent jokesters and musicians to serious leaders of the counterculture, a position confirmed by the release of *Sgt. Pepper,* which put their evolving creativity on full display. Although the other Beatles were annoyed that Paul had first revealed the group's experimentation with acid, partly because he seemed to take credit for something each of the other members had done before he had, none of them denied using the drug, which Harrison always claimed was a watershed in his own psychic development. Their drug use and *Sgt. Pepper* had made the Beatles cool; even the great rock and blues guitarist Eric Clapton, who had preconceived notions about the Beatles and had hitherto failed to regard them as serious musicians, admitted that he was impressed by the album and finally understood what all the fuss was about.

The appeal of the Beatles, however, went beyond their tacit endorsement of the psychedelic drug culture of the 1960s or even their musical wizardry. They became synonymous with a

Zeitgeist that promoted collective and shared experiences based on love, peace, and harmony. These were all appropriate concepts during 1967s Summer of Love, during which the American singer Scott McKenzie encouraged all visitors to San Francisco to "be sure to wear flowers in your hair" in a song written by John Phillips (of the Mamas and the Papas) that had been released in May. Beatles' historian Jonathan Gould writes:

> In their loyalty to one another and their autonomy from everyone else, the Beatles had come to personify an ethic of collective nonconformity that took the loneliness out of rebellion and linked the activist and hedonist wings of the emerging counterculture as few things could. (Gould 345)

The question was how to harness this collectivism to effect change in the real world as opposed to the visionary and enchanted archetype inspired by the Beatles' image, genius, and lyricism. On June 25, 1967, about three weeks after the release of *Sgt. Pepper,* the Beatles took a step in that direction by performing a new song called "All You Need is Love" on an international telecast sponsored by the BBC, the first satellite broadcast beamed globally and one that attracted 2 million viewers (Miles, *Hippie,* 239).

By 1968, however, college campuses across the United States had exploded with anti-war sentiment, nurtured by four years of discontent that had started with the Free Speech Movement at Berkeley in 1964 and was fostered by the Students for a Democratic Society (SDS) at numerous universities. The Free Speech Movement and early campus protests focused more on issues of personal freedom, such as dress codes, hair length, and restrictions on visiting hours in dorm rooms of members of the opposite sex. The focus of student activism changed with the progressive escalation of the Vietnam War. Anti-draft sentiment drove many of the protests by young men reaching or approaching the age of eligibility, but such personal concerns had also merged with the larger peace ethos of the counterculture. In 1967, US President Lyndon B. Johnson announced plans to send an additional 45,000 troops to Vietnam. The revered American folk singer Pete Seeger responded with one of his most palpably political statements with his song "Waist Deep in the Big Muddy," which he planned to perform on the popular *Smothers Brothers Comedy Hour* television show. CBS executives, however, refused to permit the full version of Seeger's song, which ended with a direct association of Johnson with "the big fool" in the song who keeps pushing his troops deeper and deeper into a river until he gets over his head and drowns in the Big Muddy.

Seeger's song proved prescient. On January 31, 1968 the North Vietnamese launched the Tet Offensive, named after the beginning of the Vietnamese New Year, which dramatically escalated the fighting in this prolonged military saga with no apparent end in sight. The war's growing unpopularity contributed heavily to Johnson's decision in March not to seek reelection. The man who seemed best poised to effect the kind of change hoped for by student idealists in the United States and to end the war in Vietnam was Bobby Kennedy, who put together a surprisingly successful presidential campaign strategy after entering the race relatively late. Kennedy was an ardent opponent of the war, referring in his campaign speeches to those dying "on the other side of the world" as an immense waste of human life, talent, and abilities, but any hopes he might capture the nomination and end the war disappeared when he was struck down by an assassin's bullet in the kitchen of the Ambassador Hotel in Los Angeles on June 5. In August, a large number of protestors gathered outside the Democratic National Convention in Chicago, only to witness the nomination of the establishment figure, Johnson's Vice-President Hubert Humphrey—instead of the underdog anti-war candidate Eugene McCarthy—and the suppression of the demonstrations in particularly brutal fashion by Chicago's Mayor Richard Daley.

Anti-war protests and resistance to established authority manifested themselves in different ways in other countries, perhaps most notably in France and Czechoslovakia. In France that May a workers' strike and street protests led by students combined to produce one of the most destructive and potentially revolutionary episodes of this particularly revolutionary year, brought on partly by the Vietnam War, partly by the political authoritarianism of the beleaguered former war hero and French President Charles de Gaulle, and partly by dissatisfaction with particular university regulations. The protests were directed against the entire capitalist social order and the materialist consumer culture it had spawned. In Czechoslovakia, the spirit of reform was inspired by the liberal protests led by Alexander Dubcek against Soviet totalitarianism, though not against communism, per se, as is often thought. The French insurrection ended relatively quickly when Prime Minister Georges Pompidou negotiated an agreement with striking workers and de Gaulle promised reforms, but not before the government and French society appeared on the verge of collapse. The Czech rebellion ended with an invasion of Prague by Russian tanks that devastated hopes throughout the Soviet bloc in Eastern Europe for reform and a loosening of Soviet control.

With political solutions having vanished in the tear gas and melees between civilians and police across several hot August nights in Chicago, disaffected youth looked to artists and musicians to further their cause. The art critic Hilton Kramer wrote in the *New York Times* in September that "[p]robably at no time since the dissolution of the political movements of the nineteen-thirties has the question of the artist's political commitment—and the related question of art's social and political utility—been on the minds of so many people in this country as it is today." Among rock fans of a certain age, the Beatles had always suffered by comparison with more politically conscious artists, particularly the American folk-rock singer Bob Dylan. To quote Sean Wilentz, "[t]he Beatles, with their odd chords, and joyful harmonies, were exciting, but what was 'She Loves You' compared to the long-stemmed word imagery in [Dylan's] 'Chimes of Freedom'?" (Wilentz 90). When Queen Elizabeth II in 1965 officially named each of the individual Beatles Members of the British Empire (MBE), a relativity meaningless honorific, but one that still carried some cachet in establishment circles, their acceptance of the award was hardly a boon to the Beatles' credentials as rebels. The granting of the award to the Liverpudlians was largely an attempt by Prime Minister Harold Wilson, a political outsider and, like the Beatles, a northern grammar school graduate, to gain additional credibility with younger voters.

According to Spitz, John hated being contrasted with the rough and tough Rolling Stones, and the portrayal of the Beatles as clean-cut altar boys by comparison (608). In contrast to the Beatles, the Rolling Stones and the Who seemed much more rebellious in their stage personas (the Beatles had stopped performing live two years earlier) and in songs like "Street Fighting Man" by the Stones and the Who's "My Generation," both of which were suffused with youthful angst. "My Generation," first released in 1965, exuded a rebellious attitude toward authority ("Why don't you just fade away?") and a celebration of youth ("I hope I die before I get old"). Yet, even though toward the beginning of "Street Fighting Man" Mick Jagger sings "summer's here and the time is right for fighting in the streets," the main message of the wrenching lyrics is contained in the chorus, which proclaims that there is nothing a poor boy can do except play in a rock band "'Cause in sleepy London town.' There's just no place for a street fighting man."

In the United States, by contrast, there was plenty of street-fighting going on in 1968; even the Civil Rights movement was yielding to calls for Black Power, which rejected the call for non-violent civil disobedience by its charismatic and idealistic leader, Martin Luther King Jr., who was assassinated on April 4. The revolutionary Black Panther Party had already formed as early as 1966 and had drawn the special attention of FBI director J. Edgar Hoover, who regarded the Black Panthers as the most significant threat to the American government. Anti-war and pro-Civil Rights sentiment in many circles transmuted to hostility toward the entire corporate and political establishment and the social structure that sustained it. This drastic turn in the leftist program would produce terrorist groups in the 1970s such as the Red Brigades in Italy, the Baader-Meinhof Gang in Germany, and the Weathermen in the United States, also known as the Weather Underground, a radical offshoot of SDS, as well as the Symbionese Liberation Army, an organization most famous for its abduction of the American heiress, Patty Hearst.

At the time of the release of the Beatles' single "Revolution" (which was actually the B side of a 45 record that featured McCartney's "Hey, Jude" as the A side), the word "revolution" itself had acquired broad political overtones that went well beyond the anti-war demonstrations in the United States, or even the more serious outbreak of violence and destruction that had accompanied the rebellion by workers and students in Paris in May. To many people in the West, the Russian Bolsheviks had hijacked the term "revolution" and given it Communist connotations, superseding the more positive associations connected to the eighteenth-century American and French Revolutions, which could be interpreted as part of a broader historical evolution of freedom and democracy, despite the excesses of the latter. The Communist Revolution that culminated in the establishment of the People's Republic of China in 1949 had furthered such associations, as had the more recent triumph of Fidel Castro in Cuba and the launching of Mao Zedong's Great Proletarian Cultural Revolution in China in 1966. The Cultural Revolution castigated those members of Chinese society who retained remnants of bourgeois sympathies and called for a return to ideological purity, interpreted in essence as unquestioning adherence to the sayings and party line of Chairman Mao.

But the Beatles were a product of a more moderate revolutionary tradition, in which even the British youth of the 1960s were eager to expand their minds, experiment with drugs, and revel in the explosion of rock-and-roll music, but not necessarily to overthrow the established order. As early as 1964, Ken Kesey, one of the leaders of the counterculture movement who, along with his followers, the Merry Pranksters, had popularized the use of LSD, had expressed disappointment that the Beatles did not recognize the opportunity they had to use their popularity and influence over young people to create a new form of civic engagement (Kramer 35–6). In this respect, the Beatles were not actually all that different from American folk icon Bob Dylan, who, despite his early Woody Guthrie-inspired protest songs, refused to accept the mantle of civic leader so many of his fans were anxious to bestow upon him. In the spring of 1968 John Lennon rejected a request by the French director Jean Luc-Godard to cast the Beatle as Leon Trotsky, a leader of the Bolshevik revolution who had become the hero of many members of the New Left. Godard, like Kesey, saw political potential in the status of rock performers; rejected by Lennon, he managed to convince the Rolling Stones to film their performance of "Sympathy for the Devil" at Olympia Studio that June. Godard took Lennon and the Beatles to task for their failure to sufficiently engage with political issues (Doggett 171).

Still, Lennon had acquired a certain political gravitas not associated with other members of the Beatles, partly because he was (wrongly) perceived as representing working-class values, but mainly as a result of his iconoclastic attitudes toward authority that placed him in the same tradition as the writers who comprised the "Angry Young Men" movement in Britain during the late 1950s and early 1960s. Discontent in Britain centered partly on concerns about government corruption, heightened by the Profumo Scandal of 1963, which involved the Secretary of State for War, John Profumo, who had an affair with a piquant prostitute named Christine Keeler and then lied to cover it up, because Keeler had previously slept with a Russian naval attaché. Many young people in the late 1950s and early 1960s channeled their innate distrust of authorities and their Cold War anxieties into the Campaign for Nuclear Disarmament (CND). Beyond that, economic and imperial anxieties about Britain falling behind and losing its place in the world provoked a general feeling of malaise that only occasionally broke through into overt radical activity. The two most radical institutions in Britain were the London School of Economics and the Hornsey College of Art (Ogersby 133). Left-wing political activists at these institutions, like their counterparts in Rome, Paris, Berkeley, and New York, were divided into different Marxist, Trotskyite, and Maoist factions, but all were committed to some version of the classless society prophesied by Marx in his 1848 *Communist Manifesto*. It was two British Trotskyites, Ali and Pat Jordan, who formed the Anti-Vietnam Committee in 1966. The Committee's outrage over the war led to the violent riots that occurred in Grosvenor Square in London on March 17, 1968.

But the Beatles, in keeping with the general direction of British political culture, were cultural leaders, not political revolutionaries. The Grosvenor Square riots did not change that. It is understandable that the minority of leftist revolutionaries in Britain would take issue with the Beatles for their failure to take a more political stand, just as it is entirely comprehensible that the song "Revolution" seemed ill-timed to those seeking to disrupt the Democratic National Convention in Chicago or those rioting in the streets of Detroit that summer. The Beatles had an audience in student radicals in France, Germany, Italy, Czechoslovakia, Mexico, South America, Australia, and other places around the world who also fell out of sync with the Beatles' failure to sanction their revolutionary stance or activities. In total, fifty- six countries around the globe experienced student revolts in 1968 alone (Siegfried 61). The politicization of the baby boom generation in many of these places resulted not just from strength in numbers but also from the increasingly high proportion of young women and men in their late teens and early twenties who now attended universities. This is critical to understanding the so-called "youth rebellion," because many of the working-class youths who did not attend college did not manifest the same level of rebelliousness or share the same left-wing politics as did university students and the older intellectuals who supported them (Siegfried 74). *Sgt. Pepper* had not only increased the Beatles' popularity worldwide, even beyond what they had achieved thus far; the melodious album also strengthened their credentials as leaders of the counterculture and raised expectations when some of their fans looked to them to take the next step with them toward political radicaliza-tion. Peter Wicke explains: "While the Vietnam War led to the radicalization of parts of the young generation in the United States as well as in Europe, the (musical revolution) followed a different path, much to the regret of the political activists' of the youth and student movements" (Wicke 119). Even the Soviet press condemned the Beatles for their lack of political engagement, when later in the year it referred to them as "respectable" businessmen, the adjective not meant as a compliment (*Soviet Critic*).

Paul later told Barry Miles that he thought John was ambivalent about revolution, which is why he included both the phrases "you can count me out" and "you can count me in" in different versions of the song "Revolution" (and in different verses of the same version). Paul thought Lennon had later given the song a political meaning he did not intend when he actually wrote it (Miles 484). Devin McKinney thought the music and tone of the song belied the lyrics, writing that "the words, all ideology, speak aphorisms, while the music, all instinct, howls violence" (McKinney 221). He described the song as "formed of distortion and sonic abrasion because it is the sound that results when the sort of lie its lyric offers is forced through the Beatles' commu-nal, instinctive sense of what is true" (McKinney 222). Tim Riley thought Lennon's interviews on the subject betrayed "ambivalence vying with principle" (Riley 413). Womack sees less ambiguity, suggesting that "John desperately wanted to release 'Revolution 1' as a single—as the Beatles' explicit statement about the violence of their age" (Womack 235).

Lennon perhaps recognized instinctively a conclusion formulated by Arthur Marwick in his study of the period many years later—that "[t]here was never any possibility of a revolution; there was never any possibility of a 'counter-culture' replacing 'bourgeois culture'" (Marwick 10). Somewhat ironically, Lennon himself said that he wrote "Revolution," at least in part because "it was about time we stopped not answering about the Vietnam War" (*Anthology* 298). His feeling, which he attributed to the sense of peace he achieved in India, that everything would be "all right" simply did not resonate with a generation, particularly in the United States, that had witnessed the assassination of Bobby Kennedy, the burning of American cities, the escalation of the Vietnam War, and the debacle that accompanied the Democratic National Convention in Chicago. In the context of the latter, Graham Nash wrote a song called "Chicago," subtitled

"We *Can* Change the World," which could have been a direct answer to Lennon's "We all want to change the world." Nash's song itself is noncommittal about whether or not change could be achieved by peaceful means, whereas Lennon's song seemed to reflect a greater awareness that violence was not the answer. Furthermore, Lennon defended the song in a response to a confrontational "Open Letter" published by John Holyand in the radical publication, the *Black Dwarf.* Holyand, who had participated in the Grosvenor Square demonstrations in March, besmirched Lennon's reputation, calling his lyrics a "bitter disappointment" and his record "no more revolutionary than Mrs. Dale's diary." Lennon penned a strongly worded defense, stating that he found Holyand's letter "patronizing," asked Holyand who he thought he was, and added for good measure "Fuck Mrs. Dale." The outspoken Lennon went on write: "You're obviously on a destruction kick. I'll tell you what's wrong with the world—people—so do you want to destroy them?" (Holyand) Clearly, Holyand had hit a nerve in his unsettling critique of Lennon's song, since he elicited such a response, one which seemed to support the interpretation of "Revolution" as anti-revolutionary.

By December 1968 the Beatles had recovered much of their credibility as cultural, if not political rebels, with the release of *The Beatles,* which soon became universally known as the White Album. This ethereal album not only contained "Revolution 1," a slower version of the single they released earlier in the year, but also "Revolution 9," a highly experimental track consisting of multi-varied sound effects and recorded speaking voices. The White Album also featured McCartney's mellow and socially conscious "Blackbird," although Hunter Davies doubts Paul was actually writing about the Civil Rights movement, as he later claimed, stating that he never heard Paul give that interpretation at the time (Davies, 283). George Harrison provided additional social commentary in his whimsical "Piggies," though the song facetiously lampooned wealthy fat cats, not, as is often thought, American police officers. In *I Me Mine* George credited his mother for suggesting the line "What they need is a damn good throttling," the last word of which he changed to "whacking" because he needed a word to rhyme with "backing" and "lacking" (Harrison, 126). It is doubtful, however, that Beatles' fans or listeners of the album drew a coherent political message from the eclectic collection of thirty songs that comprised the album. The Beatles' virtuosity was on full display in such brilliant yet diverse tracks as "Why Don't We Do It in the Road," "While My Guitar Gently Weeps," and "Happiness is a Warm Gun," but the exact meaning of these and other songs on the album was unclear to listeners, perhaps even to the Beatles themselves, despite later attempts by members of the group and music critics to explicate their texts. Lennon once compared his songs to abstract art, saying "I write lyrics that you don't realize what they mean until after." In other words, the meaning was in the ear of the beholder, ranging from Charles Manson's delusional interpretation of the album as encouragement for him to commit mass murder in the hopes of perpetuating a race war to the veneration of the album by some critics as the greatest thing the group had ever done. In fact, *New York Times* music critic Richard Goldstein thought the appeal of the White Album, and the Beatles in general, derived from the vagueness of their meanings, allowing each listener to read into their songs whatever they wanted to hear.

The Beatles still had their critics, particularly in the Soviet Union, where a lengthy critique appeared the same month in *Sovetskaya Kultura,* the official publication of the Ministry of Culture. Martinova compared the Beatles unfavorably to the politically conscious folk singers Pete Seeger and Joan Baez, not to mention Bob Dylan. She averred that "Philistines must have idols whom they can admire, whose lives they can live as if they were their own" (qtd. in *Soviet Critic*). To the Soviets, the Beatles symbolized much that was wrong with Western Civilization: its decadence, cult of fame, and lack of authenticity in a culture too influenced by celebrities and the media. Some in the Western media were no kinder in their treatment of the album or the group at this stage of their career.

Still, the release of the White Album proved a prelude to John's complete rehabilitation as the quintessential anti-war rebel in 1969, a year in which he married Yoko Ono, with whom he staged his famous "bed-in" for peace in the Amsterdam Hilton. John immortalized the incident in "The Ballad of John and Yoko," in which he predicted his own crucifixion and furthered his self-association with Jesus. He even claimed at one point to actually be Jesus. Unbeknownst to his fans, if John's life was in danger at that time it was through his own doing, with assistance from Yoko, because of their shared heroin addiction. The behavior of John and Yoko in their personal lives in 1969 was thus starkly at odds with their professed commitment to peace and humanitarianism, as long-time Beatles' associate Tony Bramwell notes in his memoir, in which he refers to Yoko wasting numerous pounds of caviar on a daily basis at one point simply because she could afford to do so (Bramwell 292). One's behavior, however, does not necessarily invalidate one's ideals, and Lennon frequently spoke out in defense of his pacifist position. When David Wigg of the BBC questioned John about his famous bed-in and what could be accomplished by people staying in bed for a week, John responded:

> Well, wouldn't it be better than producing arms and bombs? Imagine if the American army stayed in bed for a week and the Vietnamese army. Or Nixon ... and Kosygin, Chairman Mao. Imagine it, if the whole world stayed in bed. There'd be peace for a week and they might get to feel what it was like. The tension would be released (qtd. in Howlett 271).

Lennon's anti-war stance and utopian vision would gain further confirmation with the release of his iconic song "Imagine" in 1971 and his political activism in the United States, which drew the scrutiny of the FBI in the early 1970s (*The U. S. vs. John Lennon*).

Greil Marcus's assessment of the downfall of 1960s rock and roll was that it became too politically self-conscious and took upon itself a level of social responsibility that had been missing from the more exuberant and free-spirited music of the legends of 1950s rock such as Chuck Berry, Little Richard, and Buddy Holly—all heroes of and powerful influences upon the Beatles (Marcus 38). But I think Marcus would be the first to acknowledge that popular music reflects its times as much as any other artistic medium. The 1960s was a political decade, which had profound and important issues with which to reckon, from Civil Rights to Vietnam, from women's liberation to Cold War escalation and the threat of nuclear annihilation. The Beatles invariably could not remain completely oblivious to these issues and the political culture of the times, especially as they were entering the stage of young adulthood themselves as the decade progressed. But it is entirely possible that their music has remained popular—and relevant—precisely because they did not explicitly respond to the incendiary politics that characterized the decade in which they flourished. The main—perhaps the *one*—song they released in which they did directly respond to the varied political currents discussed above made it all too clear that when it came to "revolution" you could count them out—or in.

Works Cited

The Beatles. "Revolution." Apple, 1968.

———. *The Beatles.* Apple, 1968.

———. *The Beatles Anthology.* San Francisco: Chronicle Books, 2000.

Bianculli, David. *Dangerously Funny: The Uncensored Story of* The Smothers Brothers Comedy Hour. New York: Simon and Schuster, 2009.

Bramwell Tony, with Rosemary Kingsland. *Magical Mystery Tours: My Life with the Beatles.* New York: St. Martin's Press, 2005.

Davies, Hunter. *The Beatles Lyrics: The Stories Behind the Music, Including the Handwritten Drafts of More than 100 Classic Beatles Songs.* New York: Little, Brown and Company, 2014.

DeGroot, Gerard J. *The Sixties Unplugged: A Kaleidoscopic History of a Disorderly Decade.* Cambridge, MA: Harvard University Press, 2008.

Doggett, Peter. *There's a Riot Going On: Revolutionaries, Rock Stars, and the Rise and Fall of the 1960s.* Edinburgh, Cannongate, 2007.

Douglas, Susan J. *Where the Girls Are: Growing Up Female with the Mass Media.* New York: Random House, 1994.

Frontani, Michael R. *The Beatles: Image and the Media.* Jackson: University of Mississippi Press, 2007.

Goldstein, Richard. "The Beatles: Inspired Groovers." *New York Times,* December 8, 1968, p. 181. http://bluehawk.monmouth.edu:2113/hnpnewyorktimes/docview/118417369/C4F5A81D85E74956PQ/1?accountid=12532. Accessed 6 December 2016.

Gould, Jonathan. *Can't Buy Me Love: The Beatles, Britain, and America.* New York: Three Rivers Press, 2007.

Harrison, George. *I Me Mine.* New York: Simon and Schuster, 1980.

Holyand, John. 'Power to the People.' https://www.theguardian.com/music/2008/mar/15/popandrock.pressandpublishing. Accessed 16 December 2016.

Howlett, Kevin. *The Beatles: The BBC Archives 1962–1970.* New York: Harper Design, 2013.

Judt, Tony. *Postwar: A History of Europe since 1945.* New York: Penguin, 2005.

Kamow, Stanley. *Vietnam: A History,* revised ed. New York: Penguin, 1997.

Kramer, Hilton. "Art and Politics: All the Old Questions Return." *New York Times.* 22 September 1968. http://bluehawk.monmouth.edu:2113/hnpnewyorktimes/docview/118262130/fulltextPDF/1CB84952555C4CF8PQ/12?accountid=12532. Accessed 6 December 2016.

Kramer, Michael J. *The Republic of Rock: Music and Citizenship in the Sixties Counterculture.* Oxford: Oxford University Press, 2013.

Kurlansky, Mark. *1968: The Year That Rocked the World*. New York: Ballantine Books, 2004.

McKinney, Devin. *Magic Circles: The Beatles in Dream and History*. Cambridge, MA: Harvard University Press, 2003.

Marcus, Greil. *Lipstick Traces: A Secret History of the Twentieth Century*. Cambridge, MA: The Belknap Press of Harvard University Press, 1989.

Marwick, Arthur. *The Sixties: Cultural Revolution in Britain, France, Italy, and the United States, c. 1958–c. 1974*. Oxford: Oxford University Press, 1998.

Miles, Barry. *Hippie*. New York: Sterling Publishing Co., Inc., 2003.

_____. *Paul McCartney: Many Years from Now*. New York: Henry Holt and Company, 1997.

"The Monarchs of the Beatles Empire." *Saturday Evening Post,* 27 August, 1966, pp. 23–27. http://bluehawk.monmouth.edu:2867/ehost/pdfviewer/pdfviewer?vid=12&sid=d6e983b1-4f9a-4046-91f7-b8f75049fac3%40sessionmgr105&hid=129. Accessed 6 December 2016.

Norman, Philip. *John Lennon: A Life*. New York: HarperCollins, 2008.

_____. *Shout! The Beatles in their Generation*. New York: Simon and Schuster, 1981.

Osgerby, Bill. "Youth Culture." *A Companion to Contemporary Britain,* edited by Paul Addison and Harriet Jones, Blackwell, pp. 127–144.

Riley, Tim. *Lennon: The Man, the Myth, the Music—the Definitive Life*. New York: Hyperion, 2011.

The Rolling Stones. "Street Fighting Man." *Beggar's Banquet*. ABKCO Record, 1968.

Sandbrook, Dominic. *Never Had It So Good: A History of Britain from Suez to the Beatles*. London: Abacus, 2005.

_____. *White Heat: A History of Britain in the Swinging Sixties*. London: Abacus, 2006.

Siegfried, Detlef. "Understanding 1968: Youth Rebellion, Generational Change and Postindustrial Society." *Between Marx and Coca-Cola: Youth Cultures in Changing European Societies, 1960–1980,* edited by Axel Schildt and Detlef Siegfried, Berghan Books, 2006, pp. 59–81.

Simonelli, David. *Working Class Heroes: Rock Music and British Society in the 1960s and 1970s*. Lanham, MD: Lexington Books, 2013.

"Soviet Critic Asserts the Beatles Are Out of Tune With the Times." *New York Times*. 4 December 1968. http://bluehawk.monmouth.edu:2113/hnpnewyorktimes/docview/118353088/fulltextPDF/DA99A0F537814899PQ/5?accountid=12532. Accessed 6 December 2016.

Spitz, Bob. *The Beatles: The Biography*. Boston: Little, Brown and Company, 2005.

Stark, Steven D. *Meet the Beatles: A Cultural History of the Band that Shook Youth, Gender, and the World*. New York, HarperEnterainment, 2005

The U. S. vs. John Lennon. Directed by David Leaf and John Scheinfeld, Authorized Pictures, 2006.

The Who. "My Generation." Brunswick, 1965.

Wicke, Peter. "Music Dissidence, Revolution, and Commerce: Youth Culture between Mainstream and Subculture." *Between Marx and Coca-Cola: Youth Cultures in Changing European Societies, 1960–1980,* edited by Axel Schildt and Detlef Siegfried, Berghan Books, 2006, pp. 109–26.

Wilentz, Sean. *Bob Dylan in America*. New York: Doubleday, 2010.

Wise, David. "How Bobby Plans to Win It." *Saturday Evening Post,* vol. 241, issue 11, 1968, pp. 23–70. http://bluehawk.monmouth.edu:2867/ehost/pdfviewer/pdfviewer?vid=33&sid=d6e983b1-4f9a-4046-91f7-b8f75049fac3%40sessionmgr105&hid=129. Accessed 6 December 2016.

Womack, Kenneth. *Long and Winding Roads: The Evolving Artistry of the Beatles*. New York: Bloomsbury, 2007.

Post-Reading Questions for Part III

1   What was significant about the Beatles' fans who comprised their audience for their first concerts in the United States? What did their behavior reveal about American society in 1964?

2   How did the Beatlemania phase of the Beatles' popularity prepare their fans for the changing role of the Beatles in American popular culture during the later 1960s?

3   How do the explanations for Beatlemania explored by Millard relate to the readings in Part I on the general appeal of rock and roll artists for the baby boom generation? How do Ehrenreich, Hess, and Jacobs account for Beatlemania? To what degree do you find their explanation convincing? Do you agree with their statement, "Rock 'n' roll made mass hysteria almost inevitable"?

4   How did the Beatles respond to the political changes and growing revolutionary attitudes of young college students in the late 1960s? What was the significance of *The White Album* and the song "Revolution 1" for their American audience?

CONCLUSION

The Long-Term Impact of The Beatles on American Popular Culture

As 1968 turned into 1969 and the dramatic events of the past year began to recede, both the Beatles and American popular culture sought to move forward—by turning back to the past. For example, Richie Unterberger has commented on the increased presence of folk influences on *The White Album*, released in November 1968.[1] In the meantime, in the United States, emerging artists like Joni Mitchell, Crosby, Stills, & Nash, and Neil Young were among those calling attention to the continuing influence of folk on American popular music, not to mention the continued success of Bob Dylan, whose music remained centered on folk influences despite his forays into rock. Protest music, however, began to give way to more a positive vibe that culminated in the music and arts festival held near Woodstock, New York in the summer of '69. The Beatles, who had not performed live since 1966, of course, did not participate.

Instead, they continued to record in the studio, working on a collection of songs for a new album tentatively titled *Get Back*. In her late-sixties anthem, "Woodstock," inspired by the festival of the same name, Joni Mitchell encouraged her listeners to "get back to the garden." Mitchell and the Beatles used the phrase differently, but both expressed a desire to return to a state prior to all of the craziness of Beatlemania, the Vietnam War, fame, and materialistic consumerism that seemed to have spoiled a more perfect world. For the Beatles, this meant returning, not to some mythical or metaphorical garden, but to the roots of American rock and roll that had originally in-spired them and brought so much meaning and purpose to their lives. They meant for the album eventually released in 1970 under the title *Let It Be* to be an old-fashioned rock and roll album after all of their in-studio innovation and experimentation that characterized albums such as *Revolver*, *Sgt. Pepper*, and *The White Album*. One song ("One after 909") on the album was a sparse rock and roll number and one of the first songs Lennon and McCartney had ever written together.

---

1   Richie Unterberger, *Eight Miles High: Folk-Rock's Flight from Haight-Ashbury to Woodstock* (San Francisco: Backbeat Books, 2003), 247.

The later release of this album, after *Abbey Road*, the last album recorded by the Beatles as a group, muted some of the impact it might have had, especially since the released album featured the heavy-handed production values of Phil Spector. (In 2003, Paul McCartney engineered the release of an alternate version called *Let it Be … Naked*, which he thought closer to the original intent of the album.) The Beatles continued to have great commercial success with both *Abbey Road* and *Let It Be*, without directly responding to the political turmoil of the late sixties and early seventies as they had in the song "Revolution 1." The group disbanded in 1970, much to the consternation of Beatles fans in Britain, the United States, and around the world. They remained defiant in the face of demands for the group to reunite throughout the seventies until John Lennon's tragic assassination by an obsessed fan in 1980. Still, they left an exceptional mark on American popular culture and have retained both their cultural relevancy and their appeal almost a half century after their breakup.

Their influence in the past fifty years has been too wide-ranging for me to attempt a sustained analysis of it here. Innumerable American groups and artists, including Billy Joel and Bruce Springsteen just to name two highly influential artists in their own rights, have traced their initial musical inspirations directly to the Beatles. The role that the Beatles have played in countless lives of their listeners from the time of Beatlemania forward is incalculable. However, the authors whose works I have included in this volume call attention to the influence of the progenitors of the Beatles, in addition to that of the Beatles themselves.

In 1973, American director George Lucas released a movie called *American Graffiti*. The film portrayed teenage life at a time right before the Kennedy assassination, the escalation of the Vietnam War, and Beatlemania—a seemingly simpler time but one when the country was on the verge of great cultural changes. In doing so, Lucas called attention to those changes without directly dealing with them, except in a few terse updates on several characters' lives that scrolled across the screen at the film's end. The film also reminded viewers, including this high school graduate of the class of '73, how much great music existed in American popular culture before the Beatles. Our culture would not only have been poorer without it, but without the pioneers of early rock and roll, the Beatles, at least as we know them, would never have existed.